UNLOCKING OUR
SUPERPOWERS

A HANDBOOK FOR PERSONAL AND
COLLECTIVE TRANSFORMATION

KEVIN MAY

PUBLISHED BY : **STORYWEAVERS PRESS**

Copyright 2021. All rights reserved.
© Unlocking Our Superpowers.
Library of Congress : Case # 1-3806789961

Cover Design : Casey House : www.Casey-House.com
Kevin's Websites : www.KevinMayCoaching.com
www.SacredStoryWeavers.com
Cover Photo : PGH Post Gazette

The first edition of this book was published on 8-8-16 and the cover featured a Rainbow Lion, painted my friend and amazing Visionary Artist, Chelsey Crandell. This Lion was intended to represent some of the key intentions of this book, including the expression of our Greatest Potential, Creative Genius, and the reclamation of our Fully Empowered Selves. The photo I chose for this 2nd edition is a giant Peace Circle from our very first Peaceful Gathering of Hands Festival in Pittsburgh PA in 2011. This iconic image represents both the power of community, as well as the diverse and unique puzzle pieces that each of our personal paths contribute.

May this book serve as a reminder of the new chapter that is beginning for humanity, as more of us claim our birthright and worthiness to experience lives full of Beauty, Strength, Love, Service, Connection, Wholeness, Harmony, Balance, and so much more. I invite you and your community to be co-creators of this multi-faceted New and Ancient story. THANK YOU for being alive in these amazing times!

~ Kevin May

DEDICATED TO THE AWESOMENESS WHICH FOLLOWS
WHEN WE UNLOCK OUR SUPERPOWERS

TABLE OF CONTENTS

~ Unlocking Our Superpowers ~
Part One
~ Setting the Stage ~

PREFACE

I used to think that the Preface was some irrelevant and boring part of a book. I would usually skip over it, and dive into the Introduction. Well, I'm here to tell you that this is the coolest, most fascinating Preface of all time! Just kidding, but it is a very important part of this book. It outlines many reasons why this book is extremely unique and a One-of-a-Kind experience to read :

If you are reading these words right now, then chances are you grew up in the so called "Modern World." I like to call this the Mainstream Strange-Dream. I see this Mainstream Culture as quite an odd version of the ideal human life. I feel that we have lost a lot of the core values that make us human, and sadly many people have become extremely unhealthy and deeply unsatisfied with life as a result. Most of us have been taught to live a life within certain limited guidelines, but I believe there are other ways to play the "Game of Life."

For the last 12 years I have been studying Human Culture, Sociology, Anthropology, Philosophy and variety of other subjects, primarily to figure out questions like **"What on Earth is going on in this society?!" "What is the true purpose of Humanity?" "Why are we living in such an unhealthy and destructive manner?"**

I've discovered that humans have not always lived in such disharmony. Many indigenous and ancient cultures have preserved wisdom of how to live a life that is deeply connected to one's inner truth, one's community, Mother Earth, and the larger cosmos. I bow in gratitude and deeply acknowledge to the many Indigenous cultures of the past and present who live in devotion and service to the web of life. I live on the territory currently called Pittsburgh, where the Allegheny and Monongahela rivers converge into the Ohio river. This area was once stewarded by the Seneca, Shawnee, and Lenni Lenape peoples, and before that there were the Ancient Mound Builders. The Seneca referred to this area as Diondega, translated as "the forks" - representing where the 3 rivers meet. I pray that this book may be a small stepping stone in the work of honoring the ancient ways and reharmonizing our human family with all of nature.

My hope and intention is that this book is a Distillation, Synthesis, and Fresh Perspective on the best "Golden Nuggets" that I have studied, tested, and applied into my life. For me, these are not just mental concepts; they are more like living, breathing teachings, which I have lived and will continue to live every day. Many of these bits of wisdom have drastically improved my existence, and completely shifted my reality.

Through applying these "Golden Nuggets" of wisdom, I'm confident you will uncover Superpowers that you already use everyday and also begin to Unlock many new ones. So what is a "Superpower" after all? **I define a "Superpower" as a gift or skill that you possess, which can enhance your life or someone else's. These can range between very simple to very complex, from small-scale to worldwide.** One of your Superpowers could be the ability to see the beauty in others, or something as unique as a life-changing invention which transforms the whole planet forever. (I do believe that both the simple and the complex Superpowers are equally important.)

My intention is to deliver these Tools, Techniques and Stories in a simple, fun and memorable way. I believe that 99% of what I share here you already know deep down. Some of these tools may seem basic, though those ones are often the most profound. Some are more complex and esoteric. Either way, the proof is in the pudding. If it resonates, and works for you, awesome! If it doesn't - Hakuna Matata (it means no worries).

My birth name is Kevin, which could also be pronounced (Key-vin). It doesn't surprise me that my name contains the word "key", as I have always had a passion for understanding the key aspects of any topic. In this book, I will present many of the most powerful Keys that I have collected, and it is up to you to unlock the door, or perhaps realize that it has always been unlocked, and you must simply walk through it.

If you decide to Unlock your Superpowers with dedication, I am quite confident you will experience deep connection with your Authentic Self, with your friends and family, and with the entire Web of Life. This usually leads to tremendous joy, fulfillment, and gratitude.

Through implementing the insights in this book, I've tapped into some of my Superpowers, which have allowed me to successfully bike 4,500 miles across America, run 2 Crowdfunding Campaigns for Poetry Tours all around the U.S., design and lead an Online Curriculum called "Conscious Creative Expression" and create over 500

YouTube videos. These tools have also empowered me to transform a chronic pain condition called RND, which is very similar to Fibromyalgia and TMS. I don't share this to brag, but to give a glimpse of what is possible for an average human, who has tapped into their sacred Superpowers :)

To quote one of my favorite authors Ram Dass "I always talk about myself, but those of you who know - know that it's not really me - it's us. And I just use myself as a case study, because I know it better than I know everybody else's case study. Because what awes me is really how parallel our journey's are"

This book is also unique for a few other reasons :

1.   It fuses the medium of a printed and/or Ebook with the vast domain of Youtube and the internet. I invite readers to check out some of my Youtube videos at any point during the process of reading this book. I am a firm believer in receiving information in multiple formats, so that one can have both a Multisensory Experience and see a variety of unique perspectives on a topic.

As mentioned above, I've created / co-created over 500 YouTube videos in the past 11 years. Some are well-edited mini-films or interviews, some are simply video blogs walking down the sidewalk. They are not necessarily "super high quality" in audio or video, though I can promise you they are fun, and show my evolution as a human being.

I originally published this book in August of 2016. In the same way that we are all a work in progress, and constantly evolving, there are parts of this book that I wanted to update. In 2021, I revised some parts of this book and updated many of the links which had changed. Also, the first edition was composed in an older version of Adobe Acrobat. When I went to edit in the new version, the software had changed so much, that some of the formatting could not be changed. So please forgive some of the weird spacing and minor formatting issues. We are all perfectly imperfect and so is this book!

2. My goal isn't to impress you, to show off, or to be the coolest dude in the world (I've already got that title - haha). My goal is to authentically share my experiences, and trust that this is why I am here on this planet. I enjoy embarrassing myself, and I'm happy to admit my flaws (i.e. being on time) and shadows (i.e. self-judgement).

3. I debated about changing my writing style and book format in order to fit the "industry standards". For a while I tried to conform, but my soul just couldn't do it. It was blocking my creativity. So, I decided, "I'm gonna write this book how I want to write it, in a way that feels real and honest." If I don't get a publishing deal, that's okay with me. As a

fellow evolutionary friend once said "It's better to be strange, than a stranger to yourself."

On the first draft of this book, I drew all of the 5 graphics in this book by hand, which infused them with my energy in a special way. Although I did enjoy these drawings, I decided to team up with my friend Casey House who designed the graphics for the front and back of this book to revamp 2 of them, and I designed one more myself, while keeping 2 of the original drawings. I am very excited about all of them, and I encourage you to take pictures, or draw your own version of them. Each of the 5 graphics in this book have been crucial resources for me on my path of transformation.

4.   While writing this book, a few times I tried to "force the flow", and write a bunch about a specific topic. Sometimes I would get in the groove, but many times, I couldn't easily tap into the essence of that topic. Then I remembered that I have been blogging on Facebook for many years, and those are almost always written during or directly after a profound experience.

For this reason, I decided to include many Facebook posts in this book. I was often full of adrenaline, in a complete flow-state while writing these "transmissions." Thus, I believe they carry a specific energy and freshness, that I can't always just conjure up on a rainy afternoon a few years after the experience. I also include the date, and time of day that I posted them, because that shows the exact moment I shared, and may carry a synchronicity of what you were up to at that time.

5. You may notice that I don't follow classical grammar rules in this book. This is because I am deeply devoted to sharing Truth in the way that resonates with me. I choose to freely express myself, which includes unsubscribing from the mainstream "rules and restrictions." I like to capitalize words that carry a specific importance in a sentence. I also use quotations a lot, usually to demonstrate that the quoted term carries a certain understanding within Mainstream Culture or a subculture such as the "Yoga Community." I also put quotes in italics, and key sentences in bold. Lastly, I even go so far as to include smiley faces :) and "haha" moments to keep it playful.

I don't think everyone should abandon classical grammar and literary structure, though for me, and the intentions behind this book, this is how I am choosing to write. Shazaam! I claim my creative freedom!

I know that some people, including myself like to skim read books, or read them in a non-linear fashion. Both of these are A-OK by me, though I can honestly say that every page has a golden nugget in it, and I have done my best to include only the most magical information and stories. With that said, I encourage you to read through the Table of Contents and skip around to whichever chapters intrigue you most. Also, feel free to take notes, (there is some blank space from pgs. 165-170. You can also write or draw in the margins, and/or highlight parts you want to revisit. This book and this world is your playground, and I invite you to play, learn, and co-create within it! So without further ado, I will say "Scoobally Doo" and let you read on through :)

INTRODUCTION

"You've had the power all along, my dear. You just had to learn it for yourself"
~ Glinda, The Good Witch (Wizard of Oz)

Growing up, I always loved to run. From age 7 onwards, my parents let me roam the neighborhood with the group of friends who lived near my house. In our family-filled urban neighborhood called "Squirrel Hill," we would create games and use a full square mile area as our stomping grounds.

Whether it was Capture the Flag or Cops and Robbers, I thoroughly enjoyed sprinting as fast as I could to outrun whoever was chasing me. I usually had a big grin on my face as I dodged getting tagged during these epic scenarios.

In Elementary School, I put my speed to the test, and joined the Track Team. In 4th grade I trained tirelessly for the 1/2 mile race (the longest distance available.) I had a "Bowl Cut" hairstyle at the time, which bounced up and down as I moved, so my friends jokingly called me "Floppy".

I managed to transcend the teasing, and won 1st place in the City Championship with a time of 2:51. My love for running continued all throughout middle school, where my cross-country coach nicknamed me "Lickety Split" because I regularly left the competition in the dust.

In high school, I used my running skills mostly on the soccer field, which I chose to play instead of cross-country or track. Although I didn't get much varsity playing time, I enjoyed hanging with all my neighborhood homies, who were also on the soccer team. We'd crack jokes on the sidelines as we'd chow down on nachos from the snack bar.

In my junior year of high school, I began to have pains in my knees following the Fall soccer season. They didn't seem to have a link to any incident, so I thought they were probably growing pains. I shrugged them off for a month, though as they worsened my parents became concerned.

We decided to visit an Orthopedist. He recommended physical therapy and gave me a knee brace to address a condition called "Osgood Schlatters", which is basically a fancy term for growing pains.

It was challenging for me physically, emotionally, and socially. By losing my capacity to run, my sense of pride diminished, since it was tied up with my speed. A few months after getting the knee brace, I began to play Raquetball, which was more focused on the upper body.

My health took another turn when my wrists started to ache every time I would swing the racket. "What the hell is happening to me?" I often thought. I tried to strengthen my forearms and upper body through weight lifting to no avail. Around March of 2008, my knees and wrists became so persistently painful that I had to surrender all physical activity.

This is when I started to enter a state of depression. My friends developed new nicknames for me like "Cripple," and some joked that I was suffering from "OMD" (Old Man's Disease). I felt pretty much worthless. I saw several doctors about my wrists, and they couldn't find any physical damage. They said it was probably some form of Tendonitis, and gave me a wrist brace for each arm.

In April, I can vividly remember sitting in Biology class, wearing two wrist braces and one knee brace. I was debating whether I should take them all off before walking down the hallway so I wouldn't have to feel embarrassed in front of all the other kids at school. It looked a bit like I was suited up for Rollerblading!

My wrist pain continued to get more intense. It felt like a deep, numbing ache was coming from my joints. Speaking of joints, smoking marijuana with my friends after school was one of the only ways I could feel relaxed. I became a regular pot smoker, and took on a cynical and jaded view of life. I would get drunk almost every weekend to experience a brief hiatus from the pain. I got some semblance of pride from winning at drinking games like "beer pong."

A big part of me was "pissed off at the world". I felt like all my physical superpowers had disappeared, and I was left to wither away. I would often poke fun at myself and my predicament as a weird way of making peace with my painful situation.

By May, the pain had gotten so intense that I became concerned that something was seriously wrong with my body. My wrists hurt so bad that I could not write with a pencil anymore, so I simply sat in class, without doing any assignments. I slept through a large portion of my classes, because I discovered that sleep was one easy way to escape the pain.

Finally, my mom and I saw a new doctor, who diagnosed me with "RND" (Reflex Neurovascular Dystrophy). This condition implies that there is no physical damage, though the nerves are still sending "pain signals" to the brain. It is commonly called a Mind-Body Disorder.

The doctor prescribed me to three weeks of intense Physical Therapy. Luckily one of the only RND Healing Programs in the nation was located a mere five minute drive from my house! In mid-May I entered the Inpatient Unit and Intensive Healing program at The Children's Institute of Pittsburgh. I had a room all to myself, though I shared a unit with a variety of other young people recovering from mild to serious injuries / conditions.

There were a few other RND patients in my unit, though I connected most with two patients who'd recently had surgeries. First I met Jody, who I quickly became enamored with. She had been in a devastating car accident, and was learning how to walk after shattering her pelvis and some leg bones. She was very friendly and we would hang out in the common area.

I was doing six hours of intense physical therapy every day. The philosophy of the program was to "re-teach the damaged nerves how to interpret pain". I was doing countless sets of jumping jacks, leg raises, and every stretch imaginable for most of the day. Luckily the food was delicious, and we ended every day with swimming, which allowed my muscles to cool down. Also, sometimes Jody was doing her pool therapy at the same time, which meant we got to see each other in swimsuits :)

The atmosphere of this hospital-like environment was very upbeat and encouraging, though I was still in a lot of pain, and felt cynical about all the "positive thinking" they told us to do. "What am I supposed to do, pretend like the pain doesn't exist?!"

A few days into this new regimen, my body was exhausted, and my pain felt more excruciating than ever. I woke up with sharp pains in my knees. I told my physical therapist that I didn't think I could do any training. A big part of me wanted to just go home and give up, accepting myself as disabled. The physical therapists encouraged me to keep persevering and surprisingly, by lunchtime, my pain had decreased dramatically. This showed me that a big part of overcoming pain was in a positive attitude.

As a few days passed, I noticed a young Black teenager who was always playing video games. He never seemed very social, though one evening we started chatting. His name was Hassan, and he quizzed me on what type of music I listened to. We quickly realized that we both loved many of the same Rap Artists, particularly Lil' Wayne, who was my favorite rapper at the time.

We began to hang out in the common room, and see who knew more lyrics to all the popular rap songs. This seemed to help us both lighten up amidst our uncomfortable physical conditions.

I was hesitant to ask Hassan what had happened to him, though after we grew closer together, he shared his story. He was the punt returner for his local football team. One day, his team faced a Suburban squad, who all appeared to be on steroids. These giants punted the ball high in the sky. Hassan caught it, and began running towards the oncoming stampede. He sidestepped a few opponents, and then out of nowhere "SMACK!" He was brutally tackled by someone twice his size.

He hit the ground hard, and his teammates soon realized he was not getting up. He was taken in an ambulance to a local hospital, and later received the life-altering news that he had been paralyzed from the waist down!

In the blink of an eye, an active young man was given a life sentence to a wheelchair. I felt chills go down my spine as I gulped and shed tears on the inside for my new friend. I thought to myself, "How can I complain about my pain, when Hassan is handicapped for life?"

This put things in perspective for me, and I began to see my situation as less severe than before. With lots of encouragement from the nurses and all my physical therapists, I began to take on a more positive attitude. My body was extremely sore from all the weird stretches, endurance training, and swimming, but I was grateful to be making progress. I was also having fun chilling with my new friends Jody and Hassan.

By the end of 2 weeks I felt like a new human being. My body felt more agile, and I was overjoyed to reclaim my ability to run. I had one more week to go in the 3-week program. In addition to the physical therapy, I was also seeing a Psychologist and doing "Biofeedback" and meditation exercises. I was led through my first "Guided Meditation" and was literally flabbergasted by how relaxed I felt afterwards. My whole body felt like silly putty. This sparked a newfound interest in the mind-body connection.

Just before entering the Children's Institute, I received an early birthday gift - my first ever laptop! This opened a portal to a vast array of new areas of interest. I started researching meditation techniques and altered states of consciousness. YouTube was just starting to take off at this point, and I avidly explored its smorgasbord of documentaries.

My 3 weeks was quickly coming to a close at the Institute. I had grown to be close with Jody and Hassan, and it was hard to believe we would be parting ways so soon. We'd all had so much fun listening to music and sharing food together in the common room. Although we were all going through our own challenges, we helped to brighten each other's days.

On my last day of the 3 weeks, I felt like I'd been reborn. My pain level had gone from an 8 out 10, to a 2 or 3 on the scale of severity. I had a new reverence for my health, and all the friends, family, and therapists who helped me find a sense of peace once again.

I remember leaving the Institute on a Friday, and felt like I had just gotten my life back! I barely knew what to do with myself without the chronic pain. My sense of identity had previously been tied up with my depressed state, so now I had to reinvent myself. I looked up at the deep blue sky scattered with big puffy clouds, and I felt a sense of childlike wonder at the mystery of life. For the previous 4 or 5 months, I often felt like my life was cursed, and in this moment, I felt as if my life was a magnificent gift.

I had a deep yearning to learn everything I could about alternative healing techniques. In the following weeks, I began devouring documentaries and Wikipedia articles, soaking up all the knowledge I could. Although I was passionate about health and wellness, I resumed my old habits of pot smoking and partying, and because it was summer, pretty much every day was a weekend.

A few months after leaving the Institute I was playing my favorite game of Beer Pong at a party. I had a soccer game the following morning, but that didn't have much effect on my desire to get drunk and high with my friends. I got back home around 4 am, and my game began around 10am, so I decided to pull an all-nighter.

On the soccer field I felt hungover, and my teammates were poking fun at me for my lack of motor skills. After the game, I struck up a conversation about some of the cool documentaries I'd been watching on my new laptop. Unfortunately, I couldn't seem to articulate these new ideas. It was as if there was too much fog in my brain to translate my thoughts into actual words.

My teammates rarely smoked pot, and they proposed that perhaps marijuana was causing me to trip over my words, and lose track of my thoughts mid-sentence. I defended my love for smoking, and didn't appreciate them making fun of my communication skills (though in the back of mind I knew they were right).

Later that day I found myself back at the same house from the previous night, partying once again. Because I hadn't slept in over 24 hours, I felt even more tipsy with only a few beers.

When I got home from the party, I did my usual nightly routine of surfing YouTube for mind-expanding videos. I started watching some video blogs from a guy named "Vagabond Steve." He was a really cool guy, who spoke about searching for meaning in life, questioning everything, and how to escape the "Rat Race".

In one of his videos, he asked the question "How are you going to feel when you are 80 years old, sitting in a rocking chair, and you reflect on your life? Are you going to wish you spent more time at the office or watching TV? Or are you going to wish you spent more time doing things like watching the sunrise, connecting with close friends, and making a positive difference in the world?"

These questions struck a deep chord within me. As I sat in front of my glowing computer screen at 4am amidst my pitch-black bedroom, I felt like someone hit the "Pause" button on reality. I thought "What am I doing with my life?" As I scratched my head, I had the shocking realization in my 17 years on this planet, I'd never watched the sun rise over the horizon!

My heart started to race. I looked out of my bedroom window. The birds were just starting to chirp. I threw on a hoody and went downstairs and laced up my running shoes. As I jogged through the deserted streets in my neighborhood, I felt like I was coming back to life. I was determined to reclaim my sacred birthright and witness a sunrise! What sort of weird illusion full of distractions and laziness had I been living in, where I never prioritized this most basic human activity?

I arrived at Frick Park just as the sky started to lighten up. I meandered around, marveling at the grass covered in a frosty layer of dew. I had now been awake for almost 48 hours straight. A crew of dog walkers started to stroll down the main path. I went over to them and asked "Do you all do this every day?" They casually replied "Yeah, pretty much." I could hardly believe that I had been missing out on the magic of the early morning hours for my entire life!

As the clouds began to turn light purple and pink, I sat down in the wet grass on top of a hill. I was full of gratitude for the friendly dog walkers, and all of the natural beauty surrounding me. I anxiously awaited to see the sun peek over the horizon.

There were some scattered clouds in the sky. As the sun slowly rose, it was hiding behind these puffballs. Then, a burst of golden light blazed through, and it felt like it pierced right into me. WOW! The entire golden orb emerged, and I stared straight into it. It was glowing orange, and to my great surprise, I was able to maintain eye contact with no discomfort.

I remembered growing up, my parents often told me "Never stare into the sun, you'll go blind." I pondered how many other limiting beliefs I had bought into, which prevented me from living fully. (Of course my parents were trying to protect me, though perhaps this had partially prevented me from pursuing a sunrise). As the sun illuminated Frick Park, more birds, squirrels, and dogwalkers showed up to greet this brand new day. I felt like I was awakening from a dream.

Witnessing my 1st sunrise felt like a milestone accomplishment, and the beginning of a new life chapter. I was reclaiming my ability to think for myself and steer the direction of my life. I was distancing myself from the cultural norms and arbitrary societal behaviors of America. I thought to myself "There's gotta be another way to live!" I declared to myself that I would take a 2 week break from smoking pot, as a way to sharpen my brain.

Sitting atop this hill, staring into the sun, I began to reflect on my time at the Children's Institute. I thought of Hassan, who was still cooped up inside, unable to even walk on his own. I wanted to enjoy the sunrise on his behalf. Even though it was about 7am, I gave him a call on my cell phone. I got his voicemail, which was a song called "Mr. Carter" by Lil' Wayne, which we often sang together. I started to tear up, hearing this song, and reminiscing on all our good times hanging out.

He called me back a few minutes later. When I heard his voice, I felt lost for words. I asked him how he was doing. He said he was fine, still at the Institute, preparing for another back surgery. In that moment, I wished I could teleport him to the hill where I was sitting so he could experience this beautiful sunrise with me. I was feeling a whirlwind of emotion including gratitude and love for life, plus immense sadness for Hassan's inability to walk, as well as the state of modern society being so disconnected from the cycles of nature.

I tried to cheer up Hassan by cracking some jokes. It felt good to share a laugh or two together. I told him I would come visit him soon, and then we said our goodbyes. I hung up the phone, and shed some more tears. Because I still had the blessing of an able body, I felt it was my duty to be of service to others, in any way I could.

I promised myself that I was going to help make the world a better place. I didn't really know what that would look like or how I would do it, but I knew that I had to try. I wanted to reconnect to the Natural World, and stop spending so much time indoors, playing video games or watching Television. I felt deeply motivated to set aside my distractions and focus on improving myself and the world. It was time to run towards my goals with the same joy and passion that pulsed through me as a youngster playing games in my neighborhood.

The story I tell above was a big turning point for me. From the summer of 2008 onwards, I began actively pursuing the dormant Superpowers of Humanity, and finding ways to implement them in my personal life. The following chapters give a glimpse into many of my discoveries, and the trials, tribulations, and victories along the way.

THE TALE OF THE TWO TREES

The Tale of the Two Trees emerged after completing the 6-month bike tour across America with the Cultural Recyclists in 2010. We were exploring Sustainable Living, and we visited a wide variety of urban farms, ecovillages, Permaculture co-ops and everything in between. As we cycled from town to town, we were asking people: "What are the biggest challenges facing humanity and how can we solve them?"

We received answers as diverse as the many types of people we met along the journey. Some folks believed terrorism and war were the biggest issues, while others were laser-focused on solving climate change or social inequality. Who was right? We didn't form a conclusive answer, though we came up with a Map to understand the state of the world.

I've led a workshop based on this Map many times, and it always leads to very powerful and insightful conversations. In these workshops, I invite folks to imagine we are a bunch of friends sitting in a backyard. We are observing two big trees. The one on the left is totally deteriorating, with dead branches and lifeless flowers all over the ground. The tree on the right is vibrantly alive, overflowing with colorful flowers and leaves.

First I ask the audience, "**What are the biggest challenges / issues facing humanity?**" On stage, I have a big easel with a drawing of the two trees, and begin to label the branches of the dying tree, as the audience shouts out their answers to my question. After labeling the branches things like "Global Poverty, Resource Management, Political Corruption, Deforestation, etc.," I ask another question: "**What are the root causes of all these issues?**"

Next, I label the roots of the dying tree. The audience gives answers like "Disconnection from Nature, Greed, Ego Consciousness, etc." I go on to explain that on the bike trip, we explored many root causes, and our grand conclusion is that "**All the biggest issues facing humanity are a result of our BS! (Belief System)**"

Our bike troupe realized that fundamentally it is our cultural beliefs which give rise to our dysfunctional Social, Educational, Energy, and Environmental systems. If we begin to question our own BS, then everything in society will shift.

We visited many farms and ecovillages which had made the transition to a new belief system, and the outward changes were very apparent. Most had alternative energy sources, grew their own food, lived close to the land, and had more peaceful personal relationships.

Next, I ask the audience to shout out what are the new beliefs and values they would like to see to create a new human culture. I label the roots / soil of the Vibrant Tree things like "Gender Equality, Respect for Nature, Cooperation, Collaboration, Reciprocity, Sacredness."

The last part of the workshop is where we label the flowering branches of the Vibrant Tree. I enthusiastically ask "**What will the world look like, smell like, feel like, when we have shifted our BS to one that we consciously choose?**"

This is when all heaven breaks out!. Audience members shout out visions and dreams like "Giant Garden Parties, Bicycle Parades, Vertical Farms, Fire Circles, Stargazing, Smells of Flowers instead of Pollution, Kids Playing Outside, Interspecies Communication!" I label the Vibrant Tree's branches all of these beautiful manifestations.

To close the workshop, I lead an overview, showing how the Dying Tree's dysfunctional Belief System gives rise to the many "problems" in our society, and once we shift our core beliefs to more holistic, all inclusive ones, we will grow an entirely new civilization!

Here is a summary of what the group usually brainstorms for both the Dying Tree and the Thriving Tree :

DYING TREE

BIGGEST CHALLENGES FACING HUMANITY
(in no specific order) :

- Climate Change
- Ignorance
- Social Inequality / Poverty
- Diseases
- Terrorism
- Systemic Racism
- Govt. Corruption

DYSFUNCTIONAL CULTURAL BELIEFS AND VALUES

- The Material World is all that exists.
- Your Genes determine how your life will unfold.
- Humans are Separate from Nature.
- It is okay to oppress marginalized groups of people.
- Humans were Destined to Control and Dominate Nature.
- Logic, Reason, and Science are the only ways to Discover Truth.
- We must Compete for Scarce Resources.

THRIVING TREE

NEW AND ANCIENT HOLISTIC SYSTEMS

- Permaculture Villages which support Climate Stability, Healthy Soil, Water + Air.
- Higher Awareness Through Holistic Education Systems.
- New Economic Models, Local Currency, + Gift Economies.
- People of all Races, Genders, Abilities, and Sexualities have Equal Rights.
- Conflict Resolution + Mass Facilitation of all Healing Modalities.

NEW AND ANCIENT CULTURAL BELIEFS AND VALUES

- Matter Arises from the Quantum Energy Field.
- Environment and Behavior play a big role in Genetic Expression
- Humans are vitally interconnected to the whole Web of Life.
- There are many ways to perceive Truth i.e. : Logic, Intuition, Divination, etc.
- Cooperation and Collaboration empower us to live and share in abundance.

The "Tale of the Two Trees" Map is a very simple and powerful way to describe the state of the world. It gives you the Superpower of grasping the past, present, and potential future of our entire civilization! I've received so much positive feedback from people who've attended this workshop and also who've seen my videos online. They explain how they now feel they know their place in the larger Cultural Evolution, and feel motivated to keep living the "New and Ancient Cultural Values." Many people also explain that having this Map alleviates stress, because they can now see how there is a massive movement taking place on this planet, and they must simply do their little, yet important part to contribute to it. I invite you to share this map with anyone who is interested in world affairs and transforming themselves / society.
I also invite you to watch my workshop on YouTube from Burning Man on this topic called "Cultural Evolution - Kevin May"

THE POWER OF QUESTIONS

"It is not the answer that enlightens, but the question."
~ Decouvertes

I returned to live with my parents in December of 2010 after completing the 4,500 mile bike tour with the Cultural Recyclists. I was bursting with inspiration and passion to put what I had learned into practice. I got involved with the Transition Town Movement which focuses on building community and transitioning towards a localized way of living. I became an event organizer and a "point person" for sustainability and consciousness in my hometown.

I was in love with life! I was planning events with friends, making lots of YouTube videos, and staying up late in jam sessions with fellow musicians. Although I felt like I was thriving, my parents were concerned that I didn't have a "regular" paying job, and they wanted me to go back to college. After 15 months of "tasting freedom", I reentered the standardized domain of Penn State University in fall of 2011. Mind you, I signed up for some pretty awesome classes which catalyzed me to grow and think outside the box. I met an inspiring professor named Chris Uhl, author of "Developing Ecological Consciousness." I took his class called Biological Science, though many students called it "Waking Up 101."

A few weeks into the semester, I did feel like I was "waking up" to new aspects of reality. I began to see the confinements of social norms and did my best to be a "glitch in the matrix," by befriending people I wouldn't normally talk to, going dumpster diving, and living spontaneously. One day I arrived to class, and Chris gave all the students a unique assignment : Write 100 open-ended questions about absolutely anything in under 30 minutes.

This simple task had an extremely profound impact on me and my consciousness. Rather than grasping for answers, the goal was to simply ask questions. I could handle that. I dove right in. The questions flew out of me like birds cooped up in a cage. As I wrote the first 50 questions, I felt a sense of freedom and excitement, like a little kid who had been given permission to eat as many cookies as he wanted. By number 65, I started to pose some very juicy questions to myself about the course of my life. Here are the last 35 questions I wrote:

65. What would I do if I dropped out of school?

Teach workshops, be a spiritual comedian?

Would my parents support me?

Would I use food stamps?

How soon will shit hit the fan in society?

Would I live in Pittsburgh?

Would I travel w/ or like Michael Garfield?

Would people support me using PayPal?

Where would I sleep?

Couch surfing?

How would I subsist?

Sell art, t-shirts, books, stickers?

I could bike tour maybe?

Live on an ecovillage?

Am I wasting energy and opportunity if I stay in school?

How can I best give my gifts?

What can I bring to Burning Man next year?

What if mad celebrities start waking up and want to support me and my ventures? What would I spend the money on?

A center in Pittsburgh?

A center in Happy Valley?

A speaking tour?

An ecovillage?

Indigenous protection?

Should I write a book?

Or just keep making videos, which flow easier?

Why is life so crazy?

Why is the sky blue?

Are ghosts just fear vibrations?

What is love?

Is god love?

What does infinite mean?

How can I most contribute towards a more beautiful world?

What is my highest potential path?

Who am I?

What is a question?

After this assignment, I began to seriously question whether I wanted to remain at Penn State, or flap my wings into the world of possibilities I had glimpsed on the bike trip. As I sat in class day after day, I felt a deep anxiety inside of me. "This is not what I'm meant to be doing," I often thought to myself as I walked across campus. I had seen how much I could accomplish both on the bike trip and as a community organizer in Pittsburgh. Within the restrictions of school life, I felt like I was wasting time, and missing out on my destiny.

The questions above stirred in my mental crock pot for about 2 months before it was 100% clear to me that I needed to blaze my own trail outside of the college world. Much to my parents dismay, I broke the news that my plan was to leave school, and focus on creating YouTube Videos, Music, and Community Organizing. This was a massive leap of faith for me, and it certainly hasn't been easy. 8 years later I am still blazing my own trail, and this book is largely a byproduct of this exploratory journey!

Questions are so powerful because they open doorways to new possibilities. They can act as "Fear Flashlights," and shine a light of clarity, truth, and humor on a limiting story in your mind. As you pose questions to your mind's fearful perspectives, these rigid viewpoints often melt away. Questions can also assist you in discovering your deepest desires and soul calling. I especially love **"Juicy Questions", which shake the foundation of your comfort zone.**

Throughout this book, I will propose open-ended questions at the end of many sections or chapters for you to explore in your own life. **Here are a few Questions about Questions :)**

1. When have you asked a "juicy question" that made a big impact in your life?
2. What area of your life could use some investigative questioning?
3. How often do your friends and family ask you "juicy questions"?

> *" Behind every problem, there's a question trying to ask itself.*
> *Behind every question, there's an answer trying to reveal itself.*
> *Behind every answer, there's an action trying to take place.*
> *Behind every action, there's a way of life trying to be born. "*
> **~ Rev. Michael Beckwith**

PEELING AND REVEALING

Over the past 11 years, I have gone through many phases and stages of my personal Hero's journey. Along this walk, I have experimented with going by different names. I believe the name that we each go by has a profound effect on one's sense of self and personal identity.

Back in 2010, I was reading lots of Philosophy books, and thought, "Hey it would be funny if I changed my name on Facebook to Phil...Osophical." So I did. With this new alias, I felt a little bit more permission to say things I might have been afraid to say before.

Eventually I started sharing Spoken Word Poetry at lots of open mics, and I used my new alias "Phil Osophical." It worked well, so I kept with it... It was kind of nice to have a "stage name" while still going by Kevin amongst my friends. When I moved to California in 2013, many people on the west coast new me from my Poetry, and so they just assumed my name was Phil, and I was like "Whatever, I guess my name is Phil, now."

As I continued the process of asking "Juicy Questions," I began to peel back the layers of myself like an onion. After parting ways with my girlfriend (who I'd been with for almost 2 years in May of 2014), I dedicated myself to inner reflection. Society had programmed me in a zillion ways of how to dress, how to talk, how to show up in the world, and I decided to truly ask myself, "How do I actually want to present myself to the world?"

As the months passed, and I did my various Healing Practices everyday (explained in a later chapter), new revelations and transformations unfolded. When I became really honest with myself, I discovered that I was feeling sexually attracted to both males and females. For most of my teenage years, I'd been so conditioned to be homophobic that I'd completely rejected any possibility of being Bisexual. It was very liberating to realize this, though it took immense courage and a lot of time to slowly share the news with my friends and family.

Around December of 2014, I took a big leap of faith and told one of my best friends that I felt an attraction to him. I wasn't actively trying to pursue a relationship with him, but I wanted to be honest about how I was feeling. Sharing this "Radical Honesty" was like lifting a huge boulder off my back. I was slowly releasing all of the self-judgment I'd accrued from growing up in the largely homophobic subculture of my high school.

In 2015 I began uncovering my Feminine side, and realized that I definitely didn't feel like "Phil." ... One of my friends would refer to me as "Phil-O" (sounding like Phillow) and I resonated a lot more with that name.

Then I learned that Philo means "Friend" or "Love" in Greek, and that felt like a good fit. As I explored my Non-Binary/ Gender Fluid identity, Philo felt like a good mix of feminine and masculine energies.

In 2016 my Feminine side activated even more, and in meditation, I received the name Lila Rose (pronounced Lee-lah) as a representation of my feminine nature... In 2017 when I moved to Asheville, I decided to start anew and introduce myself as Lila. This felt fairly vulnerable, but it also felt very right and very liberating. I spent the whole summer deeply exploring and expressing my feminine energy. I even considered whether maybe I was trans, and just never could admit it to myself...

I had deeply suppressed my feminine side for many years, and so I needed to let her shine in her fullness...But after the summer I moved back to Florida and then found yet a new equilibrium and integration of my Masculine and Feminine sides...I decided that Philo Lila represented this new balance, and so it is the name I used online and sometimes in real life from 2018 - mid-2020.

Yet another phase began around my birthday - May 26th of 2020. I turned 29 years old, which many people relate to one's "Saturn Return," which often marks entering the next phase of adulthood and involves reassessing many fundamental aspects of life. I decided to completely return to my roots, and fully embrace myself as Kevin May in all arenas (online, offline, and in-line at the grocery store).

As I turned 29, I reflected back on my long Hero's journey of self-discovery. I felt like I had successfully integrated my feminine and masculine, light and shadow, adult and inner child aspects to a new level of wholeness. And it felt really freaking good. I was and still am very proud of myself, and immensely grateful for all the support I had a long the way.

During this whole 11 year journey, my family has always called me Kevin, and many friends as well. I have enjoyed going by Phil, Philo, Lila, or whatever people prefer, and it has given me many teachings into the multi-dimensionality of myself.

The truth is that we all perceive each other through our unique filter, and so if I have 1,000 friends, then there are 1,000 perceptions of who I am out there.

Overall, this journey of Peeling and Revealing has been full of it's ups and downs, smiles and frowns. I'm proud of myself for making it through so many challenges, obstacles, trials and tribulations. Today, and from now on, I give myself full permission to embody my femininity and my masculinity, in whatever way feels in alignment with my core. I also give myself full permission to embody and honor my inner child, and all other aspects of myself.

The journey of self-discovery is profoundly unique for all of us, so I can't really give advice as to how to go about it. But, I can offer perspectives from my journey, as well as many tools which are almost universally empowering for people on a path of self-development. This book is full of helpful tools and frameworks to explore.

SLIVER THEORY

" If the doors of perception were cleansed everything would appear as it is, infinite. "
~ **William Blake**

EVERYTHING in the universe is made of vibrating energy. This energy vibrates at different frequencies and takes on billions of different forms. Our nervous system, (which I refer to as the BodyMind System) filters and organizes information and sensory data inside our brains, and this turns into what we perceive as "reality." Ultimately, we each co-create and live in our own "reality hologram," or version of reality.

Even two people standing right beside each other who witness a car accident, will report two very different stories to the police investigators. **We all filter the millions of bits of information coming at us every second in a unique way, based upon our childhood programming, our cultural biases, biology, and psychological makeup. Each of our individual realities exists inside and is completely connected to the "Big Hologram" (our collective, shared reality.)**

This quote from the "Joe Rogan Experience Podcast" puts some of these truths into perspective :

" You can see less than 1% of the Electromagnetic Spectrum and hear less than 1% of the acoustic spectrum. As you read this, you are traveling at 220 kilometers per second across the galaxy. 90% of the cells in your body carry their own microbial DNA and are not "you." The atoms in your body are 99.9999% empty space and none of them are the ones you were born with, but they all originated in the belly of a star. Human beings have 46 chromosomes, 2 less than the common potato. The existence of the rainbow depends on the conical photoreceptors in your eyes; to animals without cones, the rainbow does not exist. So you don't just look at a rainbow, you create it. This is pretty amazing, considering that all the beautiful colors you see represent less than 1% of the Electromagnetic Spectrum. "

This information gives rise to what I call **"Sliver Theory," which states that our perception in every situation is always limited. We are usually only aware of one tiny sliver of all the possible options, possibilities, and perspectives that are potentially available.** Sliver Theory can be applied to everything from architecture styles, to ancient languages, to hip-hop artists and everything in between.

I particularly like to apply Sliver Theory to Human Culture. The Mainstream culture that most of us have grown up on is only ONE option of the many different cultures existing on this planet. There are around 100 unique tribes still in existence who are classified as "Uncontacted." These tribes have virtually zero contact with civilization. They still hunt with bows and arrows, drink from streams, and build their homes out of natural materials they harvest themselves. Who are we to say that these people are wrong or "living backwards?" "Survival International" is an amazing organization who works to protect Tribal Peoples (both contacted and uncontacted) who choose to remain in their Indigenous lifestyle, rather than the "Main-stream Strange-Dream."

I find it very valuable to see that the "Cultural Norms" we hold in America and many modernized nations are essentially arbitrary. The only reason we think it's the "one right way to live," is because we've been conditioned from day 1 to believe this. Whether it's the style of our clothes or the foods we eat, if you were to fly to a different culture on the other side of the globe, they'd probably look at you like you're crazy. They'd probably drop their jaw if you told them you drink the milk of a cow, while you'd be in shock that they eat gigantic live insects with every meal. Different strokes for different folks! Cultural norms are each a sliver on the gigantic pie of possibilities for human society.

I also apply Sliver Theory to this book "Unlocking Our Superpowers." The maps, keys, and models that I share are useful to the degree they are useful, though they are not necessarily going to capture the fullness of the human experience. These tools are just a tiny sliver in the big pizza of transformational tools that exist.

When you go to a restaurant, the "menu is not the meal", but it gives a helpful description of the delicious food you will soon enjoy. Also, "the map is not the territory," meaning that it will help guide and point the way, though in the end, LIFE IS BEYOND ALL MAPS! It's key to remember that there are always variables. After all, that is why mystics throughout the ages have referred to life as the "Great Mystery."

Whether it's maps, keys, or somewhere in between, I consider myself a "jack of all trades." I know a little bit about a lot of topics. Some areas I have studied and cultivated far more than others. Please, take what I share with a grain of salt, and don't blindly follow what I recommend. Mostly, I hope to catalyze your imagination and curiosity to explore. My goal is to share what has worked for me, and potentially inspire you to explore new topics, tools, and techniques!

~ Unlocking Our Superpowers ~

Part Two

~ Marvelous Maps ~

THE INVISIBLE PATH

BY CHARLES EISENSTEIN

I read this essay back in 2010, and it has been a major guiding force in my journey ever since. I felt as though it was directly describing the various phases of my path of transformation. I believe that using this map as a framework is equivalent to a Superpower, because it gives one a keen sense of perspective of where we've been, where we're at currently, and where we're going. With the permission of Charles, I am including it in this book, because it is such a magnificent map of the human journey. Here it is:

As the age turns, millions of people are pioneering a transition from the old world to the new. It is a journey fraught with peril and hardship and breathtaking discovery, a journey irreducibly unique for each of us. Because we are stepping out into the new, it is also profoundly uncertain and at times lonely. I cannot map out the details of anyone's individual path, but I can fortify you as you walk it and illuminate some of its universal features. My purpose is to give voice to what you have always known (without knowing it) and always believed (without believing it), so that you may breathe a sigh of relief and say, "Ah, I was right all along."

In a sense I am not describing a path at all, since there isn't one in the new territory of the pioneer. Indeed, what I am describing is a *departure* from a path, the ready-made paths laid out before us, and the creation of a new one. You know the ready-made path I'm talking about. Typified by that odious board game "Life," it begins with school, traverses the territory of marriage, kids, and career, and, if all goes well, ends in a long and comfortable retirement. This program has been crumbling for decades now, as high rates of divorce and radical career change demonstrate. I, for one, am not planning for retirement; the very concept feels alien to me, as does the notion that my Golden Years are to be any time other than right now.

I will describe seven stages of the discovery and walking of this invisible path from the old world to the new. I present them in a linear narrative, but usually their progression is not strictly linear. It is, rather, fractal: each stage interpenetrates the rest, and we may skip around a lot, revisit old territory, jump ahead to new, pass through some stages in minutes and others in years. Nonetheless, I think you will recognize some of the major landmarks in your own journey.

Stage 1 : Something is Wrong / Idealism

Idealism is a belief that a more beautiful world is possible; that the world as we know it is deficient, unworthy of our full participation. When idealism is not expressed as action, it turns into cynicism. It is no accident that both idealism and, today, cynicism are hallmarks of youth: young people, being newer to the world, less inculcated with the belief in its permanence, and less personally invested in its perpetuation, can see much more easily the possibility of a better one.

The idealism of youth is a seed of what is to come. The teenager looks out upon some aspect of the world and is outraged. "No force in the universe will make me accept a world in which this happens! I will not be complicit in it! I will not sell out!" Usually this attitude is unconscious, manifesting either as cynicism or as rage, an uncontrollable anger directed at whatever surrogate target is available. Those teenagers with the strongest idealism are often the angriest; we think there is something wrong with them and their anger problem, but really there is something right. Their protest is misdirected, but fundamentally valid.

Our culture fears youth even as we valorize it. We are afraid of that knowledge that the world we have invested in is wrong, and go to great lengths to suppress it, both within ourselves and externally as a war on youth. In a carrot-and-stick strategy, on the one hand we entice youth into complicity with the adult world, while on the other abashing it with patronizing dismissals and intimidating it with severe punishments for lashing out. And so, bought and cowed, we earn the badge of "maturity" and enter the adult world. Bought and cowed, yes, but never broken.

That knowledge of a more beautiful world lies latent within us, waiting for an event to reactivate it. Each time we encounter something unacceptable in our lives or in the world, something that arouses our indignation and protest, we feel our spark of youth being fanned into flame. We can and do put out the fires, repeatedly, but the invitation never stops coming, and it comes louder and louder until we can no longer ignore it. Then it launches us into the next stage, when we act on our indignation, whether consciously or not, and begin looking for the path out of the old world.

Stage 2 : Refusal or Withdrawal

On some level, Stage 2 is always concurrent with Stage 1, but I will describe it separately because so many people are very nearly successful in suppressing the feeling of wrongness, suppressing the intuition of a more beautiful world that is possible, and relegating it to an inconsequential realm: their weekends, their choice of music, or most insidiously, their opinions. People have very strong opinions about what is wrong with the world and what "we" should do about it, and how life "should" be lived, but don't meaningfully act upon those opinions. They like to read about what is wrong with the world and voice their concurrence. It is as if their opinions provided a vent for the indignant anger that would otherwise power real transformation.

The suppression of the desire to transcend the old world is never entirely successful. The unexpressed energy comes out in the form of anxiety, which is none other than the feeling, "Something is wrong around here and I don't know what it is." It can also fuel addiction or escapism, substitutes for the longed-for more beautiful world. Eventually, if all goes well, these props to life-as-usual fail, initiating a withdrawal from the lives we have known.

This withdrawal can take many forms. In my previous essay I discussed depression and chronic fatigue, which are unconscious or semi-conscious refusals to participate in the world. In my own life, for many years the refusal took the form of a half-hearted participation, in which I would go along with some, but not all, of the conventions of compliance. Whether in school or in work, I did just enough to get by, unwilling to fully devote myself to a world I unconsciously knew was wrong, yet not aware enough or brave enough to repudiate it fully either. If you perceive in yourself or another such "flaws" as laziness or procrastination, you may actually be seeing the signs of a valid, noble, yet unconscious refusal.

In other people, the withdrawal takes the form of self-sabotage. You get yourself fired, you engineer an argument or an accident, you inexplicably mess up, you don't take care of yourself and get sick. These are all ways of implementing a decision that we are afraid to make consciously. So if you find yourself immersed in the wrong life but lack the courage to make a break from it, don't worry! You will exit it sooner or later, whether you have the courage to or not. On this path, fear is no more the enemy than is ego or any other New Age bogeyman. A process is grabbing hold of you that is far beyond your contrivance. Your struggles are nearly superfluous as you are being born.

Another means of withdrawal happens when you just get fed up, and you snap. "I quit!" you say. Maybe you tell the boss to shove it. Maybe you drop out of school. At this moment you feel a sense of exhilaration, maybe of satori. It does not last and it does not obviate the upcoming journey on the invisible path, but it is valuable nonetheless as a reminder of your power.

A final and very telling symptom of this stage is the experience of struggle. Because you are still trying to participate and to withdraw at the same time, life becomes exhausting. You have to expend tremendous efforts to accomplish anything. You wonder why your career is stalled, why your luck is bad, why your car keeps breaking down, why nothing seems to click, when other people's careers proceed smoothly. The reason is that unconsciously, you are expelling yourself from the world you've inhabited so you can search for another one.

Stage 3 : The Search

In this stage, you are searching for something, but you don't know what it is. You begin to explore new worlds, read books you would never have been interested in before. You dabble in spirituality, in self-help books and seminars; you try different religions and different politics. You are attracted to this cause and that cause, but although they are exciting, you probably don't commit very deeply to any of them (though for a time you may convert very loudly). You try to figure things out. You want an answer, you want certainty. You want to know what to do.

Sometimes you think you have found it, but after a period of intense infatuation with Zen meditation, or Reiki, or yoga, or the Landmark Forum, or shamanic journeying, you are eventually disappointed every time. Their promise of a new life and a new self is not redeemed, despite a promising beginning, and despite seeing others whose lives seemingly *have* transformed through these. You might conclude you just didn't try hard enough, but redoubled efforts bring no further results. Yet notwithstanding the disappointments, you know something is out there. You know there is another world, another life, bigger and more beautiful than the one you were acculturated to. You just don't know what it is, and you have never experienced it. It is therefore a theoretical knowledge.

The search is in vain. Sometimes you give up for a while and attempt to recommit fully to the life you have withdrawn from. You join back in, but not for long. The self-evident wrongness of that world becomes more acute, and the relapse into depression, fatigue, self-sabotage, or addiction is quick and intense. You have no choice but to continue searching.

Stage 4 : Doubt and Despair

The third stage morphs easily back and forth into despair or doubt, a natural response to the fruitlessness of the search. You think, "There is nothing for me. I don't belong in this world." You think, "Who am I to think I could be an exception to the universal law of sacrifice and self-control for survival's sake? Why did I give up my promising future? Why didn't I devote more energy to staying with the Program? I have made a mess of my life."

In despair, the weight of the world comes crashing down on your shoulders. The various rays of hope you found in your search are extinguished in an all-encompassing darkness. Whatever political causes or spiritual groups you joined, whatever self-help programs or health regimes, all crumble under the onslaught of the powers that seem to rule this world. Quite logically, there is no hope, nor could there be any hope.

At this point, your idealism, your refusal, your search might seem like an enormous, self-indulgent error. Yet at the same time your perception of the wrongness of the world intensifies. You cannot go back, you cannot rejoin the program; but you cannot go forward either, because there is nowhere to go. Your situation is like that of a fetus at the onset of labor. The cervix has not yet opened: there is no light, no exit, no direction to escape the titanic forces bearing down upon you. Every promise of escape, every door you explored in your search phase, is proven to be a lie, a dead end. Desperately you may resume the search, hoping against hope to find it this time, only to plunge even more completely back into despair when your new guru too shows his feet of clay, when your new group shows the same ego and politicking, when your new self-help technique, your new promising lead, turns out to the yet another loop returning you to the center of the same old labyrinth.

At its most extreme, this is an unbearable condition that must nonetheless be borne. Subjectively it feels eternal. It is from such a state that we derive our descriptions of Hell: unbearable and eternal.

Stage 5 : A Glimpse

In the midst of despair, from beyond hope, from beyond possibility even, comes an unbidden glimpse of another world. It comes without figuring out an exit from doubt and despair, whose logic remains unassailable even as it becomes irrelevant. You have caught a glimpse of your destination, the thing you'd been searching for. You might observe that the effort of your search fell a million times short of the power that has finally brought you here. Your quest was impossible — yet here you are! Perhaps it comes in the form of an intense experience of your true power and gifts, of joy and healing, of unity and simplicity, of the omnipresent providence of the universe, of the presence of the divine. It could happen through a near-death experience, a tragedy in the family, a psychedelic plant or chemical, an encounter with a being from another world, a miracle. You will be left in a state of profound gratitude and awe.

This state does not last very long: sometimes just minutes, sometimes days, rarely for weeks. It disappears faster the more you try to hold on to it, and once it is gone it will not come back by trying to replicate the circumstances through which it came before. You might slip back into doubt and despair, you might live a while longer in the old world, but there is a huge difference now. After having had this glimpse, you now *know* that a more beautiful world and a more beautiful life is possible. You know it in your bones, in your cells. Even if from time to time you doubt it in your mind (for the logic of its impossibility still remains), the doubts no longer seem so real, so compelling. You are leaving that world behind.

The glimpse of a new world is not necessarily a single definable event. Well, it is, but this single event might be diffracted onto linear time, spread out over a period of months or years. When it has happened, then the existence of a new life in a new world is no longer something you've just been told about. It is not a matter of religious ideology or New Age opinion. Because it is a real knowing, sooner or later (and usually sooner) it manifests as action in the world, creative action. You begin the next stage: a walk toward the destination you have been shown.

Stage 6 : The Invisible Path

You have glimpsed your destination and felt its promise, but how do you get there? Now begins a real adventure, a journey without a path. Well-marked paths exist to becoming a lawyer, a professor, a doctor, or any other position in the old world, but there is no path toward the next unfolding of your true self. To be sure, you may still embark on a training program or something as part of a radical career change, but you realize that these structures are merely something you recruit into your own pathmaking, and not a path to your destination.

In this stage, real changes happen in your life. You may experience the end of a relationship, bankruptcy, career change, moving to a different part of the country, changes in your body, an entirely different social life and different kind of intimate relationship. You may continue to undergo various crises, but they don't have the apocalyptic, desperate feeling of the earlier stages, but are rather like birth contractions, and indeed your situation is much like that of a fetus in the birth canal, being propelled toward the light. As this phase progresses, you might even have the feeling of having been reborn in the same body (or different body). While some vestiges of your old life will remain, there is no doubt that you are in new territory. You often experience a sense of newness, freshness, vulnerability, and discovery.

The walk toward the state you now know exists is fraught with pitfalls, dead ends, thickets and swamps. You have no markers, no external indicators of the right way. I said there is no path in this new territory, but that is not strictly true. There is a path, but it is an invisible path, a path you work out yourself. Your guides are your own intuition and self-trust. You learn to ignore the voices that say a given choice is foolish, irresponsible, or selfish. Your self-trust is your *only* guide, because the voices of your old world do not know this territory. They have never been there. It is new for you. You find your own way, groping along, taking wrong turns sometimes and doubling back, only to realize that the wrong turn was not wrong after all, but the only way you could have learned the right path.

Many have preceded us into this new territory, blazing trails into new territory for the bulk of humanity to follow as the old world falls apart. We are still among the early ones, though, establishing roles that have never existed before, the roles for a new world. Only a few of them have names: healer, life coach, facilitator, and so forth. Many more are nameless, riding the vehicle of existing occupations. The form of the lawyer may remain, but she is really doing something very different. You may have encountered such people before, angels in the guise of clerks, mystics in the guise of garbage men, saints in the guise of mechanics. Any profession can be a vehicle for healing work; or you may establish an entirely new profession.

The stage of the invisible path differs from the searching stage in that now, you are actually living the new life, or learning to live it. It is no longer the wishful possibility of someone trapped in the old world and longing for the new. While doubt and despair may pay an occasional visit, they do not weigh you down, because you know better. Their logic cannot assail the felt experience of the new being that draws you down the invisible path.

Stage 7 : Arrival

Here is what it feels like to have arrived at the end of the Invisible Path:

1. You do something that makes complete sense given all that you know is wrong about the world. That doesn't mean you can claim to be saving the world. It means, though, that you can look any of the victims of the earth-wrecking, culture-wrecking, spirit-wrecking machine in the eye, unapologetically, knowing that in their heart of hearts they would have you do no differently.

2. You are living in the full expression of your gifts, doing beautiful work for which you are uniquely suited. This need not be work that is commonly recognized in vocational terms. It could be invisible work done as a father, a grandmother, a friend. You may not have a job at all, or you may have an ordinary job, or an extraordinary one, but either way your life will fully engage your gifts. You will feel that you have been of service, and happily. Indeed, you can never be fully happy if your gifts are not fully expressed and received. Ultimately, this is what drives us to search for the Invisible Path to begin with. We are here for a purpose and can never know peace until we find it.

3. You wake up most days happy and excited to live your day. You can hardly stay in bed. You are full of life, because you love the life you are living, and your energy system is therefore wide open.

4. You receive clear feedback from the world that your gifts are received, and that you are participating in the creation of the more beautiful world our hearts tell us is possible.

The journey is not over with arrival. In a way, Stage 7 is the precursor to Stage 1. We are born into a vast new world and a vast new womb, in which we grow once more until eventually we bump up against the limits of that world, too, triggering a new birth process. After a time of exhilarating development in the new world, you may become aware of an even deeper wrongness, or to phrase it more positively, of new needs for creative expression and healing. Each time you go through this process, new gifts become manifest. You have potentialities within you that will not germinate for many many cycles of time.

I am sure that the readership of this essay comprises people in each of the seven stages I have described. Indeed, because they are not necessarily linear or discrete, you might recognize a little of each inside of you. My message to you today is therefore different depending on which stage most defines your experience at the present time.

If you are in the stage of **Idealism / Something Wrong**, my message to you is: You are right! The voices of normalcy are lying. Your perception of a more beautiful world is a true perception, not immaturity or youthful naiveté. So believe, and do not succumb to cynicism.

If you are in the stage of **Refusal / Withdrawal**, I congratulate you on your strength of spirit. That is what is behind your failures, in school, in career. Your refusal is valid, noble even, especially considering you may not even know what it is you are rejecting. And I affirm that underlying feeling: "I was not put here on earth to…"

If you are in the stage of **Search**, I can only offer you a paradox. You will not find what you are looking for by searching, yet only after searching will it find you. The search itself is a kind of ritual of supplication that will bring what you are looking for into your experience. Your efforts attract it to you, even though you cannot possibly find it through your efforts.

If you are in the stage of **Despair**, there is nothing I can do for you except to intensify it. You will never get your proof that something is there. Your logic is airtight. You certainly won't find it in this essay, or from me. You are in this territory for a reason, and the only way out is through, and part of the "through" is for it to seem that there will never be a way out, and even telling you this will not help.

If you have had the **Glimpse** of a new world, then my message to you is, Yes! It is real. It is not a trick. You were shown it for a reason, and would not have been shown it if there were no way to get there.

If you are walking the **Invisible Path**, I suggest that you trust yourself. What looks like a wrong turn is part of the path too. Trust your instincts, follow your guidance, and be brave. It is OK to make mistakes, even huge mistakes. Errors and wrong turns are part of the destiny of the pioneer.

If you have already **Arrived**, then I would like to invite you to take on a new job in addition to what you are doing already. When you interact with people on other parts of the journey, your job is to have complete confidence that they will arrive too, to know it so firmly that you know it for them even when they do not know it themselves. You see others as heroic and hold a space for them to arrive. This message also goes to that part of everyone that knows the new world and is witnessing your unfolding into it.

I would like to emphasize again that these seven stages are not a monotonic progression, and certainly not an ascension from ignorance to enlightenment. They are archetypes that project themselves onto our lives, often following each other in the order I have described but sometimes all mixed together. I myself could almost say that I experience all seven on a daily basis! You might move forward to Stage 6 or Stage 7, only to discover some incomplete remnant of an earlier stage to which you circle back for completion. In fact, Stage 6 includes all the rest, and the whole cycle of seven could also be called the Invisible Path.

On the Invisible Path, there are certain crossroads, waystations, resting spots where we encounter our fellow travelers and share in the mutual knowledge that yes, we are indeed headed toward a destination that is real. I would like for this to be one of those moments.

~ Charles Eisenstein

Now can you see why I had to include this epic essay?! Having this map in your mind is quite a Superpower, because it can give you a bird's eye view of where you are at, whether you are deep in doubt or whether you are feeling fully fulfilled living your purpose. From this bird's eye view, you can then zoom into your current situation and move forward with greater clarity :) Next, I will share a map I drew of the Invisible Path, so that you can envision it in a linear, cyclical, spiral and/or fractal pattern :

THE
INVISIBLE
PATH

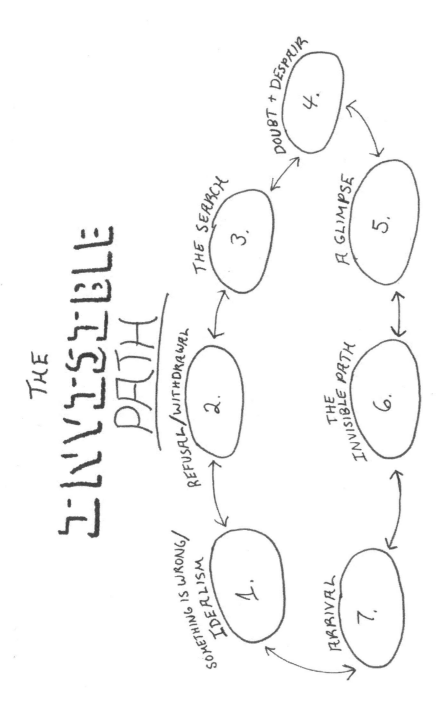

1. SOMETHING IS WRONG/ IDEALISM

2. REFUSAL/WITHDRAWAL

3. THE SEARCH

4. DOUBT + DESPAIR

5. A GLIMPSE

6. THE INVISIBLE PATH

7. ARRIVAL

THE UNCHARTED TERRITORY

As you walk the Invisible Path, (by the way this is Kevin writing now, not Charles) I invite you to envision that you are traveling in a vast territory, similar to "Middle Earth" in the Lord of the Rings. You can see giant snow-covered mountains in the distance. Billowing gray clouds are blowing in from the West. The leaves are bursting with fiery colors as they fall from the trees. Just like Frodo and his crew, during your explorations, you encounter many unique terrains, interactions, and experiences. Each offers an opportunity for growth and development.

Here are a few key metaphorical insights about the Uncharted Territory:

1. In some areas, you can only move forward by going alone, such as crossing a "Crocodile Pond." The only way to progress is to tiptoe across a narrow tree, which has fallen and formed a narrow bridge. No one can hold your hand. You must rely on your own focus, physical stamina, and inner balance.

2. Sometimes you get stuck in a swamp of quicksand. It is completely impossible to escape on your own. You must call out for help. You yell out to a distant passerby, and she throws you a long branch to pull you out. You emerge out of breath and covered in muddy sand. You are eternally grateful for the support of this kind young woman.

3. After travelling solo for large portions of the journey, you sometimes meet fellow Pioneers and share stories by a fire. Many of you have overcome similar challenges. The warmth of the fire and a small gathering of travelers nourishes your soul. This experience reminds you that although the path is invisible, you are not lost, and you are not crazy. You leave the fire feeling rejuvenated and ready to keep exploring.

4. When you reach the top of a mountain, everything seems so clear and the vision ahead looks hopeful. From this glorious view, you don't always see that you must hike all the way down the mountain, wrestle a dragon, cross three swamps, and forage for food before you can climb the next mountain. After overcoming all of these obstacles, you will have learned the proper lessons, and gained a new level of inner strength to climb this next mountain, and fulfill the vision you saw from the previous peak.

5. As you feel your way through this Middle Earth-like terrain, what other insights / metaphors can you derive from the Uncharted Territory?

SIGNS AND SYNCHRONICITIES

Amidst the Uncharted Territory, we can be guided by a wide variety of signs, omens, and synchronicities. These can come in the form of Animal Totems, Numerology sequences, hilarious synchronicities, and much more. In this section I will break down a few examples of things to look out for, and potentially keep track of :

Animal Totems : Indigenous Cultures from every corner of globe have always had a deep connection to the animal neighbors in their area. Whether or not the tribe depends on the animals for food or clothing, they still have a close relationship with these fellow creatures. In Modern Society, many of us have lost touch with all our non-human homies. Thus, it is time to reconnect with our relatives.

Many people nowadays are aware of the concept of having a "Spirit Animal." This is a particular animal that guides you throughout your entire life. Personally, I believe that usually we have multiple Spirit Animals, each with their unique qualities and strengths. In this way, you can call upon Hawk when needing to see the bigger picture, and Bear when you need to go into hibernation, for example.

Many Tribal Traditions teach that any animal or creature that crosses your path carries some sort of message for you. Different tribes have unique meanings for each animal. I have gained so much from studying these teachings, and keeping an eye out for what animals I see day to day. I believe we can also add / discern our own Meaning and Stories from our interactions with animals. I feel a deeper sense of belonging on this planet now that I am befriending and learning from every life-form around me.

If you feel a connection to study Animal Totems, I highly recommend purchasing the "Animal Medicine" cards and guidebook by Jamie Sams and David Carson. They have studied and received the direct teachings of numerous Indigenous Elders from a variety of traditions. The teachings are very practical, applicable, and stunningly accurate! It is truly medicine for the soul!

1. What wild animals / creatures have you recently interacted with?

2. Have any animals / creatures appeared in your dreamworld?

3. In either case, did you feel they were carrying a particular message?

Numerology : There are many books and essays online that give specific meanings to different numbers and sequences. I recommend exploring these on your own. Personally, I like to notice repetitive numbers on the clock or on license plates, such as 333, 444. Particularly, I love to connect with 11:11 on the clock. It feels like a moment to align myself with my intentions and deeper purpose.

Also, it is very cool to imagine viewing your time zone on the globe from an "Outer Space" perspective. Looking down, imagine that everyone looking at 11:11 represents a little light on the map. Thousands, potentially millions of people are all having that "Lightbulb Moment" at the exact same time saying "Woah it's 11:11!!" Together, we create a connected network of lights. In this sense, 11:11 serves as a tool to unify collective consciousness.

1. What numbers do you often see on the clock, licence plates, or elsewhere?

2. Do they hold any particular meaning to you?

3. What correlation do you find between numbers and Sacred Geometry?

Synchronicities : I've heard that Synchronicities can be explained as "A sequence of events that fits together perfectly." Similarly, my friend Michael once said, "No matter how crazy things in your life seem to be, a synchronicity reminds you that you're still on the path."

Essentially, it feels like you are Lucid Dreaming in real life, because you can see the magical connections and purpose behind life. A good synchronicity usually sparks a burst of laughter from everyone involved. Some call it "coincidence" which only makes sense in a universe that is inherently random and lacking unity. That is why people often say "Wow, I can't believe it!" Or "It's too good to be true." But what if the Universe is not chaotic and random?

Once you begin to believe in the interconnectivity of all things, then you see that Synchronicity is the norm. "Wow, I CAN believe it!"

Here are 3 tips to amplify your **Synchronicity Superpowers** :

1. Choose to live spontaneously, and outside normal routine when it feels right.

2. Gather with like-minded, kindred spirits / soul family, and find ways to co-create, support, and inspire each other.

3. Ask Great Spirit "How you can I be of service today?" Then, follow the trail of guidance, signs, and synchronicities.

The Secret Language of Language :
If you begin to look deeper into the English language, you will find many amazing clues into how language shapes our perception of reality. There are a few ways to do this :

1. Break down words into their parts / syllables and re-analyze them.

2. See what words are similar or rhyme together and notice the patterns.

3. Research the etymology and/or ancient meanings of certain words, prefixes, or suffixes.

One example of this is the word "Monday." One day, I was noticing how Saturday represents the planet Saturn and Sunday obviously represents the Sun. I wondered, "Maybe each day of the week connects to a different planet or astrological sign?" Without even doing any research online, I noticed that Monday in Spanish is "Lunes" and the Moon moves in "Lunar Cycles." By looking into the Secret Language of Language, my theory was that Monday used to be called "Moon-day," and over time it was shortened to Monday. I believed the same thing happened with a "Month" or a "Moonth," which is essentially the length of one Moon cycle! A quick Google search into the etymology of these words confirmed my theories to be true!

1. When have you noticed patterns or hidden meanings in language?

2. Have you looked up the etymology / meaning of your first and last name?

3. What are 3 words that you'd like to take a deeper look at?

The Discerning Guidance Superpower :
It's extremely important to keep your head on straight when following "clues." YES! The universe speaks to you in mysterious ways, and YES, it is fairly easy to get "spun out" by looking for guidance

outside of yourself all the time. "Oh my gosh, I just saw an image of Lady Gaga at 11:11pm, that must mean we are gonna be best friends!"

Sometimes, that song on the radio is speaking directly to you, but sometimes you can take things TOO LITERALLY and/or TOO PERSONALLY. The key is to use Discernment. Also, it is important to realize that for the most part, YOU create the meaning of whatever you experience. To some degree, there is "Objective Truth," but for the most part you decide what interpretation to give the events in your life. For example, take an event like a person's house burning down. A Hindu may interpret this to mean that they have bad karma due to a violent act in a past incarnation. A Christian may interpret this to mean that God is mad at them for missing church last week. An Atheist may interpret this to mean that random events unfolded, and there is no big reason to be upset. A Spiritual Optimist may interpret this to mean that one life chapter is over, and a new and exciting opportunity awaits them!

It is important to realize that when you receive clear guidance, messages, or clues, the key is to TAKE ACTION upon what you received, before looking for the next clue. Otherwise, you can go into a tailspin of following clues, and end up in a haze of confusion. Believe me, I know from experience. It's very important to trust your inner instincts, and also bounce ideas off a friend who is in a level-headed place. Sometimes a friend who is very down to Earth can knock some good sense into you :) The key is to use your Discerning Guidance Superpower!

THE INTERNAL COMPASS

(MENTAL) AIR

(SPIRITUAL) FIRE

WATER (EMOTIONAL)

EARTH (PHYSICAL)

— LOVE —
(CONNECTS EVERYTHING TOGETHER)

THE INTERNAL COMPASS

If the path is Invisible, and the territory Uncharted, then how the heck do you know which way to go? What tool could serve you in finding your way? Now is the time to utilize your Internal Compass :)

This compass is a synthesis and distillation of many Traditional Teachings, and I have found it very helpful for navigating life's labyrinths. For eons, humans all over the world

have studied the basic elements for gaining deeper insight on life. The Internal Compass as I share it, is inspired from many traditions, including Chinese Medicine, Astrology, Celtic Wisdom and the "Medicine Wheel" of many Native American Tribes. This Compass is not meant to replace any of those traditional teachings, but simply to offer a basic understanding of the 5 elements.

In many Traditional cultures, medicine is not just something to take if you're sick, it is an integral part of life. Everything in the web of life carries its own "medicine" or sacred teachings and gifts. In her guidebook Sacred Path Cards, wisdomkeeper Jamie Sams writes, "In Native American Tradition, Medicine is anything that will aid the seeker in feeling more connected and in harmony with nature and all life-forms. Anything that is healing to the body, mind and/or spirit is Medicine." (pg. 5) The Internal Compass highlights and guides you to utilize and harmonize with Medicine in its many forms :

EARTH = Physical

Key Attributes : **Grounding, Touching, Resting**

WATER = Emotional

Key Attributes : **Flowing, Cleansing, Feeling**

AIR = Mental

Key Attributes : **Thinking, Breathing, Communicating (with self and others)**

FIRE = Spiritual

Key Attributes : **Observing, Creating, Transforming**

(AIR and FIRE are classified as dominantly Generative and "Masculine")
(WATER and EARTH are classified as dominantly Receptive and "Feminine")

<u>LOVE = The Intersection Point</u>

Key Attributes : **Unifying, Balancing, Harmonizing, Understanding**

As you navigate the Uncharted Territory, you can utilize your Internal Compass to make decisions. For example, when you feel out of touch with your inner self, here are 2 exercises you can explore :

<u>Internal Compass Exercise # 1</u>

1. Pause, sit down, and enjoy some deep breaths, inhaling gratitude, exhaling worry with a big, sighing, "HAAAAAAAA."

2. Ask yourself : What do I want to receive right now? What do I want to give right now? Then, look at the compass and feel into the 5 elements, and see which ones jump out to you.

3. Whatever you are most drawn to is the Element to work with at this time. Here are some notes on the 5 elements :

- Some situations are best solved at the Air / Mental level, others may call for primarily Earth / Physical strength. If you meet a fellow traveler who is deeply sad, you'll probably utilize the Water / Emotional element to provide empathy and compassion. In other cases, you may tap into the Fire / Spiritual dimension, by calling upon Spirit Guides or Angels to assist the situation.

- Love is beneficial in all situations, and can be channelled in a variety of ways depending on what is being called forth.

Here are some ideas for connecting with each element :

Earth : Sitting / Laying on Pachamama, Eating food, Cooking, Massaging, Exercising / Lifting Weights, Holding grounding stones, Doing Grounding Meditation, Sleeping

Water : Showering, Bathing, Swimming, Drinking water / juice, tea, Cleansing, Processing Emotions / Crying, Doing Flowing Movements i.e. Dance, Yoga, Tai Chi

Air : Communicating, Finding new ideas / inspiration via music, inspiring videos, events, Doing Breathwork / Deep Breathing, Going Outside (feeling the breeze), Getting a Fan / Air Purifier / Filter for your home, Exercising your mind

Fire : Expressing your Passion in whatever way inspires you, Spiritual Practice, Lighting a Candle, Connecting to your Spirit Guides / Ancestors / Angels, Sitting / Dancing / Singing around a Fire, Expressing intense emotions

Love : Feeling your Heart, Doing what you Love, Random Acts of Kindness, Connecting with people, pets, things you love :)

Internal Compass Exercise # 2

1. Pick an element that you want to RECEIVE more of in your life.
2. Pick another element that you want to EXPRESS / GIVE more of in your life.
3. For each element, ask yourself 6 questions related to it, beginning with these 6 words :

Who?
What?
Where?
When?
Why?
How?

Example of 6 questions for EARTH :

Who embodies the Earth element in a balanced way?
What does it look like to embody Earth in a healthy way?
Where are my favorite places to commune with Mother Earth?
When during my day do I connect with Mother Earth?

Why is it important to embody the Earth element?
How can I prioritize physical touch and rest?

These are a few examples of how to formulate questions to explore how the elements interact in your journey. I invite you to create your own open-ended questions to whichever elements are most intriguing to you.

Overall, the **Internal Compass is an extremely useful tool for inner reflection, and empowers you to tune into all dimensions of yourself : Physical, Emotional, Mental, and Spiritual.** I recommend drawing your own version of the Internal Compass and referencing it at any point in your day when you want to tune in. Anytime you feel unsure of where to go or what to do, a few minutes contemplating this tool can often give you greater clarity to move forward. Through ever increasing self-awareness, you will be able to better navigate during times of ease, and times of turmoil.

~ Unlocking Our Superpowers ~

Part Three

~ Creating Our Dreams ~

THE KEYS TO CREATIVITY

1. Preparation Phase
2. Dream and Design Phase (V.A.S.T.)
3. Creative Action Phase
4. Completion Phase
3. Summary of the Keys to Creativity

PREPARATION PHASE
a. What is Creativity?
b. Genius In a Bottle
c. Encouragement
d. Personal PepTalk
e. Environment - Outer and Inner
f. Get Out The Way, Let The Universe Play
g. Imagination and Experimentation

DREAM AND DESIGN PHASE
a. V.A.S.T.

CREATIVE ACTION PHASE
a. Intention, Ritual, and Container
b. Support and Perseverance
c. Refinement and Feedback

COMPLETION PHASE
a. **Sweet Success!**
b. **The Power of Reflection**
c. **Sharing With The World**

SUMMARY OF THE KEYS TO CREATIVITY

WHAT IS CREATIVITY?

In my opinion, creativity is a key pillar of life. Throughout the ages, Spiritual Leaders from various traditions have spoken of "Honoring all Creation." Mainstream Christianity essentially teaches that "God created the world in 6 days, and on the 7th day, he rested." Through this lens, "Creation" is the entire planet and all its creatures, which God magically created eons ago, and this Creation is still here for us to enjoy.

I like to see "Creation" as not simply the physical world, which was created in the past, but more of an ever-present wellspring of diverse creations, which are evolving and interacting in new ways every moment! In the past minute, as you read this page, babies are being born, wildebeests are stampeding, a brilliant inventor is having a stroke of genius, lightning is splitting a massive oak tree in two, lovers on a beach are peering into each other's eyes. This is Creation in action! We as humans are a piece of this creation, and with our conscious minds, we can co-create with the other levels of intelligence all across this planet and galaxy! Woah! Pretty cool, eh?

In this sense, to be creative is to move in step with the epic dance party of "Creation."

There are many different definitions of **Creativity**. Personally I like to see it as **bringing something from the realm of pure imagination into an art form that can be shared. Another way to put this is : Turning the IDEAL into the REAL DEAL!**

In order to create beautifully with the rest of the Web of Life, there are **2 key elements to balance.**

1. **Your internal state, i.e. the harmony of body, mind, and soul.**
2. **Your external environment, where you are being creative.**

When these are both in an optimal state, you are best suited to create amazing things, and enjoy the process : In this chapter, I outline the "Keys to Creativity" that have supported me on my creative journey. These Keys both cover and mesh between the internal and external aspects. I also believe that Creativity and Healing are very intertwined. For example, we can express repressed emotions and pain through Spoken Word, and channel that energy in a healthy way. You will find many similarities and parallel themes between this chapter and the "Healing Process" chapter.

GENIUS IN A BOTTLE

" Every block of stone has a statue inside it. The task of the sculptor is to discover it. "
~ Michelangelo

I believe that we all have "Genius" and brilliance within us. It is merely a matter of chiseling away all the excess baggage that is blocking this genius from shining into the world. Many of us have been conditioned to "be practical" or told to "get real" when we become overly imaginative.

It breaks my heart to see so many young people shoved into cookie-cutter jobs and menial labor when I can see their amazing gifts lying dormant beneath the surface. With that said, **a crucial Key to Creativity is to Entertain the possibility that we each have genius within us.**

Can you feel it? Regardless of how much you've been conditioned, there is still a tiny spark deep down that knows you have gifts to give this world. One thing to remember is that sometimes what comes natural and obvious to you is incredibly unique and amazing to others.

Author Derek Sivers has some incredible insight on this:

On **October 16th, 2013 @ 10:49pm,** I posted this paraphrased segment from Derek Sivers' video "Obvious to You, Amazing to Others." I essentially apply what Derek expresses to my own experience :

I am often blown away by the genius put forth from musicians, thinkers, activists, and artists. "How could they have possibly created or thought of that?" I think to myself. I am humbled by their amazing capacity to share their unique gifts.

People often write to me thanking me for my creative ideas, Poetry, and videos. I appreciate the support, though I also feel that many of my insights are completely obvious.

Then I realized that "Maybe everyone's music, ideas, artwork comes natural to them, and seems completely obvious! Maybe what's obvious to me is amazing to someone else!"

Hit songwriters in interviews often admit that their most successful chart-topping song was one that they just thought was stupid and not worth recording. We are clearly a bad judge of our own creations.

We should just put it out and let the world decide. Are you holding back something that seems too OBVIOUS to share?

----

3 Questions on Genius :

1. Who do you know that expresses their Inner Genius out into the world?

2. When have you glimpsed the potential of your own Inner Genius?

3. What comes natural to you that may be amazing to others?

ENCOURAGEMENT

In high school, many of my friends teased me for wanting to be a rapper, and this left a negative imprint on me. I was very cautious not to express myself in a way that would make me the butt of a joke. I only felt comfortable being creative if I was very intoxicated at a party. Even then, I was very nervous and afraid that people would make fun of me.

When I went to college at Penn State, I connected with a new group of friends, where I felt more free to express my true self. As I hung out with these new friends, I had my first experience of a "jam session." This concept was totally new to me. "You mean… we can actually create music — not just listen to it? ... You mean we can generate fun out of thin air?!"

One night, as 6 of us sat in a friend's apartment, two played guitar, one was drumming, another shook a salt shaker, and we all sang together. We smiled and laughed together as we sang songs from the Beatles, Bob Marley, and Sublime. For the first time ever, I beatboxed into a microphone. It sounded so cool! My friends told me I was a great beatboxer. "Me - no way?" I thought to myself. They kept encouraging me, and eventually I was grooving with all the other instruments and had a huge grin on my face. With this new group of friends who actually encouraged me, I felt inspired and motivated to both create and share more often. It felt so good!

I composed my first piece of Slam Poetry in the spring of 2010. My goal was to synthesize many of the complex concepts I was learning about into a format that young people would jive with. I intertwined topics of eco-consciousness, global inequality, and meditation into what later became the title track to my 1st album "Paradigm Shifting Flowetry." Mind you, I was very nervous to share this new art form with any of my friends, because I still remembered being the butt of jokes in high school.

I practiced this piece of Slam Poetry over and over again in my head, and in front of the mirror. Once I finally had it memorized, I knew I had to break through my fears and share it. One night we were way up on a mountain near Penn State having a bonfire. People were chatting and playing music. I didn't want to change the vibe, or have all the attention on me. I looked over my piece of paper with all the lyrics written on it. Something deep within me knew it was time to share.

I asked my friends if they could pause playing music for a few minutes. I took a deep breath and recited "Paradigm Shifting Flowetry" while staring into the crackling bonfire.

Everyone seemed captivated by the lyrics. I stumbled over them a few times, but for the most part I remembered the whole thing! My friends were really impressed. They gave me warm hugs, high-fives, and "mad props." I drove home from the bonfire feeling on top of the world. I was deeply fulfilled and excited to keep sharing Slam Poetry. The encouragement was fuel for my creative fire.

On the note of Encouragement, here is what I wrote on **November 25th, 2014 @ 10:10pm** :

I'm a believer. I believe in you. I'm a believer. I believe in what you do.

I could have never accomplished all that I have in this life without the encouragement and support of so many homies. Encouragement is a priceless gift we can always give to each other. I invite you to see the incredible potential in everyone you meet, and simply by seeing it, you will help them grow and blossom.

May we all see each other with new eyes.

----
3 Questions on Encouragement :

1. What family members or friends have encouraged you in a big way?
2. What impact has their encouragement had on you?
3. Who in your life could you give more encouragement to?

THE PERSONAL PEP TALK

Although outer encouragement is helpful and feels good to receive, the ultimate foundation for your creative success lies within. You must believe in your own dreams and goals, and find ways to encourage yourself to accomplish them.

I highly recommend using your Superpower called the **"Personal Pep Talk."**

You can look at yourself in the mirror, or simply speak to yourself. You can be half-joking, or totally serious. Either way, it will help boost your confidence.

1. List 3 reasons why you're gonna do awesome in whatever endeavor you are taking on! For example "I'm gonna rock this speech on bicycles because I freaking biked across America! I'm gonna rock this speech because I practiced it 100 times! I'm gonna rock this speech because it's going to inspire lots of people to ride bikes!"

2. Visualize and feel yourself getting the results you want.

3. If a challenging situation arises, affirm that you are able to respond in a cool and collected manner.

4. Give yourself a 1-minute **Self Love Hug (Bring your hands across your chest to opposite shoulders and close your eyes)**.

5. Affirm that regardless of what happens, the key is to give it your best.

ENVIRONMENT

Reflential : This is a word I invented, which means **"The environment reflects your greatest potential. It mirrors back to you the ideal vision and lifestyle you are becoming / growing into."**

Example : Jason created his new studio to be Reflential of his love for the wilderness. He set up beautiful altars filled with feathers and stones he had found all over the globe while exploring in nature. This way, every time he entered his studio, he would feel inspired and connected to all of these amazing places and experiences.

The first group of Environmental factors I will outline here are primarily EXTERNAL, and the second group are primarily INTERNAL. They are both intertwined and often reflect each other in "mirror-aculous" ways.

EXTERNAL ENVIRONMENT

1. **LIGHTING** - The quality and quantity of light in a space profoundly impacts your state of consciousness. For example, compare how you feel in a store like Walgreen's, where you are blasted with tons of fluorescent light, with how you feel in a meditation room

where the lights are dim. As any Hollywood filmmaker will tell you, lighting is absolutely key to setting the tone of a space.

I invite you to explore different types of lamps or bulbs in your creative space. I enjoy having medium-intensity lighting when I am in an active state of creativity. Blue colored lights can also enhance the vibe. I love having a Himalayan salt and candle light when I am in a reflective or restful space. I am seriously in love with Himalayan Salt Lamps! They add such an amazing element to a creative / healing space.

1. Does your space receive direct sunlight?
2. How does direct sunlight affect your creativity?
3. What is your ideal lighting for active creativity?

2. **AIR QUALITY** - In order to have sharp mental clarity, fresh air is pivotal. I recommend having a decent air filter and/or a fan in your creative space. Also, be conscious of accumulated dust in your environment. If you are able to have fresh air from outside, that is wonderful too. Deep and conscious breathing also help to circulate oxygen throughout your body, and keep your brain in a state of relaxed focus.

3. **SMELLS** - What smells inspire you and catalyze creativity? I sometimes enjoy natural scented candles or use my Essenital Oil Diffuser. I also recommend putting 20-30 drops of your favorite Essential Oils in a spray bottle with fresh water, and creating a "spritzer" / "mister." Hey, maybe you can call it Mr. Spritzer :)

4. **FOOD / DRINK** - What tastes or foods inspire you to get into a creative state? Do you find that having a mostly empty or full stomach serves your creativity? What do you prefer to drink while you are in the creative zone?

Personally, I enjoy sipping some warm tea and having a big jug of alkaline water. My favorite teas are "Traditional Medicinals", specifically "Throat Coat", "Breathe Easy" and "Cup of Calm". There are many delicious varieties.

Pure SereniTEA Superpower : I recommend using 2 tea bags per mug of tea, instead of one. This makes it at least 77% more robust and delicious!

(see chapter called Phenomenal Food for more info on foods / drinks)

5. **SOUND** - What sound environment is ideal for you? Ambient? Music with lyrics? Loud / Quiet? What type of speakers do you have?

Laptop and phone speakers nowadays are decent quality, though real speakers with bass create an amazing vibration for being creative. I believe that the better quality the speakers, the more powerfully they can set the tone of a space and truly have a profound, transformative effect on your state of consciousness.

6. **VISUAL ATMOSPHERE** : What colors, images, artwork and other eye candy is ideal for your creative space? I like to decorate my room with pictures of people who inspire me, lots of bright colors, and images related to the goals I am working to accomplish.

I also loooooove VISIONARY ART! I recommend adding some to your Creative Space and/or ingesting this "visual food" each day on the Internet. A good place to start is to search "Visionary Art" page on different online platforms.

After returning from a Transformational Festival which was abounding with visionary art, this is what I posted on **September 27th, 2013 @ 9:29pm** :

There is a potent mind-altering substance spreading around the planet at a rapid pace. If used properly, this substance can catalyze very powerful shifts in consciousness...

What is this substance? ...
PAINT !
Visionary artwork, largely originating from transformational festivals such as Burning Man, has blasted me into other dimensions simply from staring into these epic "masterpeaces" for several minutes…

Here are a few of my favorite visionary artists. I recommend soaking up their rich imagery online, buying some prints, and/or printing out some of their magic :

Pablo Amaringo, Amanda Sage, Jah Ishka La, Krystleyez, Michael Garfield, Baron Batch, and Autumn Skye Morrison

7. **SPACE TO MOVE / DANCE** : I believe that creative energy flows best when we let it move through the whole body. Because of this, it is important to have open floor space to dance and jump around when you have a creative burst. It's also important to celebrate mini-accomplishments with a 5-minute dance party! Having decent speakers helps to pump up the jams :)

8. **OVERALL VIBE / CLEANLINESS** : What is the overall energy / feel of your creative space? If the environment you are in was food, would it be appetizing? Is there unnecessary clutter in your space? (Clutter creates stagnant energy and blocks the good vibes, bro!) Is your creative space somewhere that you truly feel "at home"?

How is the flow of energy / feng shui? In regard to this, I don't know all the in's and out's of feng shui, though from what I gather, it's beneficial to have all the elements represented. For this, I like to have some sort of living plants (Earth), a beeswax candle / Himalayan Salt Lamp (Fire), a fan / Air Purifier (Air), and one of these days I will have a fish tank (Water). And the 5th element which I call Love is a feeling that I cultivate while being creative.

You can also check out a cool guidebook called "Using Feng Shui" by Antonia Beattie.

9. **COLLABORATION** : Do you prefer to create directly with other people? Do you like to be around other people, even if you are not working together? Do other people's energy or conversations easily distract you?

INTERNAL ENVIRONMENT

1. **PACE** : What is the pace / speed you prefer to create with? I find that other people often move too quickly for me, and I prefer to go at my own pace. I like to enjoy the subtleties during the process, and stay aware of my breath. I've noticed I make silly mistakes and get unnecessarily stressed out if I try to move too fast. Also, choosing specific types of music can determine at what pace I prefer to move.

I invite you to explore different paces while working on projects in order to find your preferred sweet spot. (Your pace may be linked to how much coffee / chocolate you have consumed :)

2. **BODY-MIND STATE :** Your creative productivity has a direct correlation to how well your BodyMind System is operating. If you feel healthy and strong, you will have much better results and be able to stay in the creative zone. If you are feeling drained, mentally unclear or emotionally blocked, then it will be tough to make much progress on your projects.

Cultivating a healthy BodyMind System includes a lot of different aspects, which are covered more in the other chapters of this book. As you practice the tools offered there, I am quite confident you will see it reflected in your creativity.

Also, I don't claim to be a Sex Coach or a Kama Sutra Expert, though I know that our sexual energy is directly connected to our creativity. Personally, I notice that when I feel sexually fulfilled and my life-force energy is flowing through my lower chakras, I have more creative drive and motivation. **Here are a few questions to explore around Sexuality :**

1. Are your Sexual needs / desires being met?
2. How can you channel this energy into your creative projects?
3. Does abstaining from sexual pleasure increase your creativity?

3. **POSTURE** : To allow creative energy to flow smoothly through your BodyMind System, a healthy posture is highly recommended. As mentioned in the "Healing Process" chapter, I recommend exploring the basics of Vinyasa Yoga and/or Qi Gong to practice good posture, and to learn how energy flows throughout your system. The main keys are to have a straight spine, relaxed shoulders, and to avoid hunching.

Personally, when on the computer, I like to stand up and have my computer keyboard a few inches below my navel. This allows me to stay present in my body, and to keep my energy and blood circulating as I type and surf the web. This has been such a game-changer for me that I have officially deemed it the **"Stand-up Desk Superpower."** If you want to set one up for yourself, I invite you to be creative in finding a desk, or small shelf that is about waist height. Next, you can stack textbooks or something else, to bring your computer / notepad to the optimal height for your comfort :)

If you do prefer to sit down while typing, painting, etc. you can also explore sitting on an exercise ball or purchasing an ergonomic chair to support your posture.

4. **BREAKS** : Are you taking breaks once an hour or so to check in with your body, stretch, and/or go outside for a few minutes? This helps me to stay mentally clear, and keep the vital energy in my body flowing. I also like to have spontaneous 5-minute dance parties :)

5. **HEALTHY SLEEP** : Related to Lighting is the theme of healthy sleep. If you are not getting enough good quality sleep, this can diminish your creative abilities. Science shows us that sleeping in pitch black is ideal for the maximum production of Melatonin as well as DMT, both chemicals produced at the center of the brain in the Pineal Gland. I like to sleep with a t-shirt over my eyes to ensure that little to no light gets in to my brain as I rest.

The Pineal Gland is what many Spiritual Traditions refer to as the "Third Eye." Located in the center of the brain, this has also been called the "Seat of the Soul," and I believe that if the Pineal Gland is functioning optimally, then our Creativity shoots through the roof!

In Mainstream Society, there are several factors that have contributed to the "Calcification" of the Pineal Gland, meaning that an MRI scan would show a lump of Calcium Phosphate around this gland. The primary causes are Fluoride in water, and toxic chemicals, pesticides and preservatives in the foods we've eaten. Other studies link heavy cell phone usage, and watching television to the calcification process. As comedian Bill Hicks half-jokingly says, "Watching television is like taking black spray paint to your Third Eye."

So what can we do to reverse this process? Luckily there are many steps we can take to cleanse our Pineal Gland and experience our birthright of Creative Genius. I encourage you to do your own research online, to find which supplements and dietary habits work well for you. To get you started, here a few key foods, supplements, and practices to explore :
- Filtered, Alkalized, and/ or Spring Water
- Alkaline Diet with lots of green vegetables
- Dark and/or Raw Chocolate
- MSM
- Fasting, Cleansing, Meditation, and Intense Exercise
- Cold Showers

(A Holistic Diet is explored more in the chapter "Phenomenal Food.")

GET OUT THE WAY LET THE UNIVERSE PLAY

Once you've got your Outer and Inner Environment tuned to the right station, how do you get in the zone to create at your peak level? For me, the key is essentially to "get out of my own way."

Here's a little story I Posted on : **November 21st, 2013 @ 10:18pm** :

I listened to strictly hip-hop and rap music from age 12-17. I probably know every single lyric to over 500 gangsta rap songs. During this time I had dreams of being a rapper. I thought it would be especially cool to freestyle (to develop rhymes spontaneously in the moment).

Two years ago, I had a vision while working with a powerful plant medicine. I saw a gigantic cosmic wheel (like the one on the Price Is Right), which contained every rhyming word in the English language...

In the vision, I aligned my consciousness with this epic Rhyme Wheel, and thus I could download an immense amount of rhyming words at the snap of a finger.

After the experience, my consciousness returned to its ordinary state. I would receive awesome rhymes and wordplay, which over time I crafted into composed pieces of Poetry...but I still couldn't rhyme spontaneously like the freestyle rappers... until ...

One morning in Pittsburgh, I woke up from a dream with the rhyme repeating in my head "Get out the way, let the universe play! Get out the way, let the universe play"... I metaphorically got out of my own way and the floodgates opened up. I began joyously freestyling for the next 15 minutes.

Over the past 4 months, I have continued to get out the way and let the Universe play, and it has been extraordinarily fun to have freestyle circles with fellow rhymers and beatboxers.

Letting the Universe play through us means that we must trust what comes through us, and not be overly judgmental about it.

This story is an example of how I finally was able to "Let go and flow." Many scientists and researchers have studied various professionals from adventure sport athletes to

Fortune 500 CEOs to discover what factors determine our "peak performance." The conclusion is that we are most creative and productive when we are in "FLOW." **A state of flow is when you become totally enmeshed in the present activity.** People often describe "flow states" as losing track of time or merging with the process of life itself. Sometimes this includes tremendous effort, sometimes it requires total surrender. Sometimes it means moving fast, other times it means sitting still. The ancient teachings of Taoism essentially teach how to live in a flow state. Often called the "watercourse way," Taoism gives the metaphor of a river or stream as a great teacher. At certain points, we embody the raging rapids, at other times we embody a slow, gentle flow.

" Nature does not hurry, yet everything is accomplished. "
~ Lao Tzu (founder of Taoism)

Force is when we are not in a flow state. It is like trying to push a river. It's fruitless, and a heroic effort yields almost no results. When we are in flow, however, a gentle movement yields massive gains. It does take practice to master the art of "going with the flow." It requires tuning into the feelings and thoughts that keep us in a flow state. A flow state can be found in essentially any activity from painting, running, or making love. It is a state of dynamic balance between polarities : fast and slow, masculine and feminine, electric and magnetic, hot and cold.

The various maps and tools offered in this chapter and throughout this book will assist you in navigating the many aspects of your "flow state."

IMAGINATION AND

EXPERIMENTATION

" Possibility is as wide as the space we create to hold it. "
~ Climbing Poetree (female Spoken Word duo)

Alixa and Naima of Climbing Poetree are absolutely incredible creators, and they have certainly tapped into the **Keys of Creativity** in their own magical ways. They've inspired me to dream big and infuse passion and truth into all the words that I share. (I highly recommend checking out "Awakening by Climbing Poetree" on YouTube.)

I believe that the life we create for ourselves is as good or bad as our ability to imagine. If we think from a place of infinite possibility, then that creates the space for us to grow and evolve into our true potential.

As little kids, we have vibrant imaginations, and can envision ourselves as anything : a pro athlete, a firefighter, a rockstar, a painter. As we grow into adults, we are often conditioned to "be practical" and choose an average career or walk a path that has been laid out for us. This usually leads to a dull life, where we feel uninspired and unfulfilled. It is time to reclaim the power of imagination and turn our dreams into reality.

To reclaim imagination, you must reclaim your CURIOSITY to EXPLORE and EXPERIMENT. Before you choose a big Creative Project to devote yourself to, I invite you to spend some good ol' time just playin around!

Here are some Key Questions to get your Curiosity Gears Turning :

1. What did you enjoy doing / playing with / creating as a child?

2. Do any of those activities still intrigue you?

3. What makes you laugh? (There is always something magical to be found in what makes us laugh.)

4. What places in your hometown / region spark your curiosity / creativity?

5. What skills / arts do you find most captivating? Amazing guitarists? Breakdancers?

Now, I invite you to run some experiments. You can use the tools provided in the next section loosely while you Experiment with some mini-projects.

---- Okay, so now that you know you are a genius, you feel encouraged, you've set up your inner and outer space, and you've imagined, explored and experimented various possibilities, it's time for your "Creative Project" to emerge. First, I will guide you through the V.A.S.T. model, then I will provide tools for you to complete your project in a wonderful way. And if you don't feel like getting into the nitty gritty steps of the Creative Process right now, I invite you to skip forward to pg. 73 or hop around to other parts of this book that look interesting :)

DREAM AND DESIGN PHASE

THE V.A.S.T. MODEL

V for Vision

1. Do a Brainstorm / Heartstorm : For 15 minutes, write down all your ideas, without any limitations. Imagine that you had all the money, resources, and a team to build your vision. What would you create? Ask yourself : What vision wants to emerge through me? (I recommend writing each idea in a little thought bubble, and drawing lines and connections between them. Feel free to be creative in how you draw your ideas!)
2. After the 15 minutes is up, start to simplify your ideas into one project that you want to focus on, and literally turn the IDEAL into the REAL DEAL.
3. Dive into the specifics of this project, and outline the Who, What, Where, When, Why. What will it feel like to bring this dream into reality?

A for Assessment :

1. What are your Needs to fulfill your vision?
2. What Tools, Resources, People, Venues are you already connected to and able to use?
3. Which of these Tools, Resources, People, Venues do you want to pursue?
4. What sort of Support Structure will help you to break through Resistance and Challenges along the way? (Similar to the Vision Phase, I invite you to create an "Asset Map, where you write each Asset from the questions above in a little thought bubble, and then draw lines and connections between them.)

S for Strategy :

1. Break down all the "Action Steps" necessary to bring your Creative Project from the Ideal to the Real Deal. This process is intimately linked with step 4 of the "Timeline". The layout of your action steps is dependent on the amount of time you aim to accomplish your project. For example, if you want to finish the project in 1 month, rather than 6 months, you'll need to create some larger blocks of time devoted to Creative Action.
2. Create a Ritual and Container for you to easily get in the zone (more details on this in the next section).

T for Timeline :

1. You want to map out the dates on which you plan to complete the various parts and Action Steps of the project. It is fun to experiment with different ways of visually laying out your timeline. For example you can use a cyclical, or spiral, design and highlight each week and/or month.

Now, you've got your preparations made and project designed in the V.A.S.T. Model, so it is time for …

<u>CREATIVE ACTION !</u>

In order to turn the IDEAL into the REAL DEAL, I've outlined some key tools and aspects to explore :

a.   **Intention, Ritual and Container**
b.   **Support and Perseverance**
c.   **Refinement and Feedback**

a. Intention, Ritual and Container

Intention : What type of energy do you want to weave throughout your Creative Project? The key is to have the end goal as a part of your vision, but to also enjoy the process and let the project evolve organically as you go.

Here is an example of an intention I had for my 4-week Online Course "Conscious Creative Expression" : I intend to facilitate a fun, interactive, and transformative course, which will bring about greater clarity and creative empowerment to everyone who takes this journey with me.

Ritual and Container : In order to manifest your Creative Project, it is helpful to create a "Ritual", which makes creativity "Habitual." You need to first set aside the **Time** where you will devote yourself to this project. I recommend choosing blocks of time on your calendar, and make a creativity date with yourself. Whether it's 20 minutes or 4 hours doesn't matter so much as that you get into the zone and get your creative juices flowing. Find a time of day where you can set aside the distractions and tasks of daily life.

It is also key to have the proper **Space** to ritually work on your project. Is your Creative Environment clean and inviting, crystalline and exciting? It is also important to cultivate a healthy "Inner Environment" so that you can think clearly, and have decent posture while creating. I will also add that some of my big creative bursts have come when I felt off kilter, angry, or sad, so don't be afraid to channel all sides of yourself.

If you flip back a couple pages, you can refer back to the "Environment" section for more ideas on setting up your Creative Space.

Time and Space together form your "Creative Container" : By setting aside all distractions and carving out a block of time, you allow your Subconscious Mind/Body to relax. If you also resonate with your space, then it will be much easier to get in the zone, have fun, and be productive!

If you feel inspired, you can add to your "**Creative Ritual**" by lighting a candle, calling in your Spirit Guides / Creative Muse, and/or setting a specific intention for that block of time. Don't forget to have fun!

----

b. Support and Perseverance : Along the path of your Creative Project, you will inevitably come up against **Resistance, Naysayers, and Challenges.** Thus, it is key to have a **Support System**, and to use the **Power of Perseverance!** Your Support System and Perseverance Power go hand in hand. Both feed each other in a "Nutritious Cycle" rather than a "Vicious Cycle."

Support : Your "**Support System" is the total combination of People, Places, and Things that will empower and encourage you to keep creating despite challenges.** This system will be crucial to shield you from the inevitable onslaught of naysayers (mostly inner critics) and other obstacles in the creative process. Don't let this scare you because the challenges create the contrast necessary to maintain creative tension and continue growing.

- **Supportive People :** These are people who can see the vision you are manifesting, and will keep you accountable for the goals you set. They will encourage you to be your best. They can also serve as honest feedback on your project as you bring it into fruition (see next part on Refinement). It is sometimes helpful to have 1 or 2 friends who serve as "coaches" to cheer you on, and make sure you haven't given up on your dreams.

- These supportive people stand in stark contrast to the many people and inner critic voices that will doubt you along the way. The critics will say anything possible to demoralize you. It's as if they are throwing out bait, just patiently waiting for you to bite it. "Your idea has already been done before." "You are a crappy artist, writer, singer, etc." "You will never make any money doing this." "Nobody cares what you have to say."

- The big 2 questions are : Will you believe these limiting perceptions and bite the bait of these naysayers? Or… Will you remain firm in your creative project, trusting that your intention, vision, action plan, support team, etc. will carry it to fruition?

- **Supportive Places / Things / Activities :** I find it very helpful to take a break from my personal project and absorb some good vibes from other artists and places. What other creative projects fuel your inspiration? Go to a festival! Go to an art show! Go to a live music performance! These often serve as an injection of inspiration into your creative bloodstream, and remind you of why you are a creative being! This taps into the **"Direct Experience Superpower", which states that "What makes us feel fully alive is the felt presence of direct experience in our BodyMind System. It is crucial to discover what activities bring us deeply into the moment and a state of Wonder-standing the dance of life."**

The Power of Perseverance :

" *Life is not about how many times you fall down. It's about how many times you get back up.* "
~ **Jaime Escalante**

The Creative process often brings up a lot of our doubts and fears because the outcome is Unknown. This is very scary to the "limited self," which only feels comfortable with the familiar. Therefore, to be a creative pioneer means that you must develop a relationship with your fears, doubts, and the very real obstacles that will arise on your path.

The goal is not to conquer fear, but to keep a courageous attitude and cultivate your Perseverance Superpowers! Here are a few ideas for that :

High Tide and Low Tide : This is a concept that was shared by a good friend with potent Superpowers, Amateo Ra. **The High Tide** phase is when everything is cruising along and you are creatively expressing, having great results, and overall feeling awesome! **The Low Tide** is when things slow down, and you don't feel creative, energized or productive. This is the best time to cultivate self-care practices. Both High and Low are part of the natural ebb and flow of life. The key is to be aware of both phases, and know how to navigate each one with a level of Mastery.

Here are 3 questions for you to explore on High Tide / Low Tide :

1. For you personally, what are some signs of your High Tide and Low Tide phases?
2. How can you more masterfully navigate the High Tide mode?
3. How can you surf the Low Tides more smoothly?

Passion and Emotion : The deep passion you have to improve the world is the driving force that can reignite your motivation, when you've temporarily lost your spark. The emotions you feel — and the empathy you have towards people all over the world going through tough times — can serve as fuel for your fire.

Here are 4 questions on Passion and Emotion :

1. Why do you do what you do?
2. What cause / injustice makes your heart / stomach ache?
3. How can you use your gifts / skills to make a positive difference in the world?
4. What brings your heart the greatest joy?

----

c. Refinement and Feedback :

It is crucial to remember that you are not alone in your creativity. Sometimes I think I have to do a project all by myself, though when I open to the input and feedback of friends, I often have huge breakthroughs and realize the process is easier than I initially foresaw.

Trust the Process : It is important to let your project evolve organically. Let yourself be fairly flexible with the outcome, and trust that there is a larger creative spirit weaving through you. To co-create with this larger, mysterious force is a miraculous process. Many times I receive a vision that sparks a project, and, in addition to mapping it out, I leave space for it to evolve as I receive feedback from friends, family, spirit guides, etc.

Refinement : Remember how Michelangelo explained that the statue already exists within the piece of marble, and that you must simply chisel away the excess? This touches on **the Superpower of Refinement. It is a process of honing your craft / project until it reaches a state that truly reflects your best efforts and greatest potential.** With this in mind, it's also important to be wary of perfectionism, where you never finish a project because you are too concerned with reaching an unreachable ideal.

Refinement requires 3 main ingredients :

1. Humility : The recognition that your first attempt at anything is not usually your best, and that you must practice over and over again to cultivate a masterpiece in whatever area you focus on. We all make errors, and we all have blind spots, so it's crucial to cultivate a healthy foundation of humility.

2. Openness : You must also be humble enough to receive feedback from others and tweak your project if the outside opinion resonates with you. Friends, family, and mentors can help you see your creation from a new perspective, and potentially illuminate some of your Blind Spots.

3. Strong Internal Compass : Tying in with the first two, you must also hold strong to your core values and inner truth. You will certainly come up against naysayers who nag at you to do it their way, or they tell you "It can't be done." The key is to have a strong connection with what you know to be true, so that you can't get shaken by all the doubters.

3 Questions on Refinement and Feedback :

1. In the past, how have you responded to Feedback from others?

2. How has Feedback benefitted your creative process and how has it been a detriment?

3. What are some of your Blind Spots when it comes to Creativity? Trick question! You can't see them! Haha, just kidding, but truly we often cannot see some important aspects of our project, which is why feedback is so beneficial.

COMPLETION PHASE

a. Sweet Success!
b. The Power of Reflection
c. Sharing With The World

Sweet Success! **:** Finally finishing a project that you've poured your blood, sweat and tears into is a glorious feeling. Just like the gestation process of a human child takes 9 months, the Creative Process always takes time, and is usually full of ups and downs, smiles and frowns. In 2013, I witnessed two close friends in California hold their newborn son in the hospital. It was truly a miracle to be in the presence of this birth process. This newborn being was the result of immense love coming from both parents. I believe our Creative Projects are quite similar. To be able to stand back and say, "Wow, look what I co-created with the Universe!" is one of the greatest parts of being alive.

I spent all of October 2014 running a Crowdfunding Campaign for the "New Eyes Tour." The goal was to raise $5000 to produce a high-quality album and then tour the West Coast performing at events with a focus on inspiring young people. After the campaign was over, this is what I posted on **October 25th, 2014 @ 8:37pm :**

In my opinion, a Failure or a Success is always a matter of perception. I believe that every option on the spectrum from F- to A+ contains a unique set of lessons, and blurs the line between failure and success.

I did not reach my initial goal in dollars for the New Eyes Tour Campaign. Does this mean it was a failure? From some perspectives, it does. If we look from a different angle, then we may see Borat with his thumb up, saying "GREAT SUCCESS!"

Here is my **Recipe for Success** *:*

1. Give it your best effort.
2. Enjoy each part of the process, even the minute details.
3. Ask for support - The tribe is always stronger together.
4. Keep a sense of humor.
5. Have a clear sense of WHY you do what you do.
6. Don't get too attached to the outcomes.
7. Trust that the outcome is exactly what you need.

... I did my best to embody these principles throughout the Campaign and plan to keep it up. I am deeply grateful to all of you who added your love, support, and resources towards this co-creative project.

3 Questions on Success
1. When have you achieved the feeling of success?
2. What have you learned from situations that felt like failures?
3. How can you integrate the "Recipe for Success" into your projects?

The Power of Reflection : The process of "Reflection" is highly beneficial so that you can look back on your Creative Process and see what worked well, and what didn't work so well. Haha, when I think of reflection, I imagine Simba in the Lion King staring into the lake and seeing the image of his father Mufasa's deep voice saying, "Simba… Remember who you are!" Perhaps by deeply reflecting on your Creative Process, you can also remember who you are and your purpose on this planet. With that said, **here are some good questions to get you started on Reflecting :**

1. What did you enjoy most about the Preparation Phase?
2. What part of the Preparation Phase was most challenging?
3. What part of the Preparation Phase will you change for your next project?
4. How did the V.A.S.T. Model serve you during your project?
5. Did you keep up with your Strategy and/or Timeline?
6. Did your Vision manifest how you initially envisioned it?
7. Were you able to make consistent progress by creating a Creative Ritual?
8. How will you change your Ritual / Container for your next project?
9. How was your Support System helpful in overcoming challenges?
10. What were the biggest obstacles that you persevered through, and how did you do it?
11. What refinements did you make to your project, and how did that benefit the final outcome?
12. What outer Feedback did you receive and how did that affect your project?
13. What were 3 "magic moments" you remember from any point during your Creative Process?
14. What are the big 3 "Take Home Lessons" you learned, which you can apply to your next endeavor?

Sharing with the World : Now the time has come to share your project. I invite you to step out of shyness and embrace the honor of showing others what you've created. It may be intimidating to put your precious creation out there, but I feel that this is our duty as artists! We have truly co-created with the entire web of life, so it is only in the illusion of separation that we should hide our creations from the world.

The Keys to Creativity can be applied to a vast variety of Projects from designing a magazine, to planning a Yoga Retreat to building a sculpture for Burning Man. **Here are a few questions to ask about Sharing with the World:**

1. Where are some events, venues, or places you can share your Creative Project in person?
2. Where are some Online Resources that you can use to share your Creative Project?
3. Who are the best people to connect with who can assist you in accomplishing #1 and #2?
4. Do you feel called to Sell / Trade / and/or Gift your Project? What Energy Exchange feels most authentic to you?

SUMMARY OF THE KEYS TO CREATIVITY

Wow! What a magical process this is! I am proud of myself for persevering through years of trial and error & ups and downs to reach these understandings of Creativity. I am grateful for all the support and guidance I've received, and I'm excited to be able to share all that I've learned with you!

To bring it all together, here is a lil spontaneous Poetry :

Yo, the first key is to understand "What is Creativity?"
So you can co-create with creation, and express your divinity.

Next you gotta liberate that Genius that's been trapped in a Bottle,
So you can sing, dance, play - and move full throttle.

Receive the Encouragement of your mentors and peers,
Give Pep Talks to yourself to break through your fears.

Cultivate a good Environment, both Inner and the Outer,
This will keep you strong to overcome all the Doubters.

Cuz the Doubt dissolves, when you flow with the Tao,
All you gotta do is Be Here Now, and Allow :)

Get your third eye movin', and stretch your Imagination,
With curiosity ablaze, it's time for Experimentation.
And whaddya know, we are done with the phase of Preparation.

Now we begin to Dream and Design.
So Heartstorm and Brainstorm to get your Vision aligned.
Next you Assess how to make that Vision a Reality.
Break it down, yo! That's the way of Practicality.

Last you set everything up on a Di-vine Timeline.
Boy oh Boy, aren't you happy it's Rhyme-Time?

Got the Lights and Camera set, but you're feeling dissatisfaction,
Oh snap, yo! It's time for Creative Action!

Light your candles, call your angels, and set a strong Intention,
Create a great Container to grow your Invention.

To make progress on your project, I recommend a Ritual,
Then, "Getting in the Zone," will be easy and habitual.

Making smooth progress, give yourself a pat on the back,
Soon you'll be at the finish line, way ahead of the pack.

So, find some friends and mentors to be your System of Support,
And Persevere past the Doubters, like Michael Jordan on the court.

Refine the rough edges and be open to Feedback.
Don't do it all yourself, a "Helping Hand" - you Need that :)

Wow, you made it through the trials and tribulations.
With The Keys to Creativity guiding you through the navigations.

Now you get to taste "Sweet Success"
The big question is "Did you do your best?"
Did you infuse your Art with joy and zest?
Where can you display your art - maybe a fest?

Now, before you move off in a new direction,
Be still like Simba, it's time for quiet Reflection.

Did you bring your Vision from high in the sky,
So that now you can share it on the ground?
What moments were the most profound?
And what will you change next time around?

Anywho, I say Scoobally Doo,
Big Thanks to You for being You!
That you-nique lens
Which the You-niverse see's through!

Now, I ask that you share the Keys to Creativity
So more beings can Co-Create from now into Infinity!

(((<3)))

~ Unlocking Our Superpowers ~
Part Four
~ Healing is Cool! ~

<u>PERMISSION SLIPS AND MORPHIC FIELDS</u>

For a long time I had heard of the "Master Cleanse" and it was described as a completely life-changing experience where people who took the 10-day journey felt totally transformed on the other side. Folks reported their skin had a whole new glow, while others said their internal organs felt brand new. I had been intrigued by this 10-day cleanse for about 3 years, though I will honestly say that 10 days without solid food seemed totally impossible for me. I love eating food, and the longest I'd ever fasted was 3 days, which seemed like enough for me.

With that said, during the summer of 2015 I felt like I needed to do a cleanse. I decided to stop eating solid food, and initially only aimed to go for 3 days. After about 72 hours without food, I felt surprisingly good. I still had a lot of energy, and was feeling strong enough to do a decent dose of daily exercise. As I sat in meditation on that 3rd day, I heard the words "Master Cleanse" coming to me from who-knows-where.

It instantly resonated and I knew I had to do it. I sensed it would be very challenging, but totally worthwhile in the long run. I began doing research and decided that I would focus on cleansing my Lymphatic System (essentially the sewage system of the body, which can get backed up with toxins and chemicals if we don't flush it out. Rather than focus on the specific regimen of the "Master Cleanse", I would follow my intuition as far as what to drink and how much. My main goal was to go 10 days with no solid food.

I bought a few different types of juice to utilize during this new endeavor. Because I was focusing on cleansing my lymph, I was also putting Castor Oil all over my body every other day as a way to drain the lymph nodes. In addition, I would add some cayenne powder to apple juice each day to stimulate the lymph. The third key to draining the lymph is movement and massage. Every day I was practicing yoga, going for a light jog, and doing deep tissue massage on my body, to loosen up tight spots where the lymph can build up.

On the 5th day of the cleanse I was very proud of myself, seeing as this was 2 days longer than I'd ever been without food! My skin felt a lot healthier, and I wasn't really craving food. But could I really go another 5 days?! I needed some sort of confidence booster…

This is where the theme of "**Permission Slips**" comes in. My definition of a Permission Slip is : **A person's accomplishment, lifestyle, or way of being acting as a catalyst and piece of a living proof for another person to pursue a similar accomplishment, lifestyle, or way of being.**

I did some searching on YouTube and began watching every video I could find about success stories of people who completed the Master Cleanse. These were everyday people who used their willpower and perseverance to stick to what they intended to do. And they all had amazing results. Hearing their stories and seeing their smiling faces on YouTube during the 5th day of my cleanse served as a "Permission Slip" to inspire me to finish the cleanse.

I admit — on the 8th day I felt a bit unstable, so I ate a small salad and then meditated, which brought me back to center. I continued with only liquids after this, and began eating solid food again after a total of 11 days. I felt completely transformed: inside and out, body, mind, and soul! (If you are interested in exploring cleansing / fasting, please read the sections in the "Phenomenal Food" chapter.) FYI, in general, I do not recommend fasting for more than 3 days unless you are very experienced and have quality supervision.

Tying in directly with "Permission Slips" is a concept called **"Morphic Fields," which are essentially Energetic Imprints in the Collective Human Consciousness.** Cutting-edge scientist Rupert Sheldrake explains the concept of "Morphic Fields" in greater detail here :

"The morphic fields of social groups connect together members of the group even when they are many miles apart, and provide channels of communication through which organisms can stay in touch at a distance. They help provide an explanation for telepathy. There is now good evidence that many species of animals are telepathic, and telepathy seems to be a normal means of animal communication, as discussed in my book Dogs That Know When Their Owners are Coming Home. Telepathy is normal not

paranormal, natural not supernatural, and is also common between people, especially people who know each other well."

"This means that new patterns of behavior can spread more rapidly than would otherwise be possible. For example, if rats of a particular breed learn a new trick in Harvard, then rats of that breed should be able to learn the same trick faster all over the world, say in Edinburgh and Melbourne. There is already evidence from laboratory experiments (discussed in A New Science of Life) that this actually happens."

In the same way that we have "Muscle Memory" so that we can always remember how to ride a bike, Morphic Fields are the "Muscle Memory" of the entire Human Collective Consciousness! This means that we can potentially accomplish and acquire the same things as any human that has ever lived. What is required is research, practice, and discipline to cultivate the same energy within your BodyMind System and tap into these true Superpowers :)

For example if you want to become an Olympic runner, you'd want to study the posture, preparation strategies, sleep patterns, diet, mental attitude, etc. in order to mimic the same energetic frequencies as Marion Jones or Jesse Owens within yourself.

If you want to run a successful Life Coaching business, then you'd want to study the stories of people who have accomplished this. You could research what books these Life Coaches have read, what trainings they have under their belt, how they market themselves, etc.

Whatever it is you want to accomplish, the key is to study the Success Stories from people walking a similar path. In this way, you can tap into the "Morphic Field," and utilize a similar energy for yourself. You don't have to completely mimic or copy these people, but it can be extremely helpful to study how they behave.

I even apply "Morphic Fields" beyond the Human Consciousness to the entire Web of Life. When I'm running, I often say, "I call upon the Lion frequency." It makes me feel fast, empowered, and unstoppable (especially when I pound my chest as I run).

There are so many ways to apply the power of Permission Slips and Morphic Fields. Once you start experimenting with them, you will sense the magnitude of how powerful and real they are!

Here are a few questions to explore on Permission Slips and Morphic Fields:

1. What people inspire you and who would you like to utilize as a role model?
2. What sort of practice / routine / mantra can you develop to tap into their Morphic Field?
3. What things in your life feel out of reach or impossible? Is there a potential Permission Slip or Success Story that could change your perspective?

THE HEALING PROCESS

Table of Contents

THE HEALING PROCESS OVERVIEW

1. **My Healing Journey**
2. **The Power of the Subconscious Mind**
3. **Energetic Imprints**
4. **Everything is B.S. !**
5. **Mental Advisors**

MY HEALING JOURNEY

Back in 2014, I'd been walking the spiritual path for at least 4 years, when I finally realized that although I was constantly preaching the message of "peace and love" there were still emotions inside me like anger and sadness that I was not in touch with. As a result, I was unable to be fully at peace, and unable to love certain aspects of myself.

For the last several years, I've been actively exploring deep emotions and many modalities for expressing and integrating them. My current understanding is that we freeze emotional energy within our body anytime we don't let ourselves feel our natural, instinctual emotions. This creates a "backlog" of stored energy that causes muscle tension, and potentially disease in the body.

The blockage will remain until we give ourselves full permission to release the stored energy. The key is to connect with the feeling of the emotion, and tune into what sound, movement, or story wants to be expressed. Sometimes simply talking about a past incident with a friend is enough to clear it. In other cases, you may need to punch a pillow or yell at the top of your lungs for an hour (forreal).

There are 2 key elements necessary for every type of healing:

1. TIME: You must give yourself enough time for each session. It is essentially impossible to rush this process. It is beneficial not to put an overall timeline on the healing process because for each person, it's unique. You can certainly intend for efficiency and the most direct path towards a state of integration or wholeness, though you can't really predict how the process will unfold.

2. SPACE: You must have a Space that you feel totally comfortable to express what you need to express. For me, this is usually out in nature, in my car, or in my home. If I feel that people are watching me or judging me harshly, it is very difficult to process deep emotions. Also, I try not to disturb others with my process, so a secluded space is beneficial.

Before I get into my specific recipes for healing, here are some key concepts to explore:

THE POWER OF THE SUBCONSCIOUS MIND

In many circuses in America, they train elephants to do tricks to amuse humans. Personally, I don't agree with this weird form of abuse. Regardless, the circus trainers use a particular technique to teach the elephants to perform certain tasks.

When they are young, they tie the baby elephant's leg to a big wooden pole. This young creature pulls and pulls, day after day, trying to roam free. Eventually it associates that whenever it has a chain around its ankle, it cannot move around. This belief sets into the elephant's Subconscious Mind. When it grows up, it still associates the chain around its ankle with staying in one place. Thus, all the trainer must do is put a chain around the elephant's ankle, and it will remain in one place, even if it is not tied to anything! The elephant is extremely powerful, though its power has been co-opted by tricking its Subconscious Mind.

Related to the story of the elephant is the "**Placebo Effect.**" I will summarize my understanding of this process without citing specific scientific studies. The Placebo Effect was discovered after experiments where doctors took two groups of patients and told both groups they were receiving a pill that would cure a specific ailment such as a fever. After several days, the doctors heard back from the patients, almost everyone in both groups reported that their fever was nearly out of their system or totally gone. The miraculous thing was that only one group received a pill that actually contained medicine to cure a fever. The patients in the other group merely received a "sugar pill" (Placebo pill) with no medicinal value. **It was because they believed they were receiving a healing pill that their fever went away.** The belief itself went into their Subconscious Mind, and then their body produced the necessary antibodies to fight off the fever.

So with the **Placebo Effect, we can see that a Positive Belief accepted into the Subconscious Mind can create a Positive Outcome**, but what about a Negative Belief? This is what the cutting edge Biologist Bruce Lipton has coined the **"Nocebo Effect." This is when someone or something influences you to believe a thought that ultimately does not serve your greatest good.**

The Nocebo can affect your beliefs around personal health, beliefs around money, and/ or beliefs about other cultures. If you believe that your health is mostly determined by your genes and certain health issues like Arthritis and Cancer run in your family, then you have essentially taken a Nocebo pill, and will probably manifest Arthritis and Cancer. If you believe that "money is the root of all evil," or that it's morally virtuous to be poor, then you will most likely live in poverty. If you are taught to believe that all Muslim people are evil, then you will probably stray away from any Muslim people, and live in some degree of hate / fear due to this Nocebo belief you hold. Lastly, the story of the elephant mentioned earlier is an example of the Nocebo effect, because a deep-seated limiting belief created a negative outcome.

From age 0 to 6, as children, we are in a developmental phase where we have yet to establish a "Conscious Mind." Therefore we are essentially like blank CD Discs, being downloaded with all of the beliefs, thoughts, and behaviors of our family and social environment. We have no reference point to say "this is not what I want to believe." We just simply believe what we are told and act in a way to get our basic needs met.

Science shows that our bodies are made of approximately 75% water. Japanese scientist Masaru Emoto has demonstrated that water has "memory", meaning that it is imprinted by the energy and intention of the environment. He froze water crystals after repeatedly saying different phrases at them.

Phrases like "Harmony" and "I love you" yielded symmetrical, beautiful crystals, while "I hate you" and "Fear" yielded asymmetrical, chaotic patterns.

Our physical bodies carry an Energetic Imprint of our environmental conditions just like the water crystals. We are especially imprinted during our first six years, because we have no way to filter / discard information using our Conscious Mind.

Now, let's add in the fact that psychologists say 95% of our daily behavior is run by the Subconscious Mind. **This means that the large majority of our actions as adults are a result of the "Energetic Imprints" that we received before age 7.**

ENERGETIC IMPRINTS

During this first 6-7 years, most of us experience certain events that we consider "traumatic." In Liz Mullinar's epic TED Talk on healing trauma, she defines **"Trauma"** as **"more emotion than the brain can deal with."** The child believes that their life is threatened; his/her brain reacts to this trauma and develops differently as a result.

A key point to make is that the event can appear relatively harmless to an outsider perspective, but if the child interprets the event as very scary, he/she will react in the same way as if being chased by a pack of hyenas or some other intense experience. **Therefore it is not the event that determines a Traumatic Imprint, but each person's emotional and psychological interpretation plus their physiological response.**

" Nothing goes away until it has taught us what we need to know "
~ Pema Chodron

I describe this phenomenon of Energetic Imprints from a couple different angles, using a variety of metaphors and terminology. I believe we can grasp the process better by seeing it through a variety of related viewpoints. These have all been helpful for me to understand the process that many of us go through. I number these points as a simple way to organize them. Each numbered Point is an interrelated puzzle piece to the Healing Process.

1. For kids, energy flows naturally and freely through their BodyMind System. Swinging, dancing, laughing, and loving with ease, children are usually vibrant and enthusiastic until society teaches them to "sit down and shut up." Adults are often amazed at how much energy youngsters have. This is because they have not yet been conditioned to partially block the energy flow through their BodyMind System.

2. From a young age, you learn some things are not allowed, so you block energy flow to that part of yourself. For example if you are singing out loud too much in school, you may be consistently scolded and told to be quiet. This "pacifier" can easily develop into a blockage in your throat chakra. You learn a process of **"Resistance / Armoring"** : **where you block the natural flow of energy through your BodyMind System.**

You are passed down many of the beliefs of your parents and the society you grow up in. I call this **"Misqualified Energy": Beliefs and energetic imprints that ultimately don't resonate with one's core truth. It is helpful to imagine these like a bunch of layers of clothing that don't quite fit you.** One day, you may look in the mirror at this Misqualified Energy "clothing" and say "Woah! This is not my style anymore!" Then, the goal is to release and reprogram this Misqualified Energy.

3. A **Traumatic Event**, often causes you to freeze in time to protect yourself. Rather than the "Fight or Flight" response, this is option # 3 : **Freeze.** Like a scared bunny that "plays dead," you shut down your Sensory System during an event perceived as threatening. The key here is that the event is **"perceived as threatening."** Trauma is all about **Perception.** The event could be totally peaceful to someone else in the same situation, but if for some reason you feel in danger, your BodyMind System will react the same way as if a lion was chasing you through the plains of Botswana.

A part of yourself is essentially stuck in that moment, until you go back into it and "coach" your past self through it, telling them it's okay and they are safe. The key is to "Re-Store" this memory and fully accept that this traumatizing event did indeed happen.

To use a metaphor, imagine you have 2 cabinets inside you. Cabinet #1 is "storing" all of the Fearful, Traumatizing, Unacceptable memories. Cabinet #2 is "storing" all the Positive, Happy, Acceptable memories. In order to achieve Wholeness, we've got to Fully Accept what has happened to us, and move the memories over to cabinet #2 (thus Re-Storing ourselves).

There is a concept known as **"Soul Retrieval,"** which explains that when a traumatic event occurs, we lose touch with part of our soul, and in order to feel whole again, we must reclaim / retrieve that part of ourselves. This usually involves going back into that experience in our imagination, and viewing it from a different angle. Often times, a Healer / Shaman / Counselor will guide you into a "hypnotic state," so you can access these blurry or forgotten memories.

It is important to note that "Accepting" a memory or event does not mean that you "deserved it." This would imply that you are inherently bad, which is not true. "Accepting" a memory also does not mean that a potential Offender or Abuser was justified in their actions.

Accepting simply means that you stop resisting the fact that this event occurred. The goal is to realize that for some reason your soul chose this experience on its Journey of Evolution. The big question is : **"What is the hidden gift / lesson from this event?"** Through Acceptance and Seeing the Hidden Gift, you effectively change your Perception of the event from being Fearful to Neutral. This shifts the energy in your BodyMind System from "dis-integrated" into a state of integration. You essentially say to yourself, "Okay, I've been through some crazy shit! I am choosing to be at peace with this now." This effectively re-stores the memory into Cabinet #2 and a state of Acceptance.

4. The **Pain Body** as Eckhart Tolle describes it is **the total energy field of all our past emotional pain. This includes all the Misqualified Energy, Frozen, and Unaccepted parts of ourselves.** It is like a heavy burden we carry, and causes our Mind and Body to feel fragmented. It is comprised of all the "Resistance Energy" that we hold in our Energy field. It gets triggered anytime something shines the light of consciousness upon these unconscious, unintegrated parts of us.

(I highly recommend reading "A New Earth" by Eckhart Tolle for more about the Pain-Body and how to heal it. Tolle also has many great talks on YouTube.)

5. **When we don't EXPRESS, and instead REPRESS, then eventually we become DEPRESSED.**

There are stored emotions, and often Sound Frequencies within us, that we would have expressed if we'd had a supportive, healthy environment. Because we didn't feel safe to express them, we bottled them up, and/or believed they were unacceptable, so we stored them in the Fearful Cabinet #1. (Later in this chapter, I will provide several tools for releasing this Repressed energy.)

6. As a result of all that I just described, many of us have become partially numb, dissociated, and fragmented as adults. The wild thing is what I call the **"Acclimation Zone," where we become so acclimated to our partially numb BodyMind, that it's nearly impossible to imagine it another way.** Often we don't even know that a part of us is numb because we haven't experienced full sensation in this area since our childhood.

7. How do we heal all of this pain and numbness? **The goal is to do like Humpty Dumpty and put ourselves back together again.** In order to do this there are a few different helpful tools:
a. Expressing the repressed emotions / sounds through Catharsis.
b. Sharing your story of what happened to you with a trusted friend or counselor.
c. Retraining the BodyMind System to feel sensation and allow energy to flow.
d. Reprogramming Fearful memories and accepting that they happened, thus achieving Wholeness / Integration. This includes doing Inner Child Healing.

---- **It is often uncomfortable or painful to bring energy into these places because they've been so stiff / numb for so long. When we bring oxygen and energy into a stiff area, there is a lot of "dust and rust" that needs to be cleared off before we can feel the peace that arises from a fully functioning BodyMind System.** The tools outlined in this chapter have supported me tremendously in the process of releasing the Misqualified Energy, Armoring, and other pain that was stuck in my BodyMind, and I am supremely grateful for the state of peace and health that I now experience!

EVERYTHING IS BS! - BELIEF SYSTEM

The metaphysical teacher Bashar shares a valuable metaphor for understanding how your Beliefs and subsequently your Thoughts create your Behaviors and ultimately your Experience of Reality. He explains it like this :

1. **Beliefs** are equivalent to the blueprint of a house. They form the layout and foundation for everything else.

2. **Emotions** are equivalent to the Construction Workers who build the house. They are the E-motion (energy in motion), which provide the raw energy to create your experience of reality.

3. **Thoughts, Visual Imagery, and Behaviors** are equivalent to the Building Materials, which create the physical structure of the house (your experience of reality).

If you have harmonious beliefs, and balanced emotions, then you will have a firm foundation to utilize thoughts for a life of your own choosing. If all your beliefs have been programmed by society, and you have not questioned them, then the foundation of your reality is essentially out of your conscious control.

It is a massive step in personal empowerment to realize that **YOU CAN CHOOSE TO REPROGRAM YOUR BELIEFS.**

To put it simply, the key to exploring one's beliefs, is to dive into the Subconscious Mind. Here are some tips for doing this :

1. Begin asking yourself questions about your beliefs. Journaling is very helpful for unpacking these revelations. I recommend exploring 3 beliefs you hold related to each of these topics : God, Intimate Relationships, Money, Life Purpose, and Food.

2. A key question to ask often is "**What would I have to believe, in order to have this recurring thought / behavior?**" For example, I noticed that I had a fear of holding eye contact with others for more than a few seconds without looking away. So I asked

myself, "What belief do I hold that supports me in holding onto this fear? Unworthiness? Guilt? Fear of losing my sense of self?"

3. Then, once you identify the core belief(s), you can begin to explore new perspectives and alternative beliefs. As you identify beliefs within yourself, you can ask, "From where or whom did I receive this belief?" If you got it from a specific person, the key questions to ask are "Is this belief working for them? Are they happy, healthy, and living their life purpose?" If not, then you may want to reprogram this belief within yourself. (This chapter provides several tools for doing this. Check out the Affirmation Activations.)

4. **It is key to realize that the physical body reflects / embodies the Subconscious Mind. Your brain literally reaches down into the nerve ganglia of all your organs and ultimately every cell in your body. The mind and body are literally two aspects of ONE BIG CIRCUIT.**

5. **Thus, it is important to integrate physical, embodied practices into the process of shifting your beliefs, emotions, and realities.** (This chapter also gives a variety of Embodied Practices.)

THE MENTAL ADVISORS

" The mind is a wonderful servant, but a terrible master. "
~ Robin Sharma

" You don't have to believe everything you think. "
~ Wayne Dyer

How do you become the master of your own mind? I will share a system with you that has worked miracles in my life and in the lives of many that I've shared it with. **The Mental Advisors are societally conditioned thought patterns, which are organized into distinct "characters" and personalities.** These characters such as Worrying Wanda offer their advice and perspective, and it is up to you to decide whether to listen or not. By categorizing thought patterns in this way, it allows you to observe your mind so that you have more control over your behavior.

The metaphorical environment of the Mental Advisors is a 5-Star Hotel. You are the Manager of this hotel, and with your awareness you oversee all of the rooms and guests who come to stay in your luxurious enterprise. The 5-Star Hotel represents your mind and all your thought processes. You, the Manager, have free will to decide if the people (thoughts) who enter the lobby are worthy of staying in your hotel (mental space).

The lobby is often buzzing with stressed out and unkind travelers (Societally Conditioned Thought Patterns). You stand at the front desk and must remain alert so that you can discern whether you want these types of people staying in your 5-Star Hotel. Your job is to choose the guests who stay with you, because they determine the overall reputation and energy of your hotel. These guests represent your Consciously Chosen Thought Patterns.

As I've observed my mind for the past 12 years, I've documented and shifted many of the "guests in my hotel." Some I gently escorted out the front door and they went on their merry way. Other guests are more like needy beggars who keep coming into the lobby asking for my attention.

Below are some of the Mental Advisor personalities I've outlined. First I share a "Societally Conditioned" Thought Pattern / Mental Advisor, and then I share one or more "Consciously Chosen Alternative Thought Patterns" to replace with. Many of the

Consciously Chosen Mental Advisors are essentially Superpowers in their own right. After each Mental Advisor, I give a sense of the story that they tell you to believe in. Depending on how deep you want to go with this system, you can differentiate a Mental Advisor for each unique emotional state. The emotions held in your body (Subconscious Mind are one half of the two-part loop, which links up to the other half - the thoughts in your Conscious Mind.

The gender of these characters is pretty arbitrary, I simply chose names using alliteration or by selecting a random name. I invite you to choose new names if that feels right. Without further ado, here is one of my favorite tools in this whole book :

Examples of the Mental Advisors

------- 1. Judging Joseph - (societally conditioned)

"This person, place, or thing is annoying and fundamentally wrong. The universe must have made a mistake, so I'm going to judge and be in opposition to what I'm seeing / experiencing."

Accepting Alex - (consciously chosen alternative)

"I fully align myself with what is happening in this now moment. I choose to accept these circumstances. The Power is in the NOW :"

Discerning Danielle - (consciously chosen alternative)

"I use my Superpower of Discernment to find the best way to transform the situation I'm in, or simply leave it."

------- 2. Behind Schedule Betty - (societally conditioned)

"Oh my gosh, I'm always running late. I am behind the 8-ball, so I must hurry / worry / feel anxious to make up for it."

Right-On Time Rhonda - (consciously chosen alternative)

"I choose to believe that everything is happening right on time."

"I'm most effective in getting things done, when I take focused action in the present moment."

------- 3. Worrying Wanda / Doubt McGee - (societally conditioned)

"I love to worry and it is my greatest benefit to do so. When worrying about the past, I doubt if I made the 'correct' decision. When worrying about the present, I doubt if I'm taking the 'correct' action. When worrying about the future, I doubt if things will go as planned or if chaos will ensue."

NOTE : The following 4 consciously chosen alternatives can be utilized to replace many of the societally conditioned Mental Advisors :)

Trusting Tricia - (consciously chosen alternative)

"It is my greatest benefit to trust life. I trust that the past is past, and I accept what happened. I can learn from my actions, whether they were ideal or not. I trust the present moment, and I am empowered to take action or surrender here and now. I trust that the future will unfold as it may, and I can consciously co-create it to the degree I am able."

Fat Tony - (consciously chosen alternative)

Fat Tony is a New York cab driver who reminds you of your power to say "CTFO!" This stands for Chill-The-Ef-Out. As he drives through hectic traffic in the big city, he uses this mantra to help himself cool down, and he also shares it with anyone who is stressed out in his taxi. Whenever worry comes up in your life, I recommend imagining Fat Tony turning around from driving his Taxi and telling you, "CTFO, take a chill pill!"

Best Case Scenario Bella - (consciously chosen alternative)

Bella invites you to sing a song that goes "Best...case...scenario, Best-case-sce-nar-ioohhh," and she helps you to envision and put your creative energy

Best Case Scenario Bella - (consciously chosen alternative)

Bella invites you to sing a song that goes "Best...case...scenario, Best-case-sce-nar-ioohhh," and she helps you to envision and put your creative energy towards this positive vision. (When you envision it, and feel as if your wish is fulfilled, you become a strong magnet to attract a future that looks and feels like your wish.)

Violet Flame Superpower - (consciously chosen alternative)

The Violet Flame is a spiritual tool used for purification. You can visualize a Violet Flame burning away any thoughts that are not serving you. I like to say "I don't need this thought in my brain, so I send it into the Violet Flame!" And imagine the thought leaving my head and going into a Violet Flame above me.

------- 4. Molehill Monica - (societally conditioned)

"Whatever I want to do, whether big or small, it will be extremely difficult. It will be an uphill battle and probably take a really long time. I turn molehills into mountains."

The Shrinkmaster! - (consciously chosen alternative)

"I have the superpower of shrinking obstacles." I can turn mountains into molehills. Tasks that seem daunting turn into simple and even enjoyable activities. If I am intimidated to speak with a person, I first envision them as a gigantic dragon breathing fire. Next, I use the superpower of Shrinking to transform them into a cute pink bunny rabbit.

The 37 Second Superpower - (consciously chosen alternative)

When Molehill Monica tries to convince me that something will be difficult and/or take forever, I call upon the "37 Second Superpower." I simply tell myself "This will only take 37 seconds." Sometimes the task literally takes 37 seconds, or sometimes it's more like a few minutes. I utilize this for simple tasks that will realistically take 5 minutes or less, such as sweeping the bathroom floor, washing a few dishes, or texting a friend.

------- 5. Guilty Gerald / Shameful Shawn - (societally conditioned)

"I need to feel guilty / shameful about mistakes I made in the past. It serves me to carry this heavy burden because it is a fair punishment for what I did."

Innocent Ian - (consciously chosen alternative)

"Even if I made a mistake in the past, it is my greatest benefit to find a way to forgive myself and others. Carrying those burdens negatively affects me and distorts my present experience. I will work to make amends and heal from any wrongdoings I have done or have been done to me." I use the Affirmation "I choose to forgive myself."

Cosmic Giggle Foundation - (consciously chosen alternative)

The Cosmic Giggle Foundation is an imaginary place where you can donate your shame and guilt. The philosophy is that ultimately we are all one consciousness, so anyone or anything that appears to be judging you is really just you judging you. Therefore, there is usually no need / use for guilt or shame. You are capable of discerning what behaviors are in integrity and which are not. Perhaps one day when we are in Heaven, we will all laugh about the silly things we once felt ashamed about. For example, when I am doing yoga in public and someone drives by and makes fun of me, I can either feel ashamed, or I can donate that shame to the C.G.F. and laugh it off.

------- 6. Scarcity Samantha - (societally conditioned)

"There will never be enough. I will never be enough. There is not enough to go around. I need to hoard and control my environment, to ensure I have enough. I should be afraid to share or give away my extra resources, because it might not come back to me."

Abundance Abigail - (consciously chosen alternative)

"There is always enough to go around when I give and receive naturally. Mother Earth is plentiful. We must only respect her natural laws and there will always be enough to meet our needs. I choose to share with my community, and I know that abundance will flow back to me. I choose to see and feel the abundance of life in its many forms."

------- 7. <u>The Echo-Master</u> - (societally conditioned)

"I echo the voices of your mother, father, or friends as if they are your own thoughts." These are most often negative beliefs, insults, or limiting stories which echo through your mind and diminish your potential. For example, there was a bully in middle school who would call me "Lil Shit," and I have to mindful not to internalize negative namecalling towards myself.

<u>The Echo-Master Reprogrammed</u> - (consciously chosen alternative)

"I choose to reprogram the people and stories that I want to echo through my thoughts." "I choose stories and beliefs that enhance my potential and make me feel good about myself. I can pick from some of my favorite spiritual teachers or mentors, and/or positive statements from my friends and family."

------- 8. <u>Obligatory Olaf</u> - (societally conditioned)

Olaf says you have to follow social norms all the time and focus on being a "People Pleaser." He is always using the word "SHOULD." "Even if you feel very tired or sick, you should go to the meeting, or try to help that person out." Following Olaf's advice leads you away from your Internal Compass, and usually leaves you feeling drained.

<u>Freedom Francine</u> - (consciously chosen alternative)

Francine invites you to trust that you are completely interconnected to the web of life. Thus, if you don't feel like you have the energy to do a task, it is OK to rest. You will be supported. You are not obligated to follow the conditioning of your parents or the Mainstream Strange Dream. You are FREE to make up your own mind, your own rules, and your own decisions!

------- 9. <u>Paralysis of Analysis Patty</u> - (societally conditioned)

If Patty comes into the 5-Star Hotel of your mind, she will certainly drain your time and energy. She will weigh every hypothetical scenario over and over again, until you are lost in a labyrinth of "maybe's" and "what if's". Although it's often beneficial to see all sides of a decision, Patty gets you trapped in your head, so you can't feel the wisdom and deeper knowing of your intuition and body.

The "Boom-Done" Superpower! - (consciously chosen alternative)

This Superpower is the ultimate efficiency booster, because it assists you in making decisive decisions, so that you don't waste precious time overthinking things. When I sense I am getting into paralysis of analysis, I choose to take a deep breath, and feel into what decision feels best in my body. Then I choose. "Boom! Done!" I exclaim.

If I've got a few things to accomplish, I envision them happening in sequential order, and then say aloud "Bing, Bang, Boom!" and imagine them all being complete. This helps my brain to relax and allows me to focus on the process of completing the task at hand. This is the Bing-Bang-Boom Superpower, which was taught to me by my soul brotha, Natural.

------- 10. <u>Jukebox Josephine</u> - (can be societally conditioned and/or consciously chosen)

Josephine is the one who keeps songs playing in your head. If you listen to the radio, many of those songs are designed to be catchy, and they replay over and over again in your mind. The key is to have mastery of your mind and also what music you choose to listen to, because the lyrics and energy of songs seep into your Subconscious Mind very easily.

I choose to listen to music with conscious lyrics and positive energy. (For some recommendations check out the later chapter "The Web of Infinite Inspiration.")

Lyric Switcharoo Superpower - If you have a song stuck in your head and you don't fully resonate with the lyrics, you can utilize this Superpower to invent your own lyrics, but keep the melody. This is Alchemy at its best!

My good friend Sol Shanti revealed this Superpower to me around Moby's song "Natural Blues," that goes "Oooh Lordy, trouble so high, ain't nobody know my troubles but God, ain't nobody know my troubles but God." He switched the lyrics to "Oooh Lordy, light of my life, everybody knows your the light of my life, everybody knows your the light of my life!" ...Pretty nifty, eh? That's the Lyric Switcharoo Superpower. It's a fun one :)

------- 11. I'll Never Find an Answer Ida - (societally conditioned)

Ida tries to convince you that it will be extremely difficult or impossible to find a solution to a problem. She imagines that solutions are few and far between, and obviously she's never heard of the Internet!

Google Solution Superpower - (consciously chosen alternative)

This Superpower reminds you that many of the solutions to your so-called "problems" are literally one Google search away! It may actually take less than a minute to find an answer. Whether it's the address of an event, the name of a brand, or some odd factoid, Google is at your service 24/7/365 ! Or you can use an alternative Search Engine like Duck Duck Go or Ecosia.org

------- 12. The Naysayer Chorus - (societally conditioned)

The Naysayer Chorus comes into your Hotel Lobby singing songs of "It can't be done." They say you have to play by the rules. They say that nobody ever does it like that. They say you are setting yourself up for failure.

Because I Say So Sandra! - (consciously chosen alternative)

Sandra is a sassy girl who follows her gut instinct, heart, and intuition. She says "My way, or the highway!" She chooses to speak her truth into existence, and creates powerful ripples when she does. She sticks to her core values and is happy to be a "majority of one" if necessary.

----- Ultimately, all of these voices have a message to share with us. Often times, the conditioned thought patterns come from our brains attempting to keep us safe and to fit in with our environment. Therefore, it is important not to completely disregard a thought pattern, but rather to dissect it, and see how it may have originated. Then, consciously decide whether you want that thought pattern running in your life. And if not, then I encourage you to work on shifting your internal dialogue through journaling and daily affirmations + self-proramming.

PROCESSING ENERGY

1. Flow and Force
2. Overview of My Healing + Energy Practices
3. Movin' and Groovin (Bioenergetics)
4. Catharsis (Releasing and Reprogramming)
5. The Affirmation Activations
6. Feelization

FLOW AND FORCE

I explained the Flow State in the Keys to Creativity chapter, though I am going to restate the importance of it here because it also applies directly to the Healing Process. **A state of flow is when you become totally enmeshed in the present activity.** People often describe "flow states" as losing track of time or merging with the process of life itself. Sometimes this includes tremendous effort, sometimes it requires total surrender. Sometimes it means moving fast, other times it means sitting still. The Asian Spiritual Tradition of Taoism is sometimes called the "watercourse way," and uses the metaphor of a river or stream to describe many teachings. At certain points, we embody the raging rapids, at other times we embody a slow, gentle flow.

" Nature does not hurry, yet everything is accomplished. "

~ Lao Tzu (founder of Taoism)

Force is when we are not in a flow state. It is like trying to push a river. It's fruitless, and a heroic effort yields almost no results. Whereas when we are in flow, a gentle movement yields massive gains. It does take practice to master the art of "going with the flow." It requires tuning into the feelings and thoughts that keep us in a flow state. A flow state can be found in essentially any activity from painting, running, or making love.

It is a state of dynamic balance between polarities : fast and slow, masculine and feminine, electric and magnetic, hot and cold.

The various maps and tools offered in this chapter and throughout this book will assist you in navigating the many aspects of your "flow state." The key question to ask to access your Flow State is : "Does the way I'm performing this current action feel natural / authentic / correct?"

OVERVIEW OF MY HEALING + ENERGY PRACTICES

1. Warm up : Light jog to move the muscles and energy in my body. (Body / Ice cube begins to thaw out.)

2. Intense Exercise : I like to wear a rain jacket and a hat while exercising so that I get completely drenched in sweat and activate every cell in my body. I usually go for a jog , and also do some yoga as well as strength training consisting of push-ups, squats, and ab exercises.(Body / Ice Cube becomes liquefied and malleable.)

As I began to explore the emotions hiding deep within me, I sought out healthy ways to express them. I developed a "recipe" for processing emotions. Here is an overview :

As I described earlier, the emotions are stored in the cells of our organs and muscle tissues. In order to change the "e-motion" (energy in motion) into a more harmonious state, I have discovered a helpful metaphor to understand the process. This is called **"The Ice Cube Metaphor."** Imagine that your body is an ice cube. Frozen solid, it is extremely difficult to change its shape or structure. If you heat up this big ice cube, then it begins to liquefy, and becomes malleable and changeable. Once your body / ice cube is malleable, you can add a new imprint or design to it. Then, you can cool down your body / ice cube and it will remember some of these new imprints.

Each day I do my "Healing Practice," I am reshaping one layer of my BodyMind / Ice Cube. With this metaphor in mind, here is an overview of my Healing Practice. I will go into detail of each part later in this chapter...

3. Prayer / Intention : I say a prayer / set an intention like this: **"Great Spirit, please help me to release the next layer of my societally conditioned self, and embrace the next layer of my true, divine, empowered self."**

4. Bioenergetic Release : I tap, smack, bang my fist, or deeply massage whatever area of my body appears to have the emotional energy stuck in it. I tune into what type of sound or breath will help me to release the energy. For releasing anger, it is usually yelling at the top of my lungs. For releasing shame / guilt, it is usually a moaning or groaning sound. Sometimes I do rapid breathing, sometimes I do long slow breathing. The key is to explore this process, and get in tune with what types of Bioenergetic release works for you. (Body / Ice Cube gets reformed.)

If I sense that there is a limiting belief related to the area of my body I am exploring, I will utilize the Affirmation Activations (explained later in this chapter while doing this process. (Body / Ice Cube gets consciously re-imprinted.

5. Cool down : Gentle yoga, stretching, deep breathing, savasana, lying on Pachamama. (Body / Ice Cube slowly cools down into a slightly different, new form.)

6. Deeper Integration : This process helps to ingrain the New Beliefs and New Bioenergetic Patterns into your Subconscious Mind, and subsequently your daily life. (Body / Ice Cube re-solidifies into a new, more harmonious state of existence.) These tools are explained in greater detail later in this chapter :)

MOVIN AND GROOVIN (BIOENERGETICS)

a. Foundation : Posture + Energy Flow

b. Exercise

c. Dance

d. Yoga

e. Swimming

f. Flow Arts and Martial Arts

g. Sacred Sexuality

FOUNDATION : POSTURE + ENERGY FLOW

Before we get into the power of exercise and movement, it is key to understand the foundation to movement. This is the basic way in which we hold our bodies. There are 2 primary components to this, which both go hand in hand :

1. **The physical structure of how you hold your Bodymind.**

2. **The way in which non-physical energy flows through your Bodymind.**

I highly recommend reading / referencing Mantak Chia's monumental book : "Healing Light of the Tao : Fundamental Practices to Awaken Chi Energy." Chia gives an overview of the "Microcosmic Orbit" which is the primary way in which your Life Energy (Chi) flows up the back of the spine and then down the front of your torso to circulate once again.

I had been exploring yoga, meditation and healing for over 6 years before learning how to apply this fundamental practice! In my opinion, understanding the Microcosmic Orbit should be taught in Elementary School. What is more important than understanding how our BodyMind System operates?

I have also found Vinyasa yoga very helpful for increasing body awareness and aligning my posture. Before I began practicing yoga, I could barely tell you where certain parts of my body were located, like my pelvis, for example. After 10 or so years of being a "yogi" I have learned a tremendous amount about my BodyMind System, including my organs, glands, muscles, bones, and more :) Similar to yoga is the practice of Qi Gong, which also guides you to learn how to have proper posture, and circulate your life-energy. Lastly, I highly recommend learning about the Chakra System within your BodyMind. There are many great books available as well as some intro videos on YouTube :)

3 Questions on Posture / Energy Flow :

1. Do you consciously cultivate a healthy posture / flow of energy in your BodyMind System?

2. What practices are you most drawn to that will enhance your posture / flow of energy?

3. What parts of daily life could you bring more awareness into your posture / energy flow?

THE POWER OF EXERCISE

Throughout all of my life, exercise has been a crucial component. I have utilized regular exercise to make it over pretty much every challenge that has popped up on my path.

It is very important to have a warm-up and a cool down included in your exercise sessions. This allows your muscle tissues to loosen up before and afterwards. This will help you to maintain flexibility, build muscle easier, and reduce soreness after workouts.

I encourage you to find a warm-up that works well for you. Personally, I usually run between and 1 and 2 miles wearing my Vibram 5-Finger shoes. These shoes are absolutely amazing for reclaiming your primal running abilities. Regular shoes have so much cushion and constriction that you don't get to develop the dexterity and strength of your feet. It does take time to rebuild your natural foot strength when you first begin wearing the 5 Finger Shoes. There are many styles, and I prefer the Komodo Sport. If you get some, I recommend walking only for the first week, before you begin jogging.

After running, I usually do some sort of Strength Training. On this note, here is one of the most profound messages of this entire book :

It is quite obvious that Body Language demonstrates if a person is confident in themselves. Imagine two men walk into your office and each one is preparing to give a presentation. One man has a slouched back, droopy eyes, and his hands in his pockets.

The other guy has a straight spine, bright eyes, and his arms are energized. Before either one says a word, you can easily predict which presentation will be more effective.

Our Body Language shows and represents how we feel at a Subconscious Level. Therefore, in order to be fully Empowered and fully Conscious we must have a strong, healthy body.

Many traditions from Chinese Medicine to Shamanism explain that every part of the body has its own consciousness. **Therefore, in order to be an optimally Conscious Being, you need to wake up each part of your BodyMind System. This requires you to have Awareness, Communication, and Functionality in every muscle, organ, and area of your body.** You may say that this is a "Tall Order," but then again how can you expect to master and interact with the external world when you don't know how to use your own BodyMind System to its true capabilities?

Strength training is one of my favorite ways to cultivate Awareness, Communication, and Functionality in each part of my body. I enjoy doing some strength training outside, with the sun shining, fresh air blowing, or even sometimes in the pouring rain. I also love working out in a gym, and currently I go to Planet Fitness, which is awesome because the motto is "A Judgment-Free Zone." Whether inside or outside, I like to focus on a specific muscle group and do at least 3-4 sets to work out that area. Rather than doing a specific number of repetitions, I prefer to go until I "feel the burn" / feel that I've reached an adequate limit for that set. If you have never weightlifted before, you may feel intimidated or unsure, but I encourage you to try it out. It is so cool to wake up the strength and dexterity in areas like your forearms, lower back, and glutes, just to name a few. There is truly nothing like the magic of weightlifting!

In professional sports, sometimes opponents will try to "psyche out" the opposite team. This concept of the "psyche out" references the powerful connection between body and mind. If the mind sends a disempowering signal to the body, then the athlete will perform poorly. We can be "psyched out" by fans in the audience, or we can "psyche ourselves out" by thinking self-defeating thoughts.

This is why I choose to utilize "Empowering Mantras" while exercising to encourage my mind and body to remain in a positive, uplifted state. Rather than "Psyching myself out," I am "Psyching myself IN!" Here are some of my favorite Mantras, which I repeat during my workout (I alternate between bold and regular font, simply for contrast) :

1. Let's Go, Let's Get It, Let's Flow, Yes-I !

Let's Go, Let's Get It, Let's Flow, Yes-I !

2. Building Strength, Building Muscle,

Building Peace, Building Love

3. Right Here, Right Now,

Right Here, Right Now

4. Sat Nam, Sat Nam,

Sat Nam, Sat Nam

(This mantra is used in Kundalini Yoga, as a way to focus the mind. It translates to "Truth is my essence.")

5. Fuck Yes, Fuck Yes,

Fuck Yes, Fuck Yes

6. Focused Energy - Yes-I,

Focused Energy - Yes-I

7. Yes-I Can, Yes-I AM,

Yes-I Can, Yes-I AM !

8. Push, Push, Pull, Pull

Push, Push, Pull, Pull

9. Yes I'm strong. Yes I'm grounded. Everything is flow-ing!

Yes I'm strong. Yes I'm grounded. Everything is flow-ing!

"YES-I" is an Empowerment Mantra. It carries the vibration of self and collective empowerment. You can add "Yes-I" to any affirmation / mantra to add some extra momentum to it.

(Yes-I is also a phrase used by some Rasta's to honor the "I-n-I" aka the ONE consciousness that we all share. I don't claim to be an expert or practitioner of Rastafarianism, though I proudly say the word Yes-I as an Empowerment Mantra and beautiful sound frequency.

I can't imagine the number of times that each of the Mantras / Affirmations I listed have served as a "Grappling Hook," to pull me out of a hole / foggy state of mind. They are all extremely powerful for helping you to shift your vibration towards a greater state of strength and empowerment. I highly recommend trying them out, and creating your own :

3 Questions on Exercise :

1. Do you have a regular Exercise routine?

2. If so, how can you enhance it? If not, what would motivate / discipline you to keep with it?

3. What mantras would assist you in staying focused and motivated while exercising?

THE POWER OF DANCE

Neither of my parents were big dancers growing up, so I never really cultivated a passion for dancing. In middle school, it was "uncool" to dance in certain ways so I steered clear of truly expressing myself through this fabulous art form. The only times I really let my body groove was at school dances, where I was either "grinding" with a girl, slow dancing, or doing the Electric Slide.

It wasn't until my senior year of high school, when I began to break out of my overly self-conscious shell, that I began to let my body vibe with the music. I was invited to a Bluegrass Concert at a big outdoor pavilion. I wore my one and only Tie-Dye shirt, which was my permission slip to be a "free-spirit." I let go of worrying what others would think and just let my shoulders sway, hips twirl and legs bounce around. It felt like I was shaking out of the shackles that I had placed on myself!

As I continued on my path, for a number of years I still felt self-critical when dancing. This all changed when I began to go to "Ecstatic Dance," which is usually a big ballroom full of 50-100 people of all ages dancing however the Efff they want! There's a wide variety of music from Tribal to Electronic to Pop, to soothing. It's so freaking awesome! When I moved to Asheville, North Carolina, I began going to "Dance Church," which is a huge Ecstatic Dance event every single Sunday morning. Here are 2 posts I made that were inspired my experience there :

August 31st, 2014 @ 3:20pm :

Movement is so key for every type of healing. After one week of laying low, meditating, and barely walking or interacting with people, today I felt inspired to go to Ecstatic Dance. I let my body flow and groove in a massive dance hall with 100 other beings. The evocative music activated ancient aspects of my true self. I felt tremendous breakthroughs in the various energy blocks I've been working through.

I feel that the rest and movement are two sides of the same coin. Both are crucial for holistic health.

September 14th, 2014 @ 9:47am :

Today at Church I plan to get really sweaty and bounce around like a baboon. Everyone in our church walks into service barefoot. We pray and give praise to Life through Ecstatic Dance.

From the STATIC of the mind to the ECSTATIC of the Body. The best way to get high is to get down!

I have a dream that within the next 5 years, Ecstatic Dance will become popular on a mass scale. Every day, people of all ages and backgrounds all across the globe are realizing the profound healing benefits of this Movement Practice. I pray that we can all spread the word about the awesomeness of Ecstatic Dance! I invite you to find or start a weekly / monthly Ecstatic Dance gathering in your town. Check out www.5rhythms.com and www.Ecstaticdance.org for more information.

3 Questions on Dancing :

1. Do you have any regular dancing practice?

2. What are some of your favorite ways to move your body?

3. What type of music inspires you to dance in new ways?

YOGA

I really began practicing yoga in the end of 2010. It was 2 weeks after being hit by a car on the Bike Trip. We were staying in San Francisco, and there was a super groovy studio called "Yoga to the People." This donation based studio attracted 50 - 100 people into a massive room with a wooden floor on the 3rd floor of a downtown building. I was rehabilitating my knee after getting stitched up. With just a few classes doing as many poses as I could, I could feel my body getting stronger. When I moved back to Pittsburgh, I found the local "Yoga Hive" and began practicing vigorously, often attending 2 Vinyasa classes every day.

Since this initial love affair with yoga back in 2010, I have essentially had a daily practice. There is rarely a day that goes by without me doing some sort of yoga routine. I've experimented with many different styles. As you've probably figured out by now, I love to sweat, so hot yoga is especially near and dear to me. I did my Yoga Teacher Training at Amazing Yoga, which utilizes heaters in every sweaty class. Overall, I invite you to explore the wide array of styles, studios, and teachers to discover what styles you resonate with most.

The Extended Savasana Superpower : One of my biggest issues with doing Yoga classes in a studio is that the teacher usually gives you between 3 and 7 minutes for Savasana (the pose at the end of class where you completely relax and lay flat on your mat). I believe this is robbing you of one of the greatest opportunities for bliss, relaxation, and true union with the divine. I invite you to find time and space to allow for at least 10 minutes, ideally up to 30 minutes in this pose. I absolutely promise you that you will thank me if you try this out :) It's supremely awesome!

SWIMMING

Swimming is an excellent form of "cross training" to combine with running, strength training, yoga, etc. Swimming is great for increasing full body awareness. It can be both relaxing and extremely intense, sometimes at the same time. Swimming laps is great for endurance, and I also love to vigorously tread water in order to give my muscles a dynamic workout. Swimming also works wonders for dissolving the perceived separation between mind and body. In the water, there is only unity, and simply immersing yourself in water enhances the unity within yourself! Which way is the beach, bro? Haha, just kidding : Whether in a pool, pond, or with Mama Ocean, swimming is a phenomenal practice.

FLOW ARTS AND MARTIAL ARTS

When I speak of Flow Arts I mean activities like spinning poi, a staff, dancing with a hula-hoop, and things of that sort. Generally speaking it is moving in unison or in dynamic ways with another object outside or yourself. I am not yet super skilled in Flow Arts, though I have fantasies of becoming masterful with a staff and / or spinning fire. Going to festivals like Burning Man and seeing hundreds of coordinated fire spinners share their gift has left an indelible imprint of inspiration on my being. Personally, I love the game of "Peace Sticks," invented by my friends in Ojai, California. It's an interactive game that teaches you to be in the moment, and practice your "ninja skills." Check it out @ www.WorldPeaceTribe.com

Related to Flow Arts is the unique and beautiful realm of Martial Arts. I am also not well versed in this area, though I have friends who've experienced profound healing and growth through traditions like Aikido and Tai Chi. I believe that learning how to combat with an opponent in a conscious way can be very powerful for enhancing the strength of your BodyMind System. Your body is far more durable and strong than you may think, but until you take a few hard punches or flips, you won't realize it. The key is to do so in a safe setting with a skilled teacher, so that you do the moves correctly and don't injure yourself.

SACRED SEXUALITY

I view Sexuality as an integral part of life. We literally come from sex, and create new life through sex. One of my Spiritual Mentors often says, "Let's just accept that everything in nature is essentially having sex with everything else!" The flowers and the bees, the wind and the trees, and everything in between. In 7th grade, I went on Safari in Botswana with a friend and his family. I got a firsthand glimpse of "how they do it on the Discovery Channel." The lions, wildebeest, and other animals were getting jiggy all the time, regardless of who was watching!

I consider "Sacred Sexuality" to be the practice of sexuality in a conscious, healthy manner. This means that Consent, Setting Boundaries, and Clear Communication are key elements. Sacred Sexuality is a way to honor all the subtleties and nuances of intimacy instead of viewing sex as a means to an end, or a fleeting experience. By honoring sex as the incredible miracle that it is, you allow for deep healing, more pleasure, and even "transcendent experiences."

I am not an expert in Kama Sutra, and I am still healing a lot of conditioning around sexual shame and repression. I've dedicated myself to using clear, conscious communication with my sexual partners. Through this process, I've been able to release many fears and enjoy sexual intimacy at a deeper level.

I've included Sacred Sexuality in this chapter of "Processing Energy" because it can be an incredible tool for moving, directing, and releasing energy. As you allow the powerful currents of sexual energy to move through your body, it can help to break up stagnation, enhance blood and energy flow, as well as release tons of beneficial neurochemicals such as oxytocin and dopamine.

Although many people view it as taboo, I believe that anal pleasure is an important aspect of Sacred Sexuality. After all, why would we have so many nerves capable of feeling pleasure in and around our anuses, if they were not meant to experience pleasure? This territory is very new to me, so I won't pretend to be an expert on it. I recently got a "Sensuelle Homme Pro" (made for male prostate stimulation) which has been adding amazing vibrations to my intimate experiences. I believe that vibrating sexual toys help our entire BodyMind System raise its vibratory rate, which brings us into a state of joy, ecstasy, and optimal health. If you have resistance to anal stimulation, that is okay, but that might also be a sign that it's something to explore and learn more about.

Whether you are pleasuring yourself or exploring with a partner, I invite you to explore your desires and honor them as sacred — not something to be ashamed of. It is our birthright to experience the immense pleasure, joy, bliss, and healing that can come through this practice. Creating a sacred space or even a little ceremony for "sexy time" is a beautiful way to explore deeper. In the same way that creating the environment for creating art changes everything, you can set the tone or mood with certain elements like candles, music, incense, and dark chocolate :) You can even set an intention, or focus the energy of sex towards a specific creative project.

Here are a few questions to investigate on Sacred Sexuality :

1. What sexual desires do you have that you have not yet explored much?

2. What beliefs / limiting stories around sexuality do you have that are not serving you?

3. What sort of environment feels like it will get you and / or your partner in the mood?

<u>CATHARSIS (RELEASING AND REPROGRAMMING)</u>

a. Overview of Catharsis
b. Breathwork
c. Singing and Toning (Free Flow)
d. Tapping, Smacking, Punching, Shaking, Bouncing, and Spinning
e. Yelling and Moaning
f. Cathartic Speaking Exercise
g. Anger and Sadness Release

Catharsis is the process of releasing, purging, or purifying emotional energy. There are a wide variety of tools and techniques for doing this. In this section, I will highlight several of the ones that have worked wonders in my life. These tools and techniques build on the same philosophies discussed throughout this book. Essentially, the key is to reprogram your BodyMind System into a state of Wholeness and Integration.

Before I begin a session of Catharsis, I like to say a prayer / set an intention. One that I use often goes, **"Great Spirit, please help me to release the next layer of my societally conditioned self, and embrace the next layer of my true, divine, empowered self."** I feel it is very important to release "one layer at a time," so that you honor the entire depth of the healing process. (I explain this more later in this chapter.) You can also call in any Ancestors, Spirit Guides, or Angels that may assist you during your session. If you like to work with another person, you can ask them to hold space for you as you move and release deep emotions.

BREATHWORK

There are lots of different styles of Breathwork ranging from Pranayama to Holotropic and many more. Personally, I usually practice deep belly breathing through my mouth while I exercise. Sometimes I will fill my lungs with air and hold my breath for 5-10 seconds while doing a stretch, to enhance my breath capacity.

Your breath is an amazing tool for accessing, moving, and releasing stuck energy from anywhere in your body. I invite you to explore different breath patterns, and see which ones resonate most with you. **It is important to note that sometimes the one that is most uncomfortable is creating the most transformation, because it's moving energy, awareness, and sensation into places that have been stagnant for a long time.** I invite you to utilize your Internal Compass so you can tune into what your BodyMind truly needs. Sometimes, you may need a gentle, nurturing breath. Sometimes, you may need 20 minutes of rapid, intense breathing to release some deep-seated anger.

SINGING AND TONING (FREE FLOW)

I often turn my mantras into songs, or sing songs by my favorite Conscious Music Artists while I exercise. This helps to keep my mind focused, and my spirits high while I do a sometimes grueling physical workout. I also enjoy "Toning", which is the practice of repeating a specific tone for an extended period of time. Each of the Chakras resonates a specific frequency, and you can create these with the fabulous mechanism called your Vocal Cords! If you are moving energy through a specific area of your body, you can explore to find what tone seems to match the feeling or energy of that area. Whether Toning or Singing, these are powerful techniques for expressing, releasing, and/or moving Emotional Energy through your BodyMind System.

TAPPING, SMACKING, PUNCHING, SHAKING, BOUNCING + SPINNING

These may sound ridiculous, but they are some of the most potent practices for moving stuck energy in your BodyMind System. Tapping, Shaking, etc. allow you to literally "let go of control." By bouncing or spinning around, after about 5 minutes your rational mind (the Neocortex of your brain) releases, and allows you to flow into a trancelike state. I love to do this in a big open parking lot, grass field, or yoga studio. It feels awesome to move and bounce like a little kid!

I often run 1-2 miles wearing one or two jackets (depending on the weather), so I get really sweaty, then I do a mixture of these six things while chanting and making cathartic sounds. This is one of my favorite things to do in the whole wide world! I feel totally free and spontaneous, and I often burst out into uncontrollable laughter.

Tapping different parts of your body is a tool used in EFT (Emotional Freedom Technique), for the purpose of accessing and reprogramming cellular memories stored in different parts of the body. You can use one finger to hit a specific pressure point, or you can use all five fingers to tap a larger area of your body. EFT usually recommends repeating affirmations while tapping on a specific point or Energy Meridian. By affirming a new belief / story while tapping, you are reprogramming the cellular memories stored in that area. I invite you to explore what techniques feel best to you.

Smacking and **Punching** are essentially more intense versions of Tapping. I use these techniques to "reclaim sensation" in areas that have been partially numb / traumatized. It increases blood and energy flow very quickly. Of course, these techniques are not everyone's "cup of tea," though for me they have been very helpful in "reclaiming my power" and expressing my Primal Self. I can see how these techniques could potentially be viewed as "re-traumatizing" if you have a history of being physically abused. I have experienced some physical abuse in my past, and by smacking / punching myself consciously while affirming "I am strong, I am strong," I've been able to release old fears and reclaim both sensation and a sense of strength and groundedness in my body. Smacking moves energy and blood through the skin and surface muscles, and Punching helps to move energy through deeper muscles and even the bones / bone marrow. As mentioned earlier, everything is vibration, and so to truly release old traumas / vibrations you have to shake things up at a deep level. By doing these practices regularly in a safe container, you begin to set a new vibration into your BodyMind where you feel much more strong and grounded.

"Shake it up, baby! Twist and Shout! Shake it up, baby! C'mon and work it on out." The band Graham Blvd who sang that song back in the 1960's really knew what they were talkin' about! **Shaking, Bouncing,** and other free form movements are very powerful tools for moving and releasing stuck energy. I often practice these during an Ecstatic Dance session. I also like to do them for 5-10 minutes after jogging. Although I may look like I'm having a seizure to someone walking by, I'm really having a great time. The sign that you're doing these techniques correctly is that you will probably burst out into laughter. If you think you look ridiculous, it's because you do : Hahahah. The key is to let your muscles relax and move rhythmically up and down, side to side, and however you feel inspired. You can use a mini-trampoline, yoga ball, or do it in a swimming pool - all of which are very fun! I like to do intuitive toning / chanting while I bounce and shake.

I recently discovered a whole Training System, which teaches a technique very similar to what I've been practicing. It is called TRE (Trauma Release Exercise and to quote from the website : "TRE *is an innovative series of exercises that assist the body in releasing deep muscular patterns of stress, tension and trauma. Created by Dr. David Berceli, PhD, TRE® safely activates a natural reflex mechanism of shaking or vibrating that releases muscular tension, calming down the nervous system. When this muscular shaking/vibrating mechanism is activated in a safe and controlled environment, the body is encouraged to return back to a state of balance."*

To learn more, check out www.traumaprevention.com

Spinning is yet another Superpower tool for moving energy. You simply spin your entire body around in a circle for 1-5 minutes. This practice brings your chakras (defined as wheels of energy) into a more harmonious alignment. The Spiritual Tradition of Sufism uses Spinning as a moving meditation, and sometimes they spin for an entire hour. I love it, because it brings me deeply into the moment. As my vision gets blurry, I often enter a transcendent state of consciousness where I can sense the unity and oneness of the entire universe. Yay for spinning!

All 6 of these tools and techniques (Tapping, Smacking, Punching, Shaking, Bouncing and Spinning) assist you in changing the overall vibration of your BodyMind System towards greater harmony and balance.

YELLING AND MOANING

On this topic, here is what I posted while it was very fresh in my awareness on **November 18th, 2013 @ 11:54pm :**

I believe that yelling / screaming is a very useful and underrated tool. Sound is a powerful way to express and transmute energy.

When I was in the hospital after appendix surgery, I was in excruciating pain. My body naturally started moaning / shouting "AAAAOOOOHHH," and this actually helped the pain to go away.

It makes sense that kids scream and cry often to dispel energy that they don't want in their system...My girlfriend and I have been experimenting with this technique... Anytime we feel frustrated, angry, or even worried, we make a loud noise to express that energy. 9 times out of 10, the uncomfortable emotion passes or mostly diminishes.

I notice that if I am in a public place, I tend to hold back and not fully express the sound necessary to clear the emotion. Our societal program gives us "pacifiers" when we are young to keep us quiet, and thus as adults we become pacified as well.

I believe we must tune into our true emotions and find healthy ways to express through catharsis: whether it's yelling, moaning, intense exercise, or simply speaking our truth of what we feel. Then, we won't subconsciously build up negative emotions, until they burst out in violence or attacks.

CATHARTIC SPEAKING EXERCISE

The Cathartic Speaking Exercise gives you total permission to say whatever words, thoughts, and feelings come to mind. To start off, I set the intention / prayer of a "Bubble of Total Acceptance and Forgiveness." This way, nothing I say can harm myself or anyone that I speak about. You can also intend for the old energy you are releasing to be purified into the Violet Flame and / or give it back to Pachamama to be transmuted.

The goal is to tune into your deepest emotions, thoughts, and feelings that are often not expressed. This often includes getting in touch with your Inner Child, and speaking the thoughts / feelings that you may have had as a child but bottled inside. It feels extremely liberating to get these things off your chest and out of your system. Again, the key is to give yourself total permission to say anything and everything without holding back. I invite you to express your deep-seated fears, desires, and feelings. This means you can say Violent things such as, "I hate you, I want to kill you." You can also express all your Sexual Desires.

Of course I am not encouraging or condoning any type of violence to another being. The key here is that when we get hurt or wounded, energy gets distorted within us and by expressing these trapped energies in a safe space you set them free.

It's key to remember that the things you say aren't usually your core truth, though by letting yourself say certain things it purges that energy out of your system and often leads to a more purified state of mind.

----

3 Questions to ask yourself for the Cathartic Speaking Exercise :

1. What sound am I most afraid / ashamed to make? - That's where the juice is :)

2. What would this feeling sound like if I was to explain it without words?

3. What sound / expression would I make if I were feeling this at 5 years old?

ANGER AND SADNESS RELEASE

For much of my life, I had essentially no connection to the emotion of Anger within myself. My parents rarely expressed it in front of me, and any time it wanted to surface within me I believe I found some way to distract myself or suppress it. Around 2013, as I progressed on my Life Path, the cracks in the dam began to get bigger and I realized,

"Woah, I have a lot of anger inside me!" I began to pursue healthy ways to express everything from minor frustrations to primal rage.

Sadness often bubbles up to be released after I have moved through layers of stuck energy, and also purged some anger and frustration. The sadness sometimes mixes with deep gratitude and awe of the beauty of life. Sometimes there are specific memories or feelings connected to another person, sometimes I just feel sad for no reason.

Anger, Sadness, and a variety of interrelated emotions are usually attached to the same root feelings. The process through which I release them are very similar and also directly linked to the "Cathartic Speaking Exercise" explained earlier.

When I feel Anger coming up, I seek out a safe space to express it. Usually this is a private room in my home, in my car, or out in the woods. I will often open with a prayer like this: "Great Spirit, thank you for this day. Thank you for this life. Please help me to release what no longer serves me with ease, grace, and fierce love." (I ask for ease and grace when it's applicable, though I know that often times it is very uncomfortable and intense, which is why I prayer for "fierce love," which includes very intense sensations.)

I prefer to release anger by myself, though it may be helpful for you to have a trusted friend with you. If I'm in my car or home, I usually put on some music that helps with the process (listed at the end of this section). As the anger bubbles up, I tune into whether I want to yell, speak, move my body, or all of the above. If I'm out in the woods, I will often pick up a large branch and smash it against a rock or another branch. This helps me to tap into my primal animal self. I often yell at the top of my lungs and beat my chest like a gorilla. I've had some sessions where I literally yell for 45 minutes straight!

I also have had great success with the Affirmation Activations (listed in the next section) and declaring at full volume, "I claim my power to be strong and healthy!" "I claim my power to provide for myself!" If there is a specific person or thing I am mad about, I will utilize the Cathartic Speaking Exercise. After I feel that I've moved through a sufficient amount of anger, I will close my session by saying, "Thank you Great Spirit." Then, I close my energy field by sweeping my arms around myself 3 times in a circle and then bring my palms together. Lastly, I like to ground my energy by putting my hands and feet on Pachamama for a few minutes. It's important to let your energy settle after a big anger release session. Also, it unlocks so much energy you may feel like you can conquer the world and accomplish anything in that moment. To some degree you can, but I recommend being gentle with the integration process, and letting your system balance out for a few hours afterwards.

Releasing anger often flows easily into releasing sadness. When I need to cry, there are a few things I do. I find a space where I feel safe to let my emotions flow. It's important to have an energetically clear space so that energy can flow easily through you. I often burn some Sage or Palo Santo before and especially after the session. I usually prefer to be alone, or with one close friend who will hold a sacred space with me. I will set out a yoga mat, or blanket down, so that I can bow down on my knees. I usually say a prayer something like this, "Great Spirit, please help me to release what no longer serves me. I pray for clarity, understanding, and greater wholeness." Then, I will often put on one of the songs listed below. If there is a specific person or event I have feelings around, I will sometimes look at a few pictures of them online, or imagine them in my mind's eye. I will often repeat the Ho'oponopono prayer in connection to this person or event. Also, practicing rapid deep belly breathing through the mouth is a good way to move emotions to the surface. I like to have tissues available, and a cup if I need to spit. (I know I'm getting specific, but this is what I do, homie :) My favorite pose to cry in is where I bow down on my knees, put my forehead to the ground, and put my hands out in front of my head with my palms either cupped or touching each other. I can usually sense when I have cried enough for that session. I close it off by saying, "Thank you Great Spirit," and I close my energy field by bringing my hands to prayer position and feeling a strong bubble of protection surrounding me.

Here are 2 Artists whose music has greatly assisted me in releasing anger. Both Xavier and Trevor are very skilled on the Didgeridoo, which seems to be an excellent catalyst for releasing anger.

Xavier Rudd : Lioness Eye, Mana, Spirit Bird

Trevor Green : Essentially every song on the Album "Sacred Seed"

Listening to certain artists or songs is extremely helpful for me to let the tears flow. Here are a few of my favorite "Crying Songs" (most of which you can find on YouTube. Also check out the links in the last chapter of this book called "The Web of Infinite Inspiration")

Kevin Yazzie : Love, Hope, Good Relations, Charity

Peia : Machi, Blessed We Are, Vento

Earthwake : Dear Me, Cosmos, Johnny Appleseed
Robbie Robertson : Peyote Healing Song
Shimshai : Agua de Estrellas, Cunaq, Roots
Orka : Sirenita Bobinsana

THE AFFIRMATION ACTIVATIONS

The Affirmation Activations are a practical system for truly embodying the "Positive Affirmations" that we say to ourselves.

Many people have discovered the benefits of repeating Positive Affirmations, such as "I love and accept myself" or "I am abundant and free." Sometimes, folks will put these statements on post-it notes all over their homes. The big question is : Does saying these things over and over actually create a change in your life?

In my experience, the answer is : "You will only see new results in your life, if you truly believe these statements to be true." What does it mean to "truly believe" something? It means that you have integrated the new belief into your Subconscious Mind. The Subconscious Mind runs 95% of your behavior, and is rooted within the cells of your body.

Through studying the Subconscious Mind, Bioenergetics, and many different spiritual teachings, I've coalesced a system called the "Affirmation Activations," which are intended to penetrate the Subconscious Mind, and thus actually plant the seeds for the results we desire in our lives.

Step 1 : Do some sort of exercise / movement for at least 10 minutes to activate the circuitry and connection between the Conscious and Subconscious Mind.

Step 2 : Choose an affirmative statement that you want to cultivate in your life. Example : "I am strong and grounded."

Step 3 : Choose 1 of the Affirmation Activations (listed in the following pages) such as : "I am totally safe…"

Step 4 : Stand in a posture that matches the feeling of your affirmation. For "Generative" ones, I like to stand up strong and put my palms together or facing outwards. For "Receptive" ones, I am often laying down, or in a relaxed position. For "Transformative," there are many options. Sometimes I shout them loudly, sometimes I repeat them softly. I also enjoy repeating them in a random, routine part of my day, like walking down the stairs, and saying them aloud.

Step 5 : Combine the Affirmation Activation with your affirmative statement : "I am totally safe to be strong and grounded." The key is to DECLARE it, and feel it within the cells of your body / Subconscious Mind. It is also important to enunciate each word, for this creates a precise sound frequency and sends a clear sign to the world of what you believe. Enunciating each word causes you to use your entire mouth and both brain hemispheres, which in turn vibrates your Pineal Gland at the center of your brain. The Pineal Gland is directly linked to your state of consciousness, so these affirmations can help you tune into an empowered state of being.

Step 6 : After you say the Affirmation, deeply inhale, roll your shoulders back, and exhale, letting it sink into your body. Repeat this process 3 times, to make a deep impression within your Subconscious Mind.

Step 7 : To seal this new belief, place both hands on your heart and say "Thank you" 3 times. Between each "Thank you", take a deep inhale, do a shoulder roll, and exhale.

Step 8 : If you feel inspired, you can keep the same affirmative statement, and repeat the process with a different Affirmation Activation.

Step 9 (optional) : "YES-I" is an Empowerment Mantra. It carries the vibration of self and collective empowerent. You can add "Yes-I" to any affirmation / mantra to add some extra momentum to it. For Example :

"Yes-I am totally safe to be strong and grounded." or "Yes-I choose to believe that all is flowin."

These 9 steps are one pathway to using the Affirmation Activations. There are certainly other pathways, and I invite you to explore creating your own. Here are a few other keys to remember about the Affirmation Activations :

One Layer at a Time! - It is crucial to realize that healing happens in layers, and although it is possible to have quantum leaps, often times change doesn't happen overnight. Patience and persistence are key virtues here. I have experienced the chaos and pain that ensues from trying to rush my healing process, and now I've learned to go layer by layer.

The truth is that each layer contains unique energy, and usually has specific memories or beliefs attached to it. In relation to this, each layer holds wisdom and lessons, which can only be received if we are patient and present with the process. The healing process takes time and is exquisitely beautiful if we respect all of the subtleties of it.

I practice this by saying Affirmations like "I ask for guidance on releasing the next layer of fear." "I choose to claim the next layer of my divine, eternal self."

Gathering Evidence - I recommend gathering evidence to support the new beliefs you are implementing into your life. If your new belief is "I am totally worthy of receiving my dream job," then begin to list pieces of evidence to support this. For example : "My friend Jessica recently got hired into her dream job, and if she can do it, so can I!" Also,

"When I focused my intention and actions towards winning the film contest in 2010, my dream came true. This is another example that I am empowered and capable of success!"

It is also important to Take Action based upon your new beliefs. If you are affirming that you have an abundance of energy and vitality, then do lots of physical activities, and put your abundance of energy in service to others. As you walk around the world with the lens of your new belief, take note of little things that affirm this new reality, and watch the magic unfold before your eyes :)

Normalizing Technique - By saying the affirmations in a relaxed, average tone of voice, you "normalize" them, and tell your Subconscious Mind that it is totally natural and comfortable to accept the new belief / perspective. You can also "normalize" new beliefs by simply talking about them with friends or family. This brings the new perspective from being only in your Mental world to being spoken about by people in the Physical world. It seems so simple, but it's very powerful. Try it out!

<u>Singing Technique</u> - You can transform your Activated Affirmation into a mantra or song. You can create a simple melody, or add new lyrics to "Twinkle Twinkle Little Star" or another popular tune. This may sound silly, though some folks who did this in a workshop I led are still singing their "Twinkly Affirmations" a year or two later.

<u>First and Last 5 Minutes Superpower</u> - **This Superpower states that the 1st five minutes of your day when you wake up, and the last 5 minutes before sleep are two of the most important opportunities of your day.** This is because during these windows of time, the filter between your Subconscious and Conscious Mind is relaxed, so anything you think about marinates into your Subconscious, which is what drives 95% of your behavior. For this reason, I highly recommend practicing your personal Affirmation Activations immediately when you wake up, so that you begin your day feeling empowered and from a place of infinite potential! I love to sing my Affirmations the instant I wake up as I begin to move and dance about my home. Also, as you are settling in for sleep, review your Affirmations and the mental imagery and feeling states associated with your goals. You can do this in a journal, on a vision board, and/or in your mind, all of which allow them to plant like seeds deep into the soil of your Subconscious Mind. These beautiful images and Affirmations will eventually grow in your daily, waking reality!

The
Affirmation
Activations

I ask for guidance in...   I claim my power to...
I'm open to receive...   I choose to believe...
I allow...   I create...

(Receptive)   ## (Generative)

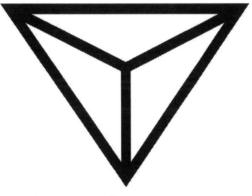

(Transformative)

It is my greatest benefit to...
It is totally safe to...
I am totally worthy to...

----- Why are these 9 Affirmation Activations so powerful? -----

They tap into 3 of the core qualities of the Universe : Receptive, Generative, and Transformative. These could be seen as the Holy Trinity : Feminine, Masculine, and the Divine Child.

RECEPTIVE

When you are feeling like you want to receive support in a particular aspect of life, it is helpful to utilize the Receptive Affirmation Activations.

"I Allow…" : Using this Activation empowers you to receive what the universe is already sending your way, but you may be subconsciously resisting at a subtle level.

"I'm Open To Receive…" : Utilizing this Activation supports you in opening your cells at a deep level to receive whatever you desire i.e. peace, clarity, pleasure, etc.

"I Ask For Guidance…" : This Activation helps you to specify what you are seeking support with. By firmly declaring it to the Universe, you will surely receive guidance. Be aware that it may not come immediately, or in the form you are expecting, but it will indeed come. I recommend keeping a journal with you, and especially by your bed, because the guidance may come in the form of dreams :)

GENERATIVE

When you want to take life by the horns and claim your power to create your own experience, the Generative Affirmation Activations are the golden ticket.

"I Choose To Believe…" : Using this Activation enables you to tap into your true power of deciding what you want to believe. Although you've been conditioned to hold certain beliefs, you can also practice rewriting them using these 4 powerful words before your new declaration.

"I Claim My Power To…" : Often times we don't realize that we can shift a situation in our lives, simply by claiming our power to steer the events, situations, and relationships in our lives. Utilizing this Activation will support you in stepping up your sovereignty and personal willpower.

"I Create…" : This simple Activation can work wonders in your life, if you choose to work with it. By declaring "I Create," you are affirming that you're an integral and empowered piece of the web of life. I dare you to dream big with your creations, because the limit is not the sky.

TRANSFORMATIVE

If you ever feel stuck in a rut, whether it be an old belief system, a stale relationship, or a traffic jam, it is a good time to use the Transformative Affirmation Activations.

"It Is My Greatest Benefit…" : At a fundamental level, you never take an action unless you believe it is somehow in your greatest benefit. Even if you are doing something that your Conscious Mind sees as harmful, deep down you have a Subconscious Belief that this action is serving you. Therefore, in order to begin taking new actions, you must affirm to your Subconscious Mind that these new habits are in your greatest benefit!

"I Am Totally Safe…" : It is unlikely that you will be able to develop a new belief or habit, unless you truly believe that it is safe to take a step into this new territory. By using this Activation, you affirm to your Subconscious Mind that everything will be okay if you integrate this new belief or action.

"I Am Totally Worthy…" : Unworthiness is one of the biggest impediments to manifestation. Whether you are desiring a new job, a fresh relationship, or inner peace, you must first believe that you are deserving of this blessing. Therefore, this Activation is crucial to unlocking your manifestation abilities!

I have literally watched areas of my life do a 180-degree turn by utilizing these 9 Affirmation Activations. They are truly remarkable keys, and I invite you to respect them as such. Please be careful what you wish for with these, because it is quite likely to manifest quicker than you think. It is also important only to shift your Belief System at a rate that feels natural and comfortable to you. Please don't try to rewrite your entire human history in one or two days. Enjoy the process, and let yourself evolve and transform organically.

"FEELIZATION"

I like to say that a Realization happens primarily in your mental brain. It is a conceptual understanding. A "Feelization" is when this realization seeps deep into the rest of your physical body.

An example of this is when I began practicing Vinyasa Yoga. Vinyasa is a style of yoga combining various asanas (postures) with rhythmic breathing. One of my instructors said that Vinyasa is sometimes defined as "the removal of inner blockages," which sounded intriguing to me.

For 75 minutes we moved through a wide variety of flowing postures. Some had me upside down and some required great flexibility. By the end, I felt exhausted. Luckily the final pose is Savasana, where you simply lay flat on the mat. In this moment I had a "Feelization." It did indeed feel like my "inner blockages" had been removed, and for the first time, I was experiencing a more unified state of being within myself. Normally, I felt my body to be a bit of a conglomeration of compartmentalized muscles, bones, organs, upper body, and lower body. As I lay on my mat, drenched in sweat, I felt my mind and all the parts of my body as completely unified and harmonious. This was a "Feelization" and it felt amazing :)

INTEGRATION TOOLS

THE IMPORTANCE OF INTEGRATION

As you do your regular "Healing Practices," it is crucial to integrate all of the new energies, insights, and transformations that you are going through. The Integration Process is often glazed over, hurried, or not fully understood. My intention for this chapter is to share the many lessons and blessings I have learned about Integration. The ultimate goal of Integration is to reclaim your birthright of wholeness. This means to have clear, fluid communication between all aspects of our BodyMind System. This chapter will provide tools for integrating and implementing the various of aspects of your Healing Practice into your daily life.

THE PERSONAL TRANSFORMATION MAP

As you cycle through the different phases of the "Personal Transformation Map", I encourage you begin to "track" Behavior / Thought patterns. Tracking is a term used in Wilderness Survival, which explains the process of following an animal's footprints (tracks) to discover information about the animal or a territory you are exploring. For example, if you notice fresh bear tracks going into a cave, you probably won't want to go in there. If you are hunting in the wild, then you are on the prowl for fresh deer footprints. When you see deer prints in the snow, you can study them to determine how far away the deer is.

Tracking is essentially the art of noticing patterns over time. The patterns can be repetitive thought patterns, body language tendencies, ways of social interaction, or situations you keep encountering in your external world. It is extremely beneficial to take note of patterns in yourself in order to grow in self-awareness. Within the 7 stages of the Personal Transformation Map, there are 2 interconnected areas where you can shine more awareness :

<u>Blind Spots</u> : **Areas of your life that are playing out on autopilot (through inertia) of which you are completely or somewhat unconscious.** For example : "Until yesterday, Bill had no idea that he was treating his wife in the same way that frustrated him so much. He would interrupt her all the time. It was only when they sat down with a therapist, who pointed out this tendency, that he was willing to look at his own behavior. Bill's "Blind Spot" was his unconscious habit of interrupting his wife while she was speaking."

<u>Numb Spots</u> : **Numb spots are areas within the body where you do not have full sensation / awareness.** It is truly incredible how we have become partially numb in different areas of our body, as a way to not feel certain emotions. It is essentially a natural defense mechanism designed to protect us, but once the event we perceive as scary has passed, we can explore the full process of "re-feeling."

Here is a brief overview of the Personal Transformation Map. It's important to remember that the process of moving through this map is often non-linear / fractal in nature. This means you can occupy multiple stages at once, skip around, and continuously revisit different stages in various areas of your life.

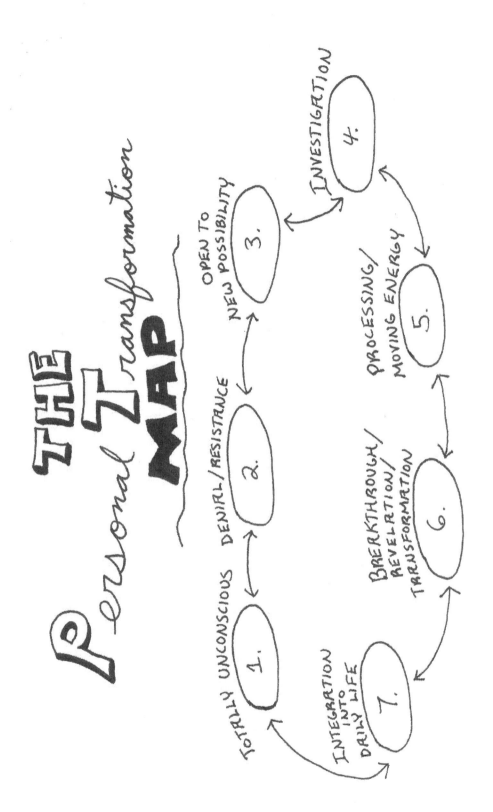

THE T
Personal Transformation
MAP

1. TOTALLY UNCONSCIOUS

2. DENIAL/RESISTANCE

3. OPEN TO NEW POSSIBILITY

4. INVESTIGATION

5. PROCESSING/MOVING ENERGY

6. BREAKTHROUGH/REVELATION/TRANSFORMATION

7. INTEGRATION INTO DAILY LIFE

1. **Totally Unconscious :** At this stage, the behavior pattern is totally outside your awareness. You may notice other people with this behavior, but the idea that you embody it too seems ludicrous.

2. **Resistance / Denial :** At this stage, someone may tell you that you are expressing a certain behavior, and you strongly deny it. "No way would I act like that!" You may even feel angry or repulsed at the idea that you act in such a way.

3. **Open to New Possibility :** At this stage, the energy shifts because you finally open to the possibility that you may occasionally demonstrate this behavior.

4. **Investigation (Internal Compass, Juicy Questions, Core Belief work) :** This is the stage where you look within and utilize your transformational tools to identify what exactly you are doing and what core beliefs are motivating it.

5. **Processing / Moving Energy :** At this stage, you actively work on Processing and Moving your energy to shift your Beliefs, BodyMind System, and Behavior.

6. **Breakthrough / Revelation / Transformation :** At this stage, you feel a shift, and have a profound breakthrough, revelation, or transformation. For example, if you've been processing to release the tension in the right side of your neck, you may finally feel some ease in this area after releasing deep-seated anger and then going for a swim. As you bask in the new level of wholeness, you will probably feel immense gratitude for this Transformation Process.

7. **Integration into Daily Life :** At this stage, you set up new habits and holistic practices to maintain your new Beliefs, BodyMind System, and Behaviors. For example, you may take space to process when anger arises rather than unconsciously acting it out, as you did in the past.

High Tide / Low Tide : It is also beneficial to keep track of the "High Tide / Low Tide" phenomenon as you move through the Personal Transformation Map. I first explained this process in the Keys to Creativity. When applied to Healing, **The High Tide** phase is when everything is cruising along and you feel empowered, as if you are turning into a Butterfly! **The Low Tide** is when things slow down, and you don't feel like you're making any progress. You doubt whether it's worthwhile to keep going. Here, you feel like a caterpillar in metamorphosis, where you are a gooey mess inside a cocoon. This is the best time to relax and cultivate self-care practices. Remember that both the High and Low Tide are part of the natural ebb and flow of life.

I recommend journaling regularly about what you are Tracking. Here are a few questions to ask yourself / journal about :

1. What repetitive Thought Patterns / Mental Advisors do you notice that are not serving your greatest good? What Thought Patterns / Mental Advisors would you rather cultivate?
2. What body language do you notice in others and/or yourself that seem odd or noteworthy?
3. What Belief Systems may be tied to these Thought Patterns / Mental Advisors / Body Language tendencies?
4. What Synchronicities, Animal Totems, Omens, etc. have you noticed that may be reflecting certain aspects of your Healing Process?

INTEGRATION TOOLS AND TECHNIQUES

Note : The tools and techniques outlined here are things I usually do "after" my normal Healing Practice is over; though sometimes they are directly integrated into my intense workout. For example, I may massage my legs for 10 minutes between doing a set of pushups and jumping jacks.

1. Journaling : It is very helpful to keep an active journal as you dive into the Healing Process and/or explore the Keys to Creativity. I like to view it as an "external hard drive" for the mind. As I write things down in my journal, I often have new insights, and it opens up new space for fresh ideas to come in. I once heard the quote "In order to see yourself, you need a mirror." Journaling can act as a mirror for you to see aspects of yourself which were previously invisible.

2. Soul Family : Another form of mirroring which has radically accelerated my healing journey is having "Soul Family" around : **close friends or family with whom you can be totally honest and authentic.** Simply speaking about what you've been going through is very powerful. It takes the process from your 1st Person perspective and Mental Level into a relationship, so you can view your process from a 3rd person view, and express on an Emotional Level. You can also receive helpful feedback and reflections that may not have occurred to you otherwise.

I tend to drive myself crazy if I try to solve all my challenges within my own mind. Usually if I just chat about it with a friend, I gain greater clarity and understanding of my situation. It helps me remember that "we are all in this together."

3. <u>Drinking Lots of Water</u> : When you are engaged in the Healing Process, you are circulating a lot of energy through your entire BodyMind System. To keep all your engines running smoothly, it is key to drink a lot of water before, during, and after your personal practice. Water helps to flush out toxins and restore a sense of peace after a potentially intense session. Coconut water can be good to replenish Electrolytes as well.

4. <u>Laying on Pachamama</u> : This practice is one of the most potent and healing aspects of my entire Healing Journey. It is one component that I feel a lot of people are missing. Mother Earth / Pachamama resonates at 7.83 Hz (the Schumann Resonance) and by laying on her surface, you harmonize with this healing frequency. This brings incredible peace and harmony to body and mind. I can't recommend this enough! I usually lay for at least 20 minutes, though sometimes for up to 2 hours. I can often feel myself becoming one with Pachamama, and I feel all the energy I moved during my practice integrate harmoniously in my being.

5. <u>Deep Rest</u> : Most of us have been conditioned to get between 7-8 hours of sleep per night. In my journey, I have experimented with many different sleep schedules. For example, I spent about 3 months sleeping for 4 hrs. per night, with a 1 hr. nap in the afternoon.

When it comes to integrating, especially after an intense session where you are clearing / reprogramming a lot, it is helpful to give yourself full permission to sleep for as long as possible. Not everyone has the time for this luxury, though if you can sculpt your life in such a way as to allow for this, it is deeply beneficial. I truly believe that your **BodyMind System knows what it needs to heal.** Thus, if you surrender to that deeper wisdom rather than projecting an idea of what you need, the results are surprising. Some days, I will easily sleep for 12 hours and wake up feeling totally rejuvenated and transformed! Oversleeping regularly can lead to grogginess, laziness, and other issues, though if you try it once a week it is usually very beneficial.

6. <u>Being in Water</u> : Water is very therapeutic and allows for powerful Body and Mind harmonization. I especially recommend a hot bath with Epsom Salts, which helps soothe sore muscles. Also, swimming in a pool, lake or in Big Mama Ocean can help you to graciously integrate new energies and dispel anything that no longer serves you.

7. Yin Yoga : This style of yoga is focused on relaxing the BodyMind System and opening the various muscle groups. The first time I experienced a Yin Yoga class at Bhakti Yoga Shala in Santa Monica, I was literally flabbergasted at how relaxed I felt. My heart melted open, and I experienced everything as love.

You can easily practice Yin Yoga at home or attend a class at a local studio. There are many great and simple Yin Yoga videos on YouTube. Be careful: it is so relaxing you may just fall asleep in Pigeon Pose. :)

8. Play / Celebration / Humor : I'll be honest - the Healing Process can often be pretty heavy. Sometimes you are working through deep-seated trauma and it can range from uncomfortable to ridiculously painful. Speaking of ridiculous, it is very helpful to keep a playful attitude while you are doing these practices. You may not be always able to laugh, though if you keep a sense of humor, it will help you stay afloat and also make it easier to communicate about your process with others.

It's great to celebrate your mini-victories, and play in spontaneous ways to activate different neural circuitry. Going to a local playground and swinging is one fun way to do this. It snaps you out of the "Healing Process" and into the simple joy found in the present moment. Pretty much anything that makes you laugh is also good medicine for integration. I like to say "Scoobally Doo" anytime I find myself getting too serious. This is a silly phrase I made up to use in many situations, and it's very fun to exclaim it! : If you drop your phone in the mud - Scoobally Doo! When no one shows up to your event - Scooablly Doo : When you can't comprehend the synchronicity unfolding in your life - Scoobally Doo!

9. Affirmative Mantras : You can also utilize the Affirmation Activations to create some mantras of your own to repeat to assist with Integration. Here are a few that I often say : "I choose to believe that everything is flowing." "I am open to receive guidance on a gracious integration."

And when I am really going through a tough spot in any part of my healing practice, I will say, "This too shall integrate. This too shall integrate. This too shall integrate." This affirmation is a remix of the common Buddhist mantra, "This too shall pass." I like it because it affirms that everything is always moving towards greater wholeness and integration. Every life experience ultimately has purpose and fits together in a beautiful way, even if I can't quite see / feel it in the moment.

10. Closing Your Energy Field : It is very important to close your Healing Practice by sealing your Energy Field / Aura. While practicing the many different Bioenergetic techniques, your energy field becomes very open and expansive. This is good and healthy, though once you return to your daily activities, I recommend setting up a healthy energetic shield. You can do this by repeating 3 times, "I close my Energy Field to all energies except my Higher Self. I call all my energy back into myself." You can also gently pat over your whole body, to feel strong and grounded in your physical body.

Lastly, I recommend "smudging" your energy field with White Sage, to clear out any left over "energetic debris" from your session, and also to assist in protecting your energy field. I like to move the White Sage smoke around the outline of my body, and also in front of each of my 7 chakras, plus my palms and feet. By doing these practices, I feel a sense of completion to my Healing Session, and ready to step into other daily activities.

Here are a few questions on Integration Tools and Techniques :

1. What Integration tools and techniques do you already practice?
2. Which new ones do you want to cultivate?
3. How can you make these new ones into Habitual Rituals?

HEALING TOUCH

(This topic is so multi-faceted, that I am giving it an individual section to dive into some of the most important aspects.)

Author Gary Chapman wrote a monumental book called **The Five Love Languages. The book explains the 5 primary ways humans give and receive love. In no particular order, they are : 1. Words of Affirmation 2. Acts of Service 3. Gifts (giving and receiving) 4. Quality Time 5. Physical Touch**

The book supports you to identify which is your primary love language. This is the form of love that makes you feel loved most deeply.

I've found that my primary love language is Physical Touch. I believe physical touch is extremely crucial to the development of healthy humans. If a baby is not touched / held enough during its first days and weeks, it can develop many disorders and potentially die.

As infants, we experience the sensation of being loved through physical touch far before we can comprehend any of the other four love languages. For this reason, I believe that receiving loving touch affects us at a Subconscious Level and helps our bodies to relax and feel at peace. When we don't experience a regular amount of physical affection, it leads to a variety of coping mechanisms.

Personally, I know that my parents loved and still love me deeply despite us speaking different love languages. Both my Mom and Dad demonstrated the other 4 Love Languages regularly, though cuddling was not something we did very often. I believe this led part of me to feel unloved and unlovable. As a result, I often felt afraid and created scary scenarios in my imagination. I thought that monsters, ghosts, aliens, robbers, and everything in between were out to get me. I truly believe that if my parents had just held me more often, I would have felt a deep sense of peace instead of being worried about all these boogie monsters. I choose not to blame my parents, or myself, for the way my childhood unfolded. I believe our souls chose each other to learn certain lessons so that we could each grow in unique ways.

Since discovering this "wound" within myself, I've been finding ways to nurture myself and help my Inner Child to feel at peace. Receiving massage and Reiki from others is very beneficial — and especially giving it to myself. Also, having a conversation with my Inner Child helps him/her to feel like his/her voice and needs are heard. (I explain this process later in this chapter.) I probably wouldn't have discovered the depth, beauty, and power of all these tools had I not experienced a lack of physical affection growing up.

Directly tied to Healing Touch is the **Healing Power of Sharing Breath**. I know this may sound odd at first, but my experience has shown me that feeling someone's breath directly is deeply therapeutic. Our breath carries the energy of our "Spirit", which is why breathing is called "re-spir-ation".To be filled with spirit is to be "in-spired."

Our breath carries a warmth — an energy that can be shared with those we are closest to. When mothers and fathers hold their children, feeling the breath of a parent reassures the child on a primal level that they are held, safe, and loved. I know my parents loved / love me deeply, though I wish I had known how much I appreciate feeling the presence of breath as a kid so I could have communicated that it was very important to me. Now as an adult, I am remembering and honoring my breath and those that I share it with.

Especially with an intimate partner, you can practice breathing directly into each other's mouths, as if you are underwater! I know it may sound weird, but I invite you to give it a try. Also, it's key to realize that this Mainstream Strangedream has conditioned us to be very judgmental of our breath. In my healing journey, I've had to shed layers of conditioning to reconnect with the natural and sacred smell / feeling of my breath, and being breathed on. When you eat nourishing foods, and have good dental health, your breath will carry a beautiful, natural aroma.

The Breath is also a key element in both giving and receiving massage. After receiving some powerful Bodywork at a Festival, here is what I wrote on **October 1st, 2014 @ 6:07pm** :

The revolution will be massaged! Out of all the healing modalities and complex meditations I've explored, good ol' Human-to-Human massage is probably my favorite. This Ancient Art balances the Mind, Body, and Soul, and reminds me that all 3 are actually 1 unified whole.

I've traveled to many transformational festivals this summer, and one of the things I am most blown away by are : The Healing Zones. Massage Therapists and Healers of all sorts come together to form a collective. They set up a sanctuary space in a Geodesic Dome or massive tent. During every day of the festival, participants enter this Sacred Space to receive a brief, yet powerful treatment.

As I hung out around the Healing Dome at Rootwire and Gratifly, I got to see so many "before" and "after" faces. It was truly astonishing to observe the shifts that would happen in people after a 20 min. Thai Massage or a little Reiki Healing.

If everyone on Earth received regular massage, our planet would become more peaceful in the blink of an eye. I'm sure of it. And the fun thing is that giving massage is healing too. As we give massage, we open ourselves to be conduits for healing chi / prana / energy.

BODYWORK / MASSAGE

Massage and Bodywork help muscle tissues to relax as well as integrate any previously blocked energy that you moved during your Healing Practice. It is usually beneficial to use light pressure after doing a lot of exercise so you don't overtax your muscles, though sometimes deep pressure is the way to go. There's nothing better than a good butt massage after an intense workout. This also helps to break up the lactic acid in the muscles. I recommend exploring these 3 types of massage :

Self-Massage : I enjoy massaging all different parts of my body throughout the day whenever I feel inspired, and I usually do a more in-depth session before bed. I often use Coconut Oil to get deep into a specific muscle area. A little bit of self-massage every day can make a huge difference in your state of well-being.

Partner Trade : I like to trade massage with one of my friends at least once a week. We get to practice intuitive massage and explore any techniques we have studied. It is a unique and fun way to connect with a friend on a nonverbal level. Depending on your preference, you can use a massage table, chair, or simply lay on the floor.

Professional Massage : I sincerely recommend experiencing a professional massage every once and awhile. Depending on your budget, you can choose how often you want to go. I see it as a positive investment in the health of mind, body, and spirit. I've experienced profound transformation on all levels through receiving professional massage.

Personally, I love Deep Tissue and Thai Massage the most. Through receiving weekly Thai Massages for 1 month from my friend Sol in Pittsburgh, my spine came into better alignment, my posture drastically improved, and I felt about 2 inches taller! Thai Massage is unique because it is usually done lying on a mat on the floor, and the practitioner essentially puts your body in yoga poses and utilizes the force of gravity to do most of the work. As you get folded into a pretzel, your body and mind relax into a state of bliss. :)

3 Questions on Bodywork / Massage :

1. When during your day can you schedule self-massage?
2. How can you integrate more partner massage trade into your life?
3. What style of Professional Massage do you feel most drawn to?

OTHER HEALING / MASSAGE MODALITIES

Reiki / Energy Healing : Reiki means "Universal Energy", and we all have the capacity to tap into it. One person simply places their hands on, or just above the recipient, and allows this healing energy to flow where it needs to go. I recommend sessions last anywhere between 5 and 75 minutes.

It is beneficial to receive a "Reiki Attunement" from a Reiki Master, though I've met plenty of people with the gift who hadn't had an Attunement. You can direct Reiki Energy to yourself, a friend, a pet, or even a turbulent situation between people. I recommend practicing on yourself on a regular basis for at least a year before giving Reiki to another person.

I've experienced deep healing through receiving Reiki. I sense that this Universal Energy helps to awaken dormant "Junk DNA" within the body, so that we can function at our highest potential. As this process happens, we gain greater awareness, sensation, and functionality in our BodyMind System.

The Tension Melter : Commonly known as "Massage Guns," these are powerful tools for releasing deep muscle tension. Please be gentle with these and ease into any painful / tight areas. There are multiple interchangeable options for putting on the end of the Tension Melter. The option with the foam ball on the end is optimal for most massages, and is my personal favorite. In the past 2 years, these devices have skyrocketed in popularity and I totally understand why! I bought mine for 90$ online, and it has worked great for the past year, but I believe it is important to use it mindfully, because they can sometimes break if you drop them. Some models like the Theragun can be up to 600$, though there are many less expensive brands, like the FlyBy version, which I highly recommend.

Homedics Shiatsu Massage Pillow : I love this massager for just kicking back and relaxing on the couch. This is a phenomenal bang for your buck! It has 2 sets of spinning shiatsu massage balls. It also has the option of adding heat, which can be very soothing! You can get in online for 40-50$.

Acupressure Mat : These devices are phenomenal for bringing increased blood and energy flow to your skin and overall body. This is definitely not everyones cup of tea, because it is a pretty intense sensation to lay on these moderately sharp acupressure points. I have the one from a company called ProSource Fit and it also comes with a small Acupressure Pillow. I freaking love this thing! It only costs 20-30$ online.

Octopus Body Massager : Also referred to as "The Tingler" or sometimes "The Orgasmatron," this amazing device is a powerful tool for relaxation. Many people only think it feels good on the scalp, though I advocate exploration of the whole body.

The Octopus Body Massager looks like an octopus and is made of an aluminum rod, with 12 rounded aluminum prongs tipped with a soft resin coating. It often catalyzes goosebumps all over the skin of whoever is receiving it. I jokingly call it the "Goosebump Inducer" and the "Road Rage Reducer" because I often use it in the car to relax.

Beginning in 2012, I started ordering OBM's in bulk online, and then selling, trading, and gifting them as I traveled the country. Between 2012 and 2015 I estimate that I distributed around 1,000 massagers, and most of them were exchanged with individuals to whom I personally gave an "Activation". It is truly an honor to witness someone receiving an OBM for the first time. They usually light up with a childlike joy and often burst into laughter. I am grateful to be able to share this healing tool with the world! There are many different styles you can purchase on Amazon or Ebay. For the best quality versions, please visit SacredStoryWeavers.com

Foam Roller : These are remarkably powerful for relaxing muscle tension in the legs and back. I'm a big fan of the the 24 in.x 6in. option. You can get them at many online stores for 15-25$

Soothing Skin Technique : The technique is to very gently caress over the skin, and aim to only touch the hair follicles on the skin's surface. If you're practicing it optimally, then you or the recipient will get goosebumps. : This simple practice works wonders for relaxing the body and mind. You can do it on yourself or with another person. You can experiment moving a few centimeters away from the skin, or going closer and actually touching the surface of the body. The key is to move slowly and be very present with the sensations as you are giving or receiving touch. The goal is to catalyze goosebumps and a deep, peaceful state of relaxation. (Some people also call this technique "Feather Touch."

I truly believe that this technique can help to heal or lessen (CPTSD symptoms. As I've worked with (CPTSD within myself, I find that the Soothing Skin Technique dissolves my anxiety, and seemingly cools down my "fight or flight response," which is usually overactive in people with (CPTSD. I pray that Holistic Techniques like this will grow in popularity and eventually reduce or replace pharmaceutical treatments for (CPTSD and other Mind-Body conditions.

INNER CHILD HEALING

In order to heal your "Inner Child", it is necessary to form a relationship and enter into communication with this innocent dimension of yourself. I learned a lot of this intuitively and also by reading Jon Bradshaw's book "Homecoming : Reclaiming and Championing Your Inner Child."

In this practice, I invite "Lil Kevin" to share how he is feeling or any memories he wants to share. Here are some examples of how I would talk with my him. First I set aside some space and time to have a conversation with my Inner Child. Just like I'm putting on a skit, I play both roles, and use my average speaking voice for my adult self, and a softer, innocent voice for my child self. Here is an example of a conversation :

Adult Self : Hey Kevin, how are you feeling today?
Lil Kevin : I'm feeling okay. I guess I'm a little sad.

Adult Self : Why are you feeling sad?
Lil Kevin : I feel like you're ignoring me. You're being too serious, and not playing with me enough.

Adult Self : Thank you for sharing this. I hear you. How would you like to play together? *Lil Kevin : I want to go swimming. And I want to play soccer. And I want to dance more.*

Adult Self : Okay, thank you for sharing what you want to do. I will do my best to schedule these activities into the next week or two.
Lil Kevin : Yay! Thank you :)

Adult Self : Is there anything else you want to share?
Lil Kevin : Yea, I wanna share how scared I was when I had to go out in public without my mommy or daddy with me. Like when I was with my babysitter, and she took me to the outdoor swimming pool, and I had to go in the locker room by myself. I felt scared.

Adult Self : Thank you for sharing this. I hear you. It is totally normal that you felt scared. I want you to know that you are safe now. I am here to protect you, love you, and take care of you.
Lil Kevin : Are you sure? Are you sure you're not gonna leave me?

Adult Self : Yes, I'm sure. I am here for you anytime you want to share anything with me.

Lil Kevin : Okay. Thank you. Can we have a hug?

Adult Self : Of course. (At this point I wrap my arms around myself and give myself a hug for at least 30 seconds)

Key Concepts to remember for Inner Child Healing :

1. Ask your Inner Child how he/she is feeling emotionally.

2. Ask them why they are feeling this way.

3. Ask them what fears / desires they want to express.

4. Assure them that you hear them, thank them for sharing, and assure them that whatever they are feeling / expressing is okay, and they are allowed to feel that way.

5. Assure them that you are able to protect / take care of them, and that they are safe now.

6. If they have specific requests that seem reasonable, you can assure them that you will do your best to meet those needs.

PAIN BODY INTEGRATION

The **Pain Body** as Eckhart Tolle describes it is **the total energy field of all our past Emotional Pain. This includes all the Misqualified Energy, Frozen, and Unaccepted parts of ourselves.** It is like a heavy burden we carry, and it causes our Mind and Body to feel fragmented. It is comprised of all the "Resistance Energy" that we hold in our Energy field. It gets triggered anytime something shines the light of consciousness upon these unconscious, unintegrated parts of ourselves. (It may be helpful to revisit the section earlier in this chapter called "Energetic Imprints.")

In order to integrate the Pain-Body, here are some tips of what has worked for me, time and time again :

1. Enter a state of "Full Body Presence." Let yourself observe the sensations in your entire body and surrounding energy field. Regardless of what sensations arise, simply **Allow them to BE**, without resistance or judgment.

2. Visualize your body as if it is made completely of golden vibrating energy. No separate organs, body parts or distinct pieces — just one continuous field of golden energy.

3. The Pain Body often manifests as a bubble of energy that feels uncomfortable or anxious. It will most likely hide in one area of your body. As you shine the light of your awareness on it, it will probably get more intensely painful. It may even move around in your body. This is a telltale sign that it is the Pain Body! The Pain Body does not want you to observe it directly. By holding your awareness on this area and not falling into victim consciousness, you are transmuting the energy. I recommend giving your Pain Body a name so you can call it out when it gets triggered. This helps you to create a space of awareness and also adds lightness and humor to your Emotional Process. I call my Pain Body "Filbert." You may want to say something like : "I've caught you Filbert. I see you. You can't hide any longer!"

4. Continue holding Full Body Presence. You are essentially diffusing the energy of the Pain Body and allowing this energy that had separated from a state of wholeness to re-integrate. You may feel like your body is becoming lighter, or even being filled with light. The "darkness" or unconsciousness of the Pain Body is being transformed into Presence and Awareness. It is truly a remarkable and beautiful process!

5. It is also important to note that the Pain Body feeds on pain, negativity, and drama. Observe any tendencies within yourself that are causing you to fuel these areas. Also, I firmly believe that the Pain Body thrives if your body is in an Acidic pH state. I recommend being mindful of which eating habits are contributing towards body acidity. Limiting / avoiding meat, fish, dairy, processed, gluten-rich, and very sugary foods is a good place to begin.

6. Communicating with friends who have an understanding of the Pain Body is another great tool for shining the light of awareness on past emotional wounds and integrating them harmoniously. This is high-level Spiritual Ninja shit right here! Hahah :) When you have a friend who is willing to hold space for you as your Pain Body gets activated, that is a priceless gift. And when you can not take your friend's behavior personally, because you can see that his / her Pain Body has taken over, you will avoid unnecessary drama.

" IS IT USEFUL? "

This is a Superpower Question right here! Teal Swan (The Spiritual Catalyst) articulates this concept very beautifully. The gist is that we must consistently ask ourselves if what we are doing / thinking / believing is actually useful. Here are two other ways to ask the same question:

1. Is this belief / thought / action constructive and/or serving my greatest good?
2. Is this belief / thought / action Beneficial or Detrimental?

It is important to be aware of those sneaky Societally Conditioned Mental Advisors such as "Scarcity Samantha." Samantha may try to sneak in and convince you that it's useful to rush eating lunch so you have more time to do other things. In truth, rushing your lunch will probably create more chaos in your mind and especially your tummy, which will make it more difficult to accomplish other tasks.

The "Mental Advisors" concept is one example of the many tools I share in this book. It is key to remember that tools are sometimes useful and sometimes unnecessary or inappropriate for a specific task or phase of life. Regularly asking the question "Is it useful?" can help you to gain clarity on the most efficient techniques for transformation.

For example, I used to say a 30-second protection prayer that I learned in Kundalini Yoga every single time I would start my car. Even if I stopped to get gas or use a rest stop, I would repeat the prayer again before I continued driving. The prayer made me feel good and connected to my higher guidance.

Eventually, there reached a point where I felt like I was just "going through the motions" when I would say the prayer. I realized that I had internalized my sense of protection and connection, and that it was no longer necessary to say the prayer every time I got in my car. Again, the key question to ask is "**Is this belief / thought / action actually useful?**"

BIOENERGETICS AND CORE ENERGETICS

After writing most of this book, I discovered two related schools of thought that cover many of these same topics covered in the Healing Process chapter. I personally intend to learn much more about both of these vast reservoirs of wisdom. I also recommend you check them out if you want to learn more, or schedule a session with a Core Energetics Practitioner :

Check out Bioenergetics by Alexander Lowen - www.lowenfoundation.org
Core Energetics - www.coreenergetics.org

THE HEALING PROCESS CONCLUSION

THE GIFT OF PAIN

Posted on October 12th, 2013 @ 11:12pm : *I am doing the best I can to integrate my week in the hospital in a light-hearted and empowering way. Honestly, it was one of the most challenging and acutely painful weeks of my life.*

Some philosophers describe life as "Consciousness playing a game to experience itself subjectively." In order for this game to happen, consciousness must venture through every type of experiential territory...from the most pleasant pleasures to the most potent pains. I feel that everyone's life is a bit of a roller coaster ride full of ups and downs, smiles and frowns. Bringing in the concept of reincarnation allows for the possibility of some "incarnations" to be far more pleasure-packed, or unbelievably uncomfortable.

I feel very blessed in my current life for so many reasons. I have the privilege to experience extraordinary things on regular basis. Some of my peaks of joy and bliss have come through adventure traveling, consistent yoga, meditation, and exercise, tantric sexuality, mindful eating, entheogenic plant medicines, and everyday miracles.

This week my consciousness seemingly decided to add a few new experiences to the Akashic database...I got to taste a wide array of flavors of pain, which rocked me to the core. I will share candidly here because I am not afraid of pain, and don't think it should be a taboo subject any longer. We all experience it, so why hide from it? I don't share this to receive pity or brownie points, but mostly because I was literally fascinated with the magnitude of pain my body could withstand...

The hospital gives a scale of 0 to 10 to rank your pain. 0 being no pain whatsoever, 10 meaning "Please God, Have Mercy on My Soul!!"

When I entered the Stanford Hospital it was about 1am. The initial pain of an infected abscess in my belly rated about a 6, pretty uncomfortable, but I could keep my swear words from coming out...36 hours later I was preparing for surgery to remove the abscess and what was left of my appendix. (My appendix ruptured a month earlier at

Bursting Man...I mean Burning Man...and I had a device to drain the fluid from the wound in my side for the following month.) The nurses forbade me from drinking water or eating anything during the 14 hours leading up to surgery. Although I snuck a few sips around 10 hrs. before, a dry throat and stomach was very uncomfortable, and I began to understand the terror of what true dehydration can feel like. Mind you, they were shooting fluids into me through IV, though these barely satiated my thirst.

Eventually I went into surgery, which was a wild warp of timespace, because I laid down in the waiting room, listening to a doctor saying "Ok, here is the anesthesia" I opened my eyes 30 seconds later with immense pain in my stomach, and quickly learned that over an hour had passed and I was out of surgery. The recovery wasn't too bad, because they gave me hefty doses of Dilaudid (also called hospital heroine) an opiate based pain-med, which left me feeling light and fuzzy...until...

12 hours after surgery I was in immense agony. It felt like I was 10 months pregnant with twin lawnmowers. The man who I shared a room with in the hospital was complaining about all the noise I was making, which was keeping him from sleeping. I couldn't help but moan swear words or sing opera notes as my pain soared above a "10", even with the painkillers.

The next morning, a new nurse came in with a unique sense of humor and some important information. She asked "Have you been passing gas?" I replied, "No, I don't think so"...She then explained that during surgery, doctors injected gas into my belly to inflate the cavity so they could maneuver their tools. She told me I needed to fart out that excess gas...

I said, "OK, lets go for a walk" Getting out of bed was borderline excruciating. I began slowly strolling down the hall in my hospital gown pushing my IV stand. I couldn't seem to push out any farts...Then I remembered that I am an excellent burp-er...I began belching incredibly loud, and it literally felt like a balloon was deflating in my belly each time. Many nurses turned and stared at these outrageous burps, but I was on a mission to relieve this pressure...

15 minutes and about 233 burps later I feel totally rejuvenated. Thank goodness this nurse informed me about the gas in my belly, and my proclivity for burping.

… After my success with burping, I thought I was in the clear. I ate a big lunch, and snacked throughout the afternoon. Then, it began to feel like I was in a Harry Potter novel… "just when Harry thought he had made it, the tides turned again." As my food

began to digest, I started to feel more discomfort in my stomach. I tried going "#2" and it felt like an L.A. traffic jam in my intestines. My girlfriend recommended I take a laxative. I'd never taken one in my life, and was fairly intimidated by them, but I wanted to release this blockage. I asked my nurse for a laxative, and she replied "OK, I will page your doctor and ask."

At this point, I had returned to the toilet, pain level at 11, begging for the Universe to allow me to shmoo. I sarcastically said to my girlfriend, "I guess my doctor is the official poo authorizer"…"Nobody shall poo without my permission!" A sense of humor was crucial for me to hold some degree of sanity. Eventually "Dr. Dumpallower" handed over some powerful laxatives…

This night I was faced with a brutal paradox: take more painkillers and increase the constipation or forego pain meds and endure the insanity… I was writhing in agony for a good portion of the night. I literally entered non-ordinary states of consciousness through this pain. It was kinda cool. Every time a burst of butt pain began, the only way to channel the energy was through groaning out a loud "UHHHHHHHHHHHHHHH" …I would rank the pain in these moments at a 27… (Luckily I had a new roommate who was more understanding of my predicament) I stumbled to the toilet several times with no luck. Finally in the morning I was able to push out one valiant fart. (I hadn't farted since surgery, some 48 hrs. previous.) This fart was a good sign, but also an entry into the gates of hell. The last few hours of undoing this internal traffic jam were truly astounding. I've had broken bones, been hit by a car, etc., but this pain of constipation surpassed them all!

The pure ecstatic joy and bliss I experienced after finally squeezing out this poo was enormously glorious! I thanked every deity I could think of. I walked back to my hospital bed a new human being. It felt as though through this process I released ancient pain, which was embedded deep in my DNA. I had been to hell and back, and lived to tell about it. My consciousness had ventured through incredibly uncomfortable terrain, and gathered lots of new experiences.

I was discharged from the hospital later that day with immense gratitude for everyone who helped me through this wild week. I give thanks for my girlfriend, all the nurses, hospital workers, and my friends and family who sent healing energy and prayers.

The lessons from this experience are still integrating, though a few I have gathered so far include:

Honor the pain. Don't be afraid of pain. Go into it. Ask it questions. The pain has a message for you. It wants to be expressed.

Keep a sense of light-heartedness and humor as much as possible. Laugh at yourself. Laugh at your challenges and obstacles. They are not as big as your mind thinks they are.

Give thanks everyday for the unfathomable blessing of a healthy, able body. So many parts and processes working on behalf of your existence is truly remarkable!

Love and forgive everyone no matter what they have done. Hurt people hurt people. You can stop the cycle with love and forgiveness.

HEALING IS COOL!

On September 13th, 2014 @ 3:20pm, I posted this passionate declaration :

It is one of my big missions in life to help make Healing "the cool thing to do."

I affirm a world where it's cooler to stay home and meditate rather than going to drink at a bar.

I affirm a world where it's cooler to cry for an hour than to "Suck it up."

I affirm a world where it's safe to express our deepest fears to our friends instead of the false strength we uphold.

I affirm a world where we always feel safe and worthy of asking for what we need.

I affirm a world where we have the resources, tools, and supportive friends around, so that we don't resort to addictions and self-sabotage.

I affirm a world where sacred plant medicines are revered and used in a ceremonial and harmonious way.

I affirm a world where Ayla Nereo, Xavier Rudd, Rising Appalachia, Chances R Good, etc. is played on the radio and all over the place.

I affirm a world where we FEEL FREE AND EMPOWERED AND JOYFUL!

What type of world do you affirm?

CONCLUSION

This post on "Affirming the World I Want to Live In" is a good summation to "The Healing Process" Chapter. My overall goal is to share a bit of my story, and all the tools and practices that have worked for me, so that more people can experiences these wonders firsthand. I'd love to see "Healing" become the cool thing for young people to do. I feel transformed a zillion times over thanks to these tools, techniques, and perspectives. I am forever grateful for all the trailblazers, pioneers, healers, teachers, guides, and others who have built a foundation for this information to be available to us!

In order to truly transform our world, we must transform inwardly. We must shine the light on all our shadows and integrate these parts of ourselves to become whole. We must see our BodyMind System as the miraculous, harmonious, and powerful temple that it truly is! I invite you to work with as many of the tools and techniques in this chapter as you like. Please remember that you are sovereign and empowered, and always use discernment when trying out new practices and perspectives. We are so blessed to have these tools at our fingertips, so let's treat them with love, respect, and gratitude as we continue on this amazing journey of life!

PHENOMENAL FOOD

INTRODUCTION

When we eat, we are quite literally transforming a substance that was previously "outside" of us into new cells of our physical bodies. This is a miracle! Eating is considered sacred and central to essentially every human culture.

Evolutionarily, foods that give us pleasure are compatible and beneficial to our physiology. This is Nature's way of guiding us to a healthy diet. If a food does not give us pleasure, then our bodies probably won't benefit much from it.

So, what does "Pleasure" truly mean?

HOLISTIC PLEASURE

I prefer using the concept of **"Holistic Pleasure" which includes a food's total effect on Body, Mind, and Spirit – not just a good flavor. Holistic Pleasure also takes into account the many qualities of the foods you ingest, Before, During, and After eating.** Also, rather than a Diet, which contains the word "Die", I prefer to call the variety of foods I eat a "Live-it", which contains the word "Live" and fills me with vitality! Since this terminology is probably new to you, I will usually write "Diet / Live-it."

Here are some criteria to consider when seeking "Holistic Pleasure." First let's take a look at the qualities of the food Before you eat :

1. Was it grown Organically? Locally (within 100 miles of your home)?

2. Does it smell appetizing?

3. How close is the food to its **Natural State**?

A food in it's most Natural State is fresh, unprocessed, and free of manmade chemicals, pesticides etc. I like to imagine a Spectrum ranging from the most Pure Natural state on the left, to the most Artificial (made in a sterile laboratory) on the right.

On this big Spectrum, each food is ranked between a Natural State and an Artificial, Laboratory-made State. A fresh, ripe apple would be at the far left side of the Spectrum, and a neon green apple flavored lollipop would be at the complete opposite side. The closer a food is to its Natural State, the more raw, life-force energy it has. As you move across the spectrum, the foods usually lose life-energy as they are processed in factories. Foods that are made in totally synthetic environments such as Laffy Taffy contain essentially zero natural life-force energy. Most artificial foods require more energy for your body to process. Thus, you are actually losing energy by eating these foods.

Rating your foods on this Spectrum is a powerful tool for integrating lots of natural and organic foods into your life.

------ **Now let's look at the qualities of the food During and After eating :)**

4. Was the food prepared / cooked with love and attention?

5. How are the flavors, colors, and texture combinations?

6. What effect does the food cause in your mind and body? Upliftment? Deep satisfaction? Comfort? Grounding? Does this food remind you of childhood, or a fond memory from your past?

7. Do you feel more energized or less energized after the meal? Do you experience any unusual sensations after i.e. headaches, sluggishness, brain fog?

8. During the following 24 hours do you have healthy bowel movements?

-------- **These are all important aspects to explore in achieving a unique diet / live-it that works for you and provides you with the utmost Holistic Pleasure :)**

A VARIETY OF VIEWPOINTS

There are many different philosophies for discovering what foods are most beneficial for our unique bodies. I have explored several of these, and I invite you to explore them as well. I'm not going to be overly assertive that one is better than another. The important thing is to discover what works for you, and in this dynamic and evolving world, what works for you is often changing too.

It has taken me a lot of exploration and experimentation to find my personal connection with the foods that give me Holistic Pleasure. To be honest, it has been challenging for me to discern the ideal Diet / Live-it for myself. I deeply resonate with Veganism, which I followed 99% for about 7 months in 2016. I feel a greater sense of mental clarity and spiritual connection when I don't consume a lot of animal products. On the other hand, my body seems to feel stronger, and more grounded, when I follow more of a Paleo lifestyle.

I do believe it's very important to incorporate lots of living foods close to their Natural State into your diet / live-it, whether you are eating Vegetarian, Vegan, or Animal Products. It's always key to get a good dose of vitamins, nutrients, fats and proteins. I encourage you to do your research to find a diversity of sources for these. My favorite Plant-Based fats and protein sources are avocados, coconuts, almonds, sunflower seeds, pumpkin seeds, chia seeds, and hemp seeds. Yummy :)

If you are enthusiastic about incorporating more Plant-Based foods into your life, there are wide variety of resources online. Firstly, I recommend watching some of Ralph Smart aka Infinite Waters' YouTube videos on Veganism. Secondly, there are many books which can guide you through the transition process into a more plant-based Diet / Live-it. With all that said, I am not 100% convinced that an entirely Vegan Diet / Live-it is ideal for everyone. Here are some other Diet / Live-it philosophies which myself or close friends of mine highly recommend :

- **Eating according to your Blood type :** *www.dadamo.com*

- **Macrobiotic :** *www.kushiinstitute.org/what-is-macrobiotics*

- **Paleo :** *www.Paleoleap.com*

- **Vegan :** *www.veganhealth.org/articles/intro*

THE BLISS OF EATING!

In the modern world there are often distractions which hinder our ability to be present while cooking / eating. How can we use our Evolutionary Instincts to follow pleasure if we are not fully present and aware of the sensations in our body while we are eating?

Here are some tips for bringing more awareness, sensation, and bliss into your meals!

1. Set aside extra time to prepare / enjoy your meal, so you can eat slower and really taste each bite.

2. Try eating in an environment with very few distractions.

3. Set down your utensil in between bites.

4. Become more conscious of your breathing while eating (many ancient traditions recommend this too). This infuses your food and digestion with fresh air and prana / energy.

5. Chew with your eyes closed and also chew thoroughly (to break down the food, so that you receive the most nutrients).

6. Experiment with making sounds to express your authentic pleasure while you enjoy your food. Mmmmmmm :)

Because many of us have become disassociated and disconnected from our food, we have become confused about what foods give us true Holistic Pleasure. We have created substitute desires and pleasures. Also, we often attempt to meet other basic Human Needs through food. Here are some examples :

1. We crave Excitement / Adventure and substitute these things with eating at a restaurant, or with very spicy and flavorful foods.

2. We crave Intimacy + Human Connection, though we substitute this with sweet, fatty comfort foods and desserts.

3. We crave Aliveness + Mental Stimulation and substitute this with very sweet treats or stimulating superfoods, which often lead to a crash or a dependency.

4. We desire Spiritual Connection + Fulfillment, and try to fill the void by overeating.

5. We fear the intensity of emotions like fear, loneliness, anger, sadness, etc. so we distract / numb ourselves by eating and snacking.

------- I have explored all of these habits at different phases of my life, and although I've made a lot of progress on my path of Holistic Pleasure, I still often meet challenges. It takes a lot of self-love and discipline / blissipline to reprogram yourself towards Holistic Pleasure.

How do we address these Substitute Desires and Distractions?

1. Awareness is the main key. I recommend "Tracking" your eating habits and patterns, and journaling regularly if that resonates with you. You can also utilize the "Personal Transformation Map" from the Healing Process chapter.

2. Having friends and family who are also cultivating Holistic Pleasure is very beneficial. This way you can make meals / eat together and support each other's successes while also discussing the challenges you are each experiencing.

I am extremely grateful for Charles Eisenstein and his book "The Yoga of Eating," which laid much of the foundation and inspiration for all that I share around the topic of Holistic Pleasure. I highly recommend you check out "The Yoga of Eating" as well the 2 hr. Audio seminar on his website :
www.CharlesEisenstein.net/project/yoga-of-eating-seminar-2006/

THE POWER OF CLEANSING

From age 0-18 or so, I pretty much ate whatever my parents and friends were eating, without tuning into what my body was truly asking for. Over the past 6 years, I've slowly gotten to know my deep desires and what makes me feel optimally healthy. Fasting and cleansing has supported me in "re-setting" my system and purifying the many organs in my body. After eating a lot of junk food and artificial ingredients, these cleanses are basically like cleaning the pipes of your body.

For the past few years, I've aimed to do a 2-3 day cleanse once each season (Fall, Winter, Spring, Summer). Doing this helps the body to have a clean slate for each new phase of the year.

As usual, I invite you to explore the variety of cleanses available at your local Health Food Store to find what resonates with you. I've had success with several relatively simple cleanses :

1. 3 Day Water and Laxative Cleanse : Simply drink water and 1-2 cups of Smooth Move Tea (Traditional Medicinals) to totally empty out your intestines, and give your digestive system a break! Whew! The sense of emptiness can be scary at first, but I've come to love the feeling of having no food in my body.

You can also do a self-administered Enema on the nights of day 2 and 3. This helps to clear out anything stuck inside your intestines / colon. I bought the "Faultless Goodhealth Douche / Enema Combination" kit from CVS. You can find this exact one or a similar version at essentially any Drugstore.

Here's what I wrote shortly after a Colon Cleanse on **August 21st, 2014 @ 2:21pm :**

I am currently in a state of ecstatic gratitude and awe at the miracle of existence. I've been doing a Colon Cleanse for the past 4 days, and HOLY CANOLI !!! My first 2 self-administered enemas were nothing short of glorious. It feels like ancient muck and toxic sludge has been released from my being, and replaced with profound mental and bodily clarity, ease and grace. I'll be celebrating this cleanse for all eternity.

----

2. Paragon Cleanse and Candigon Cleanse : Both of these are approximately 40$ kits that you can purchase at most Health Foods Stores. Paragon is highly effective at killing parasites in your gut, and Candigon gets rid of Candida, which is an unhealthy fungus that often grows in the intestines if you eat a lot of processed foods and/or animal products.

Both of these Cleansing Kits are made by a company called RenewLife, and renewing life is exactly what they do! I prefer to use "OregaMax" pills from the Company called "North American Herb and Spice" rather than the pills that come with the Paragon / Candigon kit. I've experienced tremendous transformation through using these kits, and felt a huge shift in mental clarity, and peace within my body.

3. Psyllium and Bentonite Cleanse : Bentonite Clay is usually made of Volcanic ash, and is used to absorb and pull toxins out of the body. It also has an abundance of minerals such as magnesium, copper, iron, and potassium. Psyllium Husk powder is pure fiber and acts as a gentle laxative, to pull the clay through your system, leaving your insides cleansed and purified :) I recommend mixing 1 tablespoon of each in 4 oz. of water before bed every night. If you are doing a specific cleanse, you can add this epic combination in, to amplify your results. The brand Yerba Prima makes high-quality Bentonite Clay and Psyllium Husk powders. If this sounds appealing to you, I invite you to do your own research and try it for one week and gauge the results.

4. Hulda Clarke Liver Cleanse : This is a simple, yet powerful cleanse developed by Dr. Hulda Clarke. I've done it at least 4 times, and every time, I feel so much lighter and clearer afterwards. I generally follow the steps given online. Here's an overview of what I do :

I fast with only water or tea for usually 48 hours. When I am getting close to bedtime on the 2nd day, I mix 2 tablespoons of Epsom Salt (laxative) with some kind of juice — usually Orange Juice or Coconut Water. I drink this, then repeat the same thing 2 hours later. Then I drink ½ cup of Extra Virgin Olive Oil (preferably refrigerated to reduce the taste) with 10-20 drops of Black Walnut Extract (to kill parasites coming from the liver) and a bit of Orange Juice to balance the flavor. The Olive Oil flushes out the many toxins and "stones" made of bile contained within the liver. Then I go to bed, and let this brew work its magic inside of me.

If you decide to do this cleanse, prepare to visit the toilet many times during the night after you drink the Olive Oil. If it is your first or second time, you may see little green "stones" in the toilet, which are condensed bile and toxins that have been stored in your liver. Yum! On the 3rd day, you can ease back into eating foods. I recommend steamed veggies and/or a light salad to begin with. I encourage you to research more online if this cleanse intrigues you. It has been a major gamechanger for me!

5. Black Cumin Seed Oil (Deva) : This is one of the most powerful Antioxidants on the planet! In all my experimentation with supplements and Superfoods, this is one of the absolute best. It is great to ingest a small amount daily and especially to use in conjunction with a cleanse. Black Cumin Seed oil has been used for centuries, and can be traced back to Ancient Egypt (aka Kemet). It has been studied extensively and been shown to aid in treating a huge variety of ailments from indigestion to cancer. I recommend buying a variety of Black Cumin Seed Oil that is 100% Vegan (many brands are not) from a brand called Deva in the capsule form. Or if you want to drink the oil straight (a Tsp. at a time) I recommend the company Amazing Herbs Wow, this stuff is truly amazing!

6. Silence Fast : This is a bit different than the other types of fasting and cleansing. For this one, you simply abstain from speaking for a specific period of time. I recommend attempting to go for at least 24 hours. I have had countless revelations while doing Silence Fasts. It is a great way to view your "Mental Advisors" because they begin to chatter a lot when you're in a social situation, and not speaking as you normally would. It is also fun to observe how other people behave from this silent perspective. Some people may get very frustrated that you won't talk to them - haha. Of course, use your best judgment to discern where and when to do a Silence fast. I recommend finding a day and activity where you will be around friends in a relaxed, yet social environment. I usually signal to people that I'm not speaking by either whispering in their ear, having a small piece of paper to write on, or by hand gesturing that my mouth is shut. Most people will figure it out pretty quickly and respect what you are doing. Overall, it's a very fun experiment and a good change of pace :)

With any fasting or cleansing, I encourage you to use your Internal Compass and your level-headed judgment. Be gentle with yourself during the process. I recommend getting lots of rest, and not engaging in too much social or work activities while doing a fast. May you enjoy the glorious transformations ahead of you through fasting and cleansing :)

SACRED WATER

Our bodies are made of approximately 75% water, which mirrors the fact that our planet is covered about 75% with this same sacred substance. Personally, I advocate that we all revere water, and strive to ingest the best quality possible. From many years of exploration, I have found a few key elements that I feel are most important to have in water.

1. **Fluoride Free :** If you do a small amount of research, it becomes pretty obvious that Fluoride does far more harm than good, and the bottom line is that we don't want to be drinking it. Therefore, it is a top priority to filter out the fluoride in your water and/or find a source that never had it added in the first place.

2. **Spring Water / Alkaline Water :** Spring water is naturally alkaline, meaning that is a pH value above 7. Alkaline water is a powerful antioxidant that contributes to the vibrant health of all your organs, tissues, and bodily functions. Spring water is also naturally Fluoride free - yay :)

If you can find a Spring close to where you live, that has been tested to be safe to drink, then you are blessed to experience "Pure, Living Water!" There is an awesome website designed exactly for this : ***www.findaspring.com***

3. **Filtering Systems :** In all my research, I have found two Water Filters that stand above the rest. The first is the Kangen Water Machine, which uses Electrolysis and Filtration to make regular tap water purified, alkaline, and ionized, all of which create both delicious and nutritious water. The Kangen Water Machine also causes the water to form into a "Hexagonal Structure" at a molecular level. I don't claim to fully understand all the science behind this, but intuitively, I sense that the process of Electrolysis brings the water molecules to a higher vibrational state, where they mirror the 6-sided Flower of Life, which is the geometrical pattern underlying essentially all patterns of nature.

The other system that I have tried and enjoyed is called the "Echo H2 Water Filtration System." This is another Electrolysis system that dissolves molecular Hydrogen into the water, which has been shown to convert the toxic free radicals into benevolent water molecules in the cells of your body. I have a few close friends who swear by the Echo H2 system, and said that they could feel their body detoxing and upgrading in the first weeks of drinking this filtered water. I have yet to drink only this water over an extended period of time, though I am quite confident that this is one of the best filters on the market.

If you're not able to afford one of these 1000$+ filters, I recommend a Berkey filtration system, which are only a couple hundred dollars. Until I live near a bubbling spring or purchase a Kangen or Echo Machine, I will primarily drink Reverse Osmosis + Alkalized Water. I have 2 5 gallon jugs that I bring to a local store to fill up. Then I always add Trace Mineral Drops...

4. **Trace Mineral Drops** : Regardless of what type of water you choose to drink, I highly recommend adding ConcenTrace "Trace Mineral Drops." This product contains over 72 naturally occurring Trace Minerals from the Great Salt Lake with 99% of the Sodium removed. You simply add a few drops to your water, and you receive a wide variety of natural vitamins and minerals such as Manganese, Selenium, and Chromium (just to name a few). Another alternative to the Trace Mineral Drops is to add a sprinkle of Pink Himalayan Salt to your water. :)

Overall, water is extremely sacred for me. May the waters inside us and outside us continue to flow, and may we all bow in reverence to the rivers, streams, oceans, and every drop in between :) There are 2 songs about water that are near and dear to my heart. I invite you to check out both of them :

1. "Yawanawa" by Chances R Good :
www.chancesrgood.bandcamp.com/album/earth-tones

2. "Water Blessing Song Grand Invocation" by Nalini Blossom (and Loli Cosmica) on YouTube

3. If you search through the playlists on my YouTube Channel "Kevin May and Sacred StoryWeavers," I have a playlist called "#WaterisLife Songs/Videos Honoring Water."

SOAKING AND SPROUTING

Only in the past year, have I fully "digested" the benefits of soaking and sprouting many of the foods I eat. Upon research, it is pretty obvious why soaking and sprouting makes so much sense. In the natural world, seeds and nuts are protected by certain natural enzymes, which protect that seed from early germination. This is an evolutionary advantage, because the plant (say a sunflower) can spread its seeds through the natural world, without them growing instantly. This way they can propagate and travel to a nearby ecosystem through the wind, a stream, or in the belly of a Robin.

Thus, in order to replicate the germination process (which normally happens in the moist soil), soaking and sprouting are very beneficial. This process removes the "protective shell" in the form of certain enzymes like phytic acid, which can wreak havoc on your digestive system. Soaking and sprouting also multiplies beneficial Vitamins and Enzymes within, and makes them more bio-available (meaning your body can receive it).

Aside from this "scientific" side, they simply taste awesome! The key is to get raw, high quality nuts and seeds (and some beans / grains too), and soak them (in high-quality water), according to the charts you can find online. (Search "soaking nuts and seeds chart".) I primarily soak Sunflower Seeds and Almonds. I soak almonds for about 12 hrs., whereas Sunflower Seeds only need 6-8 hrs. I rinse the water 3 times throughout the process, to remove all the stuff I don't want in my belly.

Sunflower seeds are pretty easy to sprout, which releases even more natural goodness. You simply drain the water and leave them in a bowl or jar (covered by a breathable cloth) for 2 days, stirring them with a spoon twice a day, until the sprouts pop out! If you have a dehydrator, you can preserve your new creations, and add different spices to them. Personally, I haven't delved into the world of dehydration yet, though I have friends who swear by it.

THE GOODNESS GRACIOUS
SALAD

This salad has totally revolutionized my relationship to food over the past 2 years. After my morning exercise, I love to nourish my mind body and soul with this magnificent medley of yumminess. I've eaten some rendition of the Goodness Gracious salad on a regular basis since April of 2014, and it still fills me with bliss, gratitude, vitality, and Holistic Pleasure! The key elements of the Goodness Gracious Salad are :

1. It's composed of almost entirely raw, sprouted, or fermented ingredients. I prefer essentially every item to be labeled USDA Organic. The main 3 items that are usually non-organic are avocados, green powder, and hemp seeds.
2. This salad must be delicious enough to make you say "Goodness Gracious." This sets it apart from all other salads, because it will fill you with nourishment and pleasure. The salad combines an assortment of colors, textures, shapes, and flavors and results in a stupendous synergy of deliciousness!

Here are the steps to crafting one for yourself and/or a friend :

1. Acquire a large, deep bowl to mix everything together without spilling. Grab a fork, spoon, sharp knife, cutting board, measuring cup, and tablespoon.
2. Add dressing ingredients into bowl and stir thoroughly. The goal is to create a nice, creamy texture :)
3. Chop all the veggies how you like them. I highly recommend using a Kyocera Ceramic Knife.
4. Add to bowl, mix thoroughly for 1-2 min. so all the veggies are smothered in dressing. Next you can add toppings.
5. Enjoy this flavorful and nourishing blend - goodness gracious!

Dressing :

1/8 cup Red Wine Vinegar (I prefer Napa Valley Naturals)

1/3 cup Water

1/2 TSP Himalayan salt

2 TBSP Tahini

1 TSP Turmeric and 1 TSP Black Pepper

Optional : 3 TBSP Chia Seeds (soaked in water in fridge)

Veggies :

1 Bunch Romaine Hearts (chopped) or 2 handfuls of Spinach

1/2 Sliced Cucumber (I always peel off the skin, which often has wax on it)

1/2 Avocado

Optional Add-ons :

1 Handful of Arugula

1 Chopped Green Onion

1 TBSP of Sauerkraut (I prefer Farmhouse Culture's Horseradish Leek)

Chopped Radishes

Handful of Alfalfa Sprouts

Any other yummy organic veggies :)

Toppings :

2 Tablespoons of

1. Hemp Seeds
2. Sunflower Seeds (Usually that I've soaked and/or sprouted)
3. Pumpkin Seeds (I prefer GoRaw's Sprouted version)

--- Feel free to shift the portions of ingredients as you experiment and find your unique version of the Goodness Gracious Salad. The key is to make it extremely delicious and nutritious, so keep experimenting until you find your favorite style!

---- Salad Remix Options

I invite you to experiment and explore adding or subtracting various ingredients to find your personal favorites :

Add on's / Substitutes for Dressing :

1 TSP Oregano

2 TBSP Almond Butter

2 TBSP Sunflower Butter

1 TBSP Coconut Manna

1 TSP of Organic, Vegan Pesto

Add on's / Substitutes to Veggies :

1/2 an Onion (sautéed in Coconut Oil)

1/2 Crown of Steamed Broccoli

3 Leaves of Kale (steamed)

1/2 Beet (steamed)

1/2 Tomato

Add-on's to Toppings

2 TBSP Flax Oil

Handful of mixed nuts / seeds

Kale Chips

Whatever inspires you, and fills you with Holistic Pleasure :)

THE GOODNESS GRACIOUS SMOOTHIE

I've been in love with smoothies ever since my childhood, when my mom would buy me a Strawberry Banana smoothie every time we would go to a festival Downtown. The combination of coolness, smoothness and sweetness filled every cell in my being with satisfaction. Ever since my youth, I've been studying, experimenting, and mastering the art of smoothie creation. I'm proud to announce that I've come up with an epic recipe for the Goodness Gracious Smoothie, which is supremely nutritious and delicious!

Key Ingredients :

8 oz of water (refrigerated for coolness)

½ Scoop of Garden of Life Raw Fit Protein (Vanilla Bean Flavor)

2 TBSP of Roasted, Salted Pistachios

4 Leaves of Organic Romaine Hearts or 2 Handfuls of Organic Spinach

½ Banana (refrigerated for coolness)

3 TBSP Soaked Chia Seeds (I soak and store them in the fridge overnight)

2 TBSP of Soaked or Sprouted Sunflower Seeds

Optional Yummy Add-on's

3 squares of "Green and Black's" Dark Mint Chocolate

A couple dashes of Cinnamon

A big scoop of Almond Butter (or your favorite nut butter)

¼ Scoop of your favorite Green Powder / Superfood powder

As with everything, I encourage you to experiment and explore to find the version of the Goodness Gracious Smoothie that resonates most with you. Besides the ingredients, all you need is a decent blender and you are good to go! I prefer this recipe because it's delicious, sweet, creamy, and relatively low in sugar. It is also packed with protein, and ingredients in their Natural State, which fill me with good energy. Oh my goodness gracious I'm in love with these smoothies!

CONCLUSION

Overall, food is an integral part of everyone's life. Food brings people together, and reminds us that we are nourished by a loving universe every time we eat. I invite you to develop one or more "Food Blessings" which you say before your meal to infuse love and gratitude into all the molecules of your food. Sometimes I will sing to my food and/or send Reiki energy into it. I usually pray that my food nourish a clear mind, a loving heart, and a strong, muscular body.

Rather than a "Die-t", the tools outlined here can guide you towards a "Live-it," which leads to Holistic Health and Vitality. There are countless philosophies on food, and I encourage you to explore them at your leisure. I also recommend trusting your Internal

Compass to guide you to the amazingness of Holistic Pleasure. Remember to tune into the qualities of your food Before, During, and After eating to gain a full picture of how you are interacting with the food. Personally, I am most happy and healthy eating a mostly Vegan "Live-it," with nearly 100% Organic Ingredients that are close to their Natural State on the spectrum I explained earlier. I am honored and grateful to receive this nourishment from Pachamama, the 5 elements, and all the stewards who contribute to this food reaching my kitchen. I also wish you well if you choose to pursue any of the fasting / cleansing recommendations listed earlier. These have truly transformed me from the inside out :) Also, I invite you to have fun experimenting with soaking, sprouting, and creating your own version of the Goodness Gracious Salad! Overall, I am grateful to share all that has supported and inspired me about Food, and I trust that you will find your own unique and beautiful relationship with the pillar of life that is the food you eat. The truth is that everybody is "you-nique" and requires "you-nique" foods and regimens.

May you have a wonderful journey with Phenomenal Food, filled with nourishment, vitality, and Holistic Pleasure! Enjoy the yumminess :)

SPACIOUSNESS IS GRACIOUSNESS

The next few pages is a space to fill with any notes, drawings, revelations, dreams, ideas that you would like. Let your imagination run wild!

~ Unlocking Our Superpowers ~
Part Five
~ Love Locally, Connect Globally ~

HEART MEDICINE

INTRODUCTION

The Heart is at the center of essentially every Spiritual Tradition throughout our planet's history. The wide array of feelings that we experience through our heart creates the ineffably incredible journey of being Human! Modern science has recently shown that the Heart is not just a "pump for blood", but that our hearts have neurons (brain cells), and thus we can literally "think with our hearts!"

Connecting with my heart and the themes associated with it have enhanced my life in innumerable ways. In this chapter, I will highlight a few aspects of the Heart that I am most inspired by. I invite you to explore the marvelous magic that can be felt with that beautiful vessel inside your chest :)

GRATITUDE ATTITUDE

" A grateful heart sits at a continuous feast. "
~ Anonymous

Gratitude is truly a central pillar to having an awesome and wholesome life. If you cultivate an "attitude of gratitude," then you can make it through the toughest challenges, and soar even higher when times are good. Many books and teachings are out there on how to cultivate gratitude. One unique tool that a mentor of mine has shared is called **"The Altar of Your Heart."**

This is a metaphorical altar, where instead of placing physical knick-knacks and gifts from your travels, you place profound memories, moments of connection, and cherished experiences.

Any time you experience something that touches you deeply, you can say to yourself, "I place this upon the altar of my heart." As you cultivate this practice, you can then tune into your Heart Altar, and go back into these warm, treasured memories. If you feel inspired, you can create a Heart Altar Journal, where you write down the magical details of each experience, so you can relish in the subtleties, which may slip your mind otherwise :)

In some sense, every experience of your life is stored in the Altar of your Heart, and upon your final breaths, you will experience a "Flashback / Life Review" where you get to relive all of these gems. Though, if you don't want to wait until the end of this life, you can visit your Heart Altar more often!

THE POWER OF FORGIVENESS

Forgiveness is one of the most potent Superpowers that we have available to us as Humans. It often feels like invisible thorns are lifted out of my heart as I forgive myself and others.

In all my reading, I have not found a better summation of Forgiveness than from Israeli writer, Eitan Press :

"After being hurt it's easy to hold a grudge, to psychologically hold on to the thorn we believe was put in our heart by whomever hurt us, and to point the finger of blame at whomever we believe to be guilty. Besides individuals, a person could also blame "the system" or "society." What I have learned is that to hold a grudge against someone takes energy, like if I were holding a heavy object against a wall, I would have to exert effort to maintain the object there. If someone wanted to give me hug, or if I wanted to paint or cook, I wouldn't be able to because my hands would be occupied holding that object there. So too, when I am holding a grudge against someone, I have to burn psychological calories to keep that grudge there. That is energy I could be using for something else, to be more loving in a relationship, to engage in acts of creativity or kindness, but until I put down that grudge, that energy is stuck maintaining a wound from the past.

Forgiveness is putting down the thorn of anger in our heart, allowing that wound to heal and opening our hands."

It is important to note that forgiveness often comes only after we release the anger, frustration, sadness, and other emotion attached to the experience that caused us to carry a grudge. I recommend working on each issue through the "Healing Process" tools outlined in that chapter. For example, if you are holding a grudge towards your sister, you can explore what memories are attached to that feeling. What does your inner child want to express? Where in your body is the grudge being stored? As you exercise, stretch, and massage that area, you can tap into that feeling and/or memory. As you gain greater clarity on why you are holding the grudge, you can practice catharsis on your own and/or share some Radical Honesty with the person involved.

Questions on Forgiveness :

1. What burdens / grudges are you still carrying that are potentially weighing you down?

2. How would you like to express the feelings related to the grudge? Yelling? Talking to the person? Letting your Inner Child Speak?

3. What changes do you notice in your BodyMind System after expressing how you feel and/or forgiving yourself and others?

SWEET SURRENDER

" When you surrender, the universe moves. "
~ Granny Earth

September 18th, 2014 @ 6:51pm : *Sometimes surrender is the most powerful action we can take. Trusting the larger Evolutionary process we are embedded in takes a lot of the pressure off. May we all find peace, clarity, and understanding in the eye of the storm, however it may appear.*

When it feels like "crunchtime" and we need to finish a project or accomplish a task in a limited amount of time, our rational mind usually tells us to "go, go, go" and use force and willpower to achieve the goal. Sometimes grinding it out works, but often times it leads to hitting brick walls and burnouts.

There is another approach that doesn't make sense to the rational mind. This is to let all the hurries and worries fall by the wayside, and relax into "Sweet Surrender."

A simple example of this happened back in 2013 when I was one of the main organizers for a big event in my hometown of Pittsburgh. The event was a few days away, and I was up to my eyeballs in stress trying to pull everything together. (Mind you, 99% of the stress was caused by my own mind, not external circumstances.) I was making phone calls, sending emails, and checking in with other organizers.

We were unsure if we would have enough tents and volunteers for all of the different activities.

The pressure was building inside of me, and the Universe / God pretty much forced me into a state of surrender. My body was full of stress and anxiety. I rode my bike to my local sanctuary of Frick Park. As I rode by a big mud pond, it looked surprisingly attractive. I took off my shirt and shoes, and slowly walked into this gooey pond. The mud oozed between my toes, and it felt like my worries were melting away one by one. I burst into laughter! People walking by were in awe, and I cracked a smile and waved to these confused dog walkers. I decided to surrender even deeper. I let myself flop back into the mud like I was falling into a pile of leaves. I laughed out loud and felt like a free, little child!

The mud brought me into a playful state, relaxed my muscles, and helped me surrender all the worries that were previously rushing through my head. I decided to let go of most of my to-do list, and simply trust that I didn't necessarily have to check in with every other person helping to organize the event.

On the morning of the Peaceful Gathering of Hands I was focused and certainly in "action mode," though I felt relaxed, like I was in the eye of the storm. As the lead organizer of the event, everyone was counting on me to pull many of the strings together, and although I did a lot of leading, much of it flowed effortlessly. For example, we were concerned if we had enough tents for every station at the festival. Out of the blue, a man new to our community network walks over and asks for assistance to carry in a massive 30 x 20 ft. tent - the biggest tent we'd ever had! This gigantic tent was able to serve several purposes, and made the event much more visible, which attracted even more participants :)

I was also concerned that we wouldn't have enough people to set up everything, though plenty of new participants enthusiastically jumped on board to help — and also volunteer — during the event. Overall, the day was a consistent flow of beautiful synchronicities and blessings. As we all surrendered to the harmony and magic weaving through the event, everything unfolded smoothly. That year, 2013, we made a 20 minute documentary about the festival called "Cultivating Community : Peaceful Gathering of Hands," which I invite you to watch on YouTube :)

Sometimes surrendering means completely letting go of all effort and flopping down on the couch, or into a mud pit. Other times, it means taking action, but in a state of surrender, where you take decisive action moment to moment, and trust that you are being guided by Great Spirit / God / The Universe / Life. Either way, it allows you to be more connected to your heart, rather than being wrapped up in the worries of your mind. I call this **"Flexing your Surrender Muscle,"** and it certainly qualifies as a Superpower.

Questions on Surrender :
1. When was a time that you chose to surrender rather than trying to force things to happen?
2. What changes in your BodyMind System did you notice when you surrendered?
3. What areas of your life / situations could you flex your surrender muscle more?

" You must give up the life you planned in order to have the life that is waiting for you. "

~ Joseph Campbell

DARK NIGHT OF THE SOUL

" If you're really listening, if you're awake to the poignant beauty of the world, your heart breaks regularly. In fact, your heart is made to break; its purpose is to burst open Again and Again so it can hold evermore wonders. "

~ Andrew Harvey

November 24th, 2015 @ 3:43pm :

If you're going through Hell - keep going!.. I didn't fully understand this quote until I dove deeper into my Inner Healing Journey.

There is always light at the end of the tunnel. Our pain is never in vain. We have never been abandoned by The Universe.

Many of us are healing wounds, which have been festering in humanity for thousands of years. This process is incredibly challenging. It can be insanely painful, and I mean RIDICULOUSLY and outrageously painful. AND it is the great work that we are here for. We were made for this shit! hahah

The pain purifies us like fire. We are left with deeper compassion, peace, and understanding than we could previously imagine.

So, whenever you find yourself in a tough situation, I invite you to both surrender and keep on pushin!

Lovin you all so much. (((♥)))

The "Dark Night of the Soul" is when you are tested to your ultimate limits and feel like everything is crashing down around you. These are some of the most difficult experiences of your entire life, but this is what makes the journey of being human so profound and valuable. As the Facebook post above explains, "If you're going through Hell - keep going." The only way through a dark night of the soul is to keep on going, even when it seems hopeless. Sometimes it requires surrender to the higher guiding forces of life. Sometimes perseverance requires every ounce of effort and will-power within you. I invite you to utilize your Internal Compass whenever you find yourself in a Dark Night of the Soul. Blessed be :)

SELF-LOVE

On Valentine's Day, **February 14th, 2015** I posted this message about the importance of loving oneself. I feel that I summed up my views on it quite well :

I believe Self-Love is the foundation for loving anyone or anything.

It's important to distinguish between Self-Love and Narcissism. I see Narcissism as a substitute for self-love. Narcissism is based on things, labels, accomplishments etc. - all of which are conditional and subject to change. Narcissism implies separation from the rest of life.

Self-love is unconditional acceptance. It is based on our deeper essence, which is unified with all of existence.

On this Valentine's Day, I invite us all to commit deeper to our Self-Love practices. If you feel inspired, please post a picture of you hugging yourself.

----

3 Questions on Self - Love :

1. How do you prefer to show love for yourself daily?
2. What aspects of yourself do you find most difficult to love / accept?
3. How can you cultivate greater love, acceptance, and self-nurturing habits?

SERVICE AND PURPOSE

What are we supposed to do once we tap into these incredible Superpowers? I believe the next step is to put them into service to benefit some aspect of the Web of Life. As we become more empowered, we are able to support friends and family on their journeys. Countless beings have extended their energy to support me on my path, and thus I have grown and evolved to a point where I am able to contribute in a big way to the collective. Here are three different posts I made, when this theme was very present in me and flowing through my veins :

November 27th, 2014 (Thanksgiving) @ 6:14pm :

Many authors and spiritual teachers have written about the power of gratitude, but what are we supposed to do with all this gratitude? One of my mentors always says "Place it on the altar of your heart. And if you are feeling inspired, channel it into service."

I believe that gratitude is like the fuel we can use to transform our world. When we truly receive all the blessings around us, we fill up our cup, and then the only natural thing to do is SHARE.

I invite you to step aboard the Great Gratitude Train. Every time you feel thankful, blessed, or grateful, do something kind or helpful for somebody else. There are many beings on this planet going through tough times. We can all do our part to spread positive vibrations and raise up the collective.

All aboard the Great Gratitude Train! (((♥))) Please invite your friends to ride too!

I posted this on **October 13th, 2013 @ 10:42pm :**

After spending a year in the jungle with Shipibo shamans, a friend of mine returned to the "Developed World". I asked him what he thinks is the biggest challenge facing America. He replied "Most Americans are spiritually starving."

What does it mean to be "spiritually starving"? To me, it means to be disconnected from one's inner truth, disconnected from deep relationships with other beings, out of harmony with the Earth, and the larger order of the Universe.

This spiritual starvation then leads to always seeking outside of oneself for fulfillment, truth, love, guidance, etc. when for the most part we can find these things within. Our mainstream culture, built upon outdated "myth-perceptions" leads us astray in so many ways.

How do we reconnect with ourselves, each other, and the Earth? I believe there are hundreds of ways to do this. I do it by waking up every day and exercising, practicing yoga on the Earth, meditating, singing, chanting, laughing, etc. I strive to eat / drink / consume the best quality, organic food, water, music and information possible. I have gained immense knowledge from reading "spiritual" books, and listening / watching thousands of videos on these topics. These teachings have inspired me to trust my inner truth, while simultaneously learning from the external world.

A key factor for spiritual nourishment is also service to other beings. Once one realizes that everything is intricately interwoven, service to others is not only obvious, but also profoundly fulfilling and fun. Once you deeply devote yourself to a path of service, opportunities will sprout up everywhere to lend a hand or heart.

As we truly nourish our own spirit, we inspire others to do the same. Together, we are awakening and healing this beautiful planet. I see more proof of this everyday.

Posted on January 6th, 2015 @ 9:37pm :

I was a benchwarmer for most of my high school soccer career. I would sweat my butt off at every practice session, ride the bus an hour away, do all the warm-ups, and then sit on the bench as my teammates played the actual game.

This is a very unique feeling. I knew I had skills, and I had a strong desire to take off my warm-up gear, and step onto the soccer field. "Put me in coach, put me in coach!" was often replaying through my head. But for the better part of 3 years, I sat on the bench at every single Varsity soccer game. I often felt demoralized and useless, and vented this energy in unhealthy ways like snacking and partying.

Finally, my senior year, I had climbed the ranks, built more muscle, and was ready for the big leagues. It was such a LIBERATING and FULFILLING experience to feel like I was actually unleashing my full potential and being UTILIZED. I wasn't necessarily an All-Star, though I started as a Varsity player and helped lead my team to win the City Championship.

This metaphor applies to many of us. We each carry tremendous potential inside of us to fully share our gifts with the world. Yet many of us still feel like we are watching from the sidelines. Then, we need an outlet for this energy, so we plug it into distractions of all sorts.

The solution I recommend is to wake up and ask "How can I utilize my gifts to be of service today?" Then, simply take action. Self-doubt is paralyzing 99% of the time. We will learn along the way.

It's time to step on the playing field.

When it comes to Service and Purpose, the goal is to find your "Sweet Spot." This is where these 3 categories all overlap :

1. What gifts, skills, and talents do you possess and feel inspired to share?
2. What is a cause you care deeply about making a difference in?
3. How can you provide value in a way that generates income / sustenance for you?

If you find a situation where you can apply your gifts to make a positive difference and get paid for it, then you are living in the "Sweet Spot." An example of this is my friend who goes by "Shine." His passion is to teach an interactive game called "Peace Sticks" that builds mindfulness, body awareness and eco-consciousness. His goal was to inspire young people all over the world to cultivate both inner peace and work for World Peace. Last, he connected with some Youth Programs and Rehab Centers who hired him and his team to come and teach the youth "Peace Sticks." Hooray! He found the "Sweet Spot."

Questions on Service and Purpose:

1. When was a time where you volunteered or supported a cause that was greater than you?
2. How did you feel after this experience?
3. What are some potential ideas for a "Sweet Spot" that would sound exciting and fulfilling to you?
4. Who do you know personally who is living in, or close to their "Sweet Spot?"

TRUTHSPEAKING / RADICAL HONESTY

Flashback to when I was a freshman at Penn State. I had been watching a lot of YouTube videos of people discussing concepts from a book I'd recently read called "Ishmael." The main message of the book is that "there is no one right way to live," and that Western Civilization is simply one option, out of thousands of possibilities. The book discusses how there are many Indigenous cultures still existing on this planet, and living in an amazing reciprocal relationship with their environment.

One of the video bloggers explained that a new movie called "Avatar" had the same message as *Ishmael*. I had seen some previews for this film, but I was surprised to hear that a mainstream film would have such radical ideas in it. I decided to check it out for myself. During Thanksgiving break, I was home in Pittsburgh and went to the movies for the first time in about a year. The special effects in this film were incredible, though it was the message that truly blew me away! This movie struck a deep chord in my heart, and did indeed echo the truth that "there is no one right way to live."

A week later, a few of my friends who hadn't seen Avatar invited me to go see it again. I decided that this movie was worth seeing twice. As I was sitting in the theater, I felt like this film was speaking directly to my soul. I was very passionate about protecting the wisdom and cultures of Indigenous Tribes. The Na'vi indigenous tribe in the film was fighting for their survival against the industrial, imperialistic culture from Earth.

Near the end of the movie, I felt my heart begin to race. "I wonder if the people in the audience understand that these same types of battles are happening right now all across our planet,?" I thought to myself. It felt as though the spirit of our planet, Mother Earth, was compelling me to somehow spread this message to the audience. I got chills up and down my spine. I decided it was my duty to speak up on behalf of not only the Indigenous Tribes of Earth, but also the birds, trees, and animals, whose voices are not heard by most "civilized folks."

As the movie concluded, I walked down the aisle, knees shaking - to the very front of the movie theater. The lights came on, and I shouted to the whole crowd "Hey everyone, I know you may think this is just a movie, but this story is REAL. There are tribes of people similar to the Na'vi struggling to survive all across our planet RIGHT NOW! We need to wake up to this reality, and protect these cultures from going extinct!

We don't have to destroy these cultures, all we need to do is change the way we think! If you don't believe me, check out a group called Survival International"

A lot of people were frozen in their chairs. They looked at me like I was a glitch in the matrix. A few people snickered at me. A few people clapped. As I walked back over to my friends, my adrenaline was pumping full force. I felt FULLY ALIVE. This is what I had been waiting to do for all my life : Stand up for what I believe in. It felt so good. My friends were awestruck. They didn't know what to say.

As we left the movie theater, I felt like I had reclaimed a part of my soul, and also stepped up into my sacred duty as a steward of this planet. This was one of the first times I utilized my superpower of "Truthspeaking."

Truthspeaking can also be a powerful tool in 1-on-1 relationships. As one person becomes vulnerable and shares a deep truth about themselves, it gives permission for the other person to share as well. This often leads to the "thinning of the veils" - where the normal boundaries and walls of "protection" that we often hold up, come tumbling down. The result is a deep sense of connection and it feels like you are peering into the soul of the other being.

Posted on January 25th 2015 @ 8:42pm :

I think that many of us are afraid to express our full, raw, and authentic selves. Instead we "Beat Around The Bush", telling half-truths, policing ourselves, and end up feeling only half-alive. It seems there is some deep rooted fear around "Telling the Truth, the whole Truth, and nothing but the Truth."

For me, this fear manifests through only partially expressing my needs / desires. Instead of just telling it straight up, I may give a vague or indecisive request. Also, in my deep inner healing process, I've learned that "In order to get it ALL OUT, I have to go ALL OUT." This means yelling as loud as I possibly can, stomping the ground with as much ferocity as I can muster, and crying every single tear that is ready to release.

What would happen if we were totally HONEST and VULNERABLE? Would we end up in a state of failure, rejection, or abandonment? I doubt it. Usually when I courageously speak from a vulnerable place, whoever hears me is inspired to share some of their unspoken stories. Truth leads to more truth.

Even if people do reject or abandon us for being RAW, that is better than ABANDONING and REJECTING ourselves and what we know to be true.

Mainstream Society has conditioned us to "police ourselves", and to be polite, so that we don't rock the boat. I proudly say "F*^#@K THAT!" It feels horrible to not express our natural instincts and desires. Just look at the animals in the zoo. They have been robbed of their most basic birthright : To be themselves.

It's time for us to break out of the Human Zoo. I invite and encourage us all to express our full, primal selves. Whether it's speaking up for a Cause we believe in, telling our intimate partner our true desires, or leaving a situation that is not serving us, THE TRUTH SHALL SET US FREE!

And so it is.

3 Questions on Truthspeaking / Radical Honesty :

1. When was a time that you felt like you wanted to speak your truth, but you held back?
2. What would it take for you to share Radical Honesty more often?
3. What message of truth do you feel called to share with the world?

BRINGING LOVE INTO THE WORLD

Now that you've got your Heart activated and pulsing with love and gratitude, let's spread the love out into the world! No longer need we keep our love sheltered in small yoga studios, backyard gatherings, and living rooms. Let's take this love to the streets :)

On the note of breaking social norms, here is what I posted on **September 26th, 2013 at 6:51pm :**

Today I discovered a powerful game for transforming the world. I decided that every person I interact with throughout the day, I will ask them their name, tell them mine in exchange, and do my best to be fully present with them.

First, I did it with a chef who made a salad for me. He seemed so surprised that I genuinely honored him as a human being with a unique story and purpose. As I ate my salad outside the cafe, he came out and struck up a conversation with me, as if we were old friends.

Later today in Berkeley, California, I noticed a lot of people living on the streets. I realized I had an extra pillow, which was not being used, so I decided to find someone to gift it to. I found an older man sitting on a plastic milk crate, so I walked up and introduced myself. The man's name was Smitty, and he graciously received my offering of the pillow with a smile on his face. I walked away grateful to have helped brighten his day.

In the hustle and bustle of modern civilization, we often forget that the people we interact with are real human beings, not just robotic objects doing various services for us. Even making eye contact with a "stranger" for more than a millisecond can change someone's state of being, and make them feel "seen".

I challenge you to try this "game" out for at least one day. Although I'm calling it a game, the key is to be authentic and genuine, and realize that we are all equals in this crazy world together. Whether it's a bus driver, store clerk, or security guard, just simply take a few moments to commune with this being and honor their life upon this Earth...but beware: this practice might cause unforeseen miracles to happen in your life.

Happy Thursday...and please share this game if it resonates with you.

Another fun way to bring love into the world is by giving Free Hugs. I often offer these to people who I meet at the grocery store or at a local event. It is a great way to break down social norms, and increase genuine human connection. If the person seems open to it, I will also offer a "Heart to Heart Hug," which is where you lean to the opposite person's left side (rather than the usual right side) and connect the magnetic field between your hearts. To me, this feels like the most cozy style of hug, and usually leaves both people feeling warm and fuzzy :)

If you want to spice it up even more, you can make a colorful Free Hugs shirt or sign. Recently, my friends and I in Delray have been going out in public with a "Free Group Hugs" sign. A group of us stand on a busy street corner holding onto each other's shoulders. As people of all ages, shapes, sizes, and backgrounds walk by, we offer them "Free Group Hugs." Whether they accept or not, they usually crack a smile, and it snaps them into the present moment. Many people who join in on a group hug say it made their night, and they often want to take a picture with us!

Let's keep sharing the love vibrations with the world, and growing the Conscious Co-Creative Culture represented by the Thriving Tree in the "Tale of the Two Trees!

CONCLUSION

Growing up in the Mainstream Strange Dream, many of us have become disconnected from the magic, innocence, and wisdom of our hearts. I pray that the tools in this chapter can assist you in rekindling that sacred fire within your chest.

May you cultivate an Attitude of Gratitude into Infinitude.
May you remove the thorns from your heart through the power of Forgiveness.
May you relax into sweet and remember that "When you surrender, the Universe moves."
May you persevere through the darkest of darkness, even when it seems hopeless. There is light at the end of the tunnel :)
May you love yourself more and more every day, and in doing so bring love into the lives of everyone you interact with.
May you find a purpose and way to be of service that fulfills your soul and brings joy to your heart :)
May you say what you mean, and mean what you say. May you speak your truth, even when your voice shakes!
May you bring your unique vibration of Love into the world through hugs, smiles, art, music, and million other ways! Hooray!

(((<3)))

PACHAMAMA RECONNECTION

1. Overview
2. The Golden Hours
3. Your Sacred Sanctuary
4. Connecting to the 7 Directions
5. Laying with Pachamama
6. The Permaculture Revolution!
7. Inspired Pachamama Posts
8. Concluding Questions

Many tribes in South America refer to Mother Earth as "**Pachamama**," which comes from the Quechua people and language. I honor and acknowledge all the work that the Indigenous people of South America have done to keep their connection with Pachamama, even amidst colonization and industrialization. I resonate deeply with this name, so I choose to use it too. Rather than seeing the Earth as an object, by calling her "Pachamama" I am honoring that she is a living, sovereign being. Of course this is "up for debate" in the scientific community, though I believe she has her own feelings, thoughts, and purpose, and that these are all intimately linked with the feelings, thoughts, and purposes of us humans and all other creatures. Some people also use the name "Gaia", which I like, though I prefer Pachamama. Another option is to create / receive your own name for her.

I believe that seeing Pachamama as an object allows us to destroy her beauty, and see ourselves as separate from her. There is a big difference in relationship when we simply switch the language we use. By saying "the" Earth, we are implying that she is an object. Imagine if you spoke about a family member like they are an object. For example, say you are sitting in a room with your sister Maria, and you referred to her as "the sister," rather than saying her actual name. Wouldn't that feel weird and distance you from your sister?

By reconnecting with Pachamama, it brings about a shift in consciousness and allows you to see the unified web of life with greater clarity. Over the last 7 years, I've been consciously deepening my link with Pachamama. Here are a few simple Superpowers I've learned along the way :

The Golden Hours : These are the magical windows of time during the first and last hours of the sun shining above the horizon. As the sun rises and sets, it illuminates all of creation with a mystical, mythical, and magical Golden Glow : I also like to call this "Gold Time."

All throughout history, sunrise and sunset have stirred the human soul and imagination. It is a time of Earth and Sky, Dark and Light coming into union. Many say that the "veils are thin" at these times, meaning that the boundary blurs between the Material and Spiritual world as well.

I recommend enjoying and communing with the Golden Hours at every opportunity. I love being surrounded by wilderness if possible, though even in a busy city you can find the peace and magic of these times. It is so cool to see humans, birds, and trees "in a new light" - literally! **The Golden Hours are a great time to meditate, practice yoga, or simply appreciate the beauty of life :)**

Your Sacred Sanctuary : As you connect deeper with Pachamama and all her creatures, it is highly beneficial to have a place near your home where you can go to retreat, tune in, and power up. **The goal is to find / cultivate a place where you can feel safe, free, and connected to the web of life.**

Your Sacred Sanctuary can be at a park, deep in the woods, or in your backyard. A good way to find this place is by locating an **"Elder Tree."** These are most likely the oldest living beings in your neighborhood / city! These will usually be the largest, most powerful trees in the area. You can use your intuition to sense which ones are the oldest. I truly believe these trees contain immense wisdom. In many Indigenous Tribes, sacred ceremonies and events were held in the presence of one or more "Elder Trees." Simply being in the energy field of such a tree-being for 20 minutes can put you in a heightened state of consciousness! No wonder Buddha got enlightened : he was chillin under a super wise tree!

Ideally, your Sacred Sanctuary will be a place where you won't be disturbed or distracted by other humans. This way you can connect with all the awesome non-humans like trees, flowers, birds, and squirrels! The test to see if you feel safe there is : "Can you sing loudly and do semi-awkward yoga poses without feeling self-conscious and anxious?" And the bigger test is "Can you fall into a deep sleep there without being afraid the cops will wake you up?" If you don't pass one or either of these tests, then you won't be able to enter a deep enough state of peace to experience the full magic of Pachamama.

I also recommend researching what Indigenous People live or lived in your bioregion before colonization displaced and disrupted their sacred life-ways. Native-land.ca is a good place to begin, and also www.landback.org .

I recommend bringing a journal and pen with you whenever you feel inspired. I guarantee you will receive creative insights and inspiration, and as I always say "A Notebook is an External Hard Drive for the mind!" As you go to your **Sacred Sanctuary** more often, here are some **questions** to ask :

1. What other creatures live in this place i.e. plants, animals, insects, fungi, birds?

2. What are these creatures teaching you / communicating to you? (I highly recommend utilizing the absolutely amazing "Medicine Cards" by Jamie Sams and David Carson.)

3. What subtleties and changes do you notice in this environment throughout the different times of day i.e. morning, afternoon, evening, nighttime?

4. How does your BodyMind System feel different when you are in your Sacred Sanctuary?

Connecting to the 7 Directions : Indigenous Tribes all over this planet have always been connected to the 7 Sacred Directions. To quote some Poetry from my 1st Album: "East, West, North, South, Up, Down, and the One-Within, let this rhyme remind, so we never Forget-Again." Your Heart Center is the 7th direction, where all the other 6 directions come into Unity.

As you deepen your relationship with Pachamama, it is helpful to establish a sense of where you are in relation to the 7 directions. Through this process, I am now able to estimate what time of day it is by where the sun is in the sky. It is also much easier to navigate while driving if I know the 4 directions and how they apply to the city I'm in and its road system. Overall, it gives me a sense of my primal awareness. No longer am I a robot in a foreign environment, but I feel like "Yes, I am home on this planet, and I know how to navigate it!"

To deepen your connection with the "Up" direction, you can also study Astrology and/or Astronomy. I also invite you to cultivate your **"Mama Luna Connection", which is your relationship and interaction with the Moon Cycles.** In the same way that the tides of the ocean are dictated by the magnetism of the moon, so too are the waters inside our bodies (our emotions) affected by the lunar cycles. This is why historically full moons are tied to people having wild emotions and becoming "luna-tics." Also, in the same way that I have gotten closer to Pachamama by using that name, I like to switch from saying "the moon" to "Mama Luna," which implies a personal connection.

It is so much fun to align with each New Moon and set intentions during this time. I especially enjoy gathering with soul family and affirming each other's intentions. Then as Mama Luna moves through her cycle to becoming full, you can work and play to manifest your intention. On the Full Moon, you can get a clear reflection of what dreams have come to fruition. For great insights on your evolving relationship with Mama Luna and all the stars, I recommend exploring www.MysticMamma.com.

If you want to dive super deep with all 7 directions, you can study the work of Tom Brown Jr. and his "Tracker School," which teaches you how to navigate and survive out in the wilderness.

As you link up with the 7 Directions, I also recommend utilizing your "Internal Compass" and the exercises connected to it, back in that chapter. This will help you to realize the ancient Hermetic principle that states, "As above, so below. As without, so within."

Here are a few questions to explore regularly :

1. Where does your home and bed lay in relation to the 4 directions?

2. How does the Sun and Moon illuminate the various areas around and inside your home?

3. How does your feeling walking upon Pachamama change, when you are in tune with the 7 directions?

Laying with Pachamama : It cracks me up to hear these "Scientific Studies" with new findings advocating that humans walk barefoot on the Earth. They call it "Earthing!" - hahahah. Go figure! "You mean to tell me that standing on the actual living surface of the planet I live on is beneficial? But why?"

As sad as it is, many people go large portions of their life without walking barefoot on Pachamama, let alone actually laying down in the grass. Both walking barefoot and laying for 30 minutes or more on Pachamama have been extraordinarily healing for me.

According to the Scientific Studies, Earthing allows you to draw electrons in from the Earth, which neutralize harmful "free radicals", which in turn decreases inflammation in the body. You can also discharge excess electrical charges in your body into the negatively charged Energy field of Pachamama. Lastly, you can harmonize with the "Schumann Resonances", which are the frequencies that our planet is vibrating at. The most powerful and palpable is 7.83 Hz (cycles per second).

An article online discussing the Schumann Resonance noted a study where :

"Professor R. Wever from the Max Planck Institute was interested in the effects of the Schumann resonance on human beings, and carried out tests on volunteers in an underground bunker which completely screened out magnetic fields, including the Schumann resonance of 7.8 Hz.

After four weeks underground the volunteers were suffering from emotional distress and migraine headaches. After a brief exposure to 7.8 Hz, the symptoms of dis-ease cleared up and volunteers felt healthy again. The same problems of depression and illness were reported by the first astronauts and cosmonauts, who, out in space, also were no longer exposed to the Schumann waves. To counter this, modern space crafts are said to contain a device which simulates the Schumann waves of 7.8 Hz."

Regardless of what the scientific studies show, I know from thousands of personal experiences that having direct contact with Pachamama is healing and beneficial. Countless times I have felt stressed out and overwhelmed, and simply walking barefoot, or laying down in the grass for 20 minutes, I felt totally recharged! It is truly amazing. I recommend connecting with Pachamama for a minimum of 20 minutes a day. You can also go out for 5 minute periods several times a day. I envision a world where this is a top priority for all humans, and cities will be filled with parks and natural spaces for "Earthing." YAY for reconnecting with Pachamama!

The Permaculture Revolution! : Permaculture is so freaking awesome :) I can't hold back my enthusiasm for this amazing way of life! During the Cultural Recyclists bike trip across America, we visited many Permaculture Farms and Gardens, and it filled me with enough inspiration to last a lifetime. Previous to this, I had studied sustainability and how to solve climate change, but now it all became REAL! The solutions jumped out of the books and landed right in front of my face. As I dug my hands in the rich, warm, dark soil, I could feel the reality and beauty of the Permaculture Revolution. So, what exactly is Permaculture?

Through Industrialization and the development of highly populated cities, many humans have essentially cut themselves out of the web of life, both mentally and physically. **Permaculture is an entire philosophy and way of life that re-weaves humans into the interconnected web of existence. By studying the basic laws and principles of nature, Permaculturists have applied what they've learned to gardening, designing homes, and all aspects of life. The goal is to design a "Permanent Culture," which is in harmony with all life and actually regenerates the planet, rather than degrading it.**

If you are sincere about reconnecting with Pachamama, then you gotta tap into your Permaculture Superpowers! Here are 3 ways to get involved with Permaculture :

1. Read "Gaia's Garden" by Toby Hemenway and watch the incredibly inspiring film "Inhabit : A Permaculture Perspective."

2. Books and films are awesome, but If you want to TRULY experience Permaculture, you've gotta visit a local farm and get a tour. Search online for a farm that is close to your home. Check out the "Regional" section on www.Permies.com and also the "Communities Directory" on www.ic.org .

3. The deepest dive is to volunteer on a Permaculture Farm and/or get your Permaculture Design Certificate, which essentially gives you the official title of a "Permaculturalist"!

Inspired Pachamama Posts : Throughout the past few years, there have been a few times where I had a profound experience with Pachamama. I share these Facebook posts to transmit the spirit that was flowing through me :

---- **October 28th, 2013 at 10:08pm :**

One day I was strolling in a local park with a friend. We were walking on the same concrete path as usual, chatting about the mysteries of life. As our conversation developed, I paused, and looked down at the path. For most of my life, I had always subconsciously identified with the concrete path as "where I am supposed to walk".

Though in this moment, I began to feel more connected to the grass that was beside the path, rather than the part of the Earth that was paved over. This realization then led to a stronger consciousness shift, where I felt totally harmonized with all of the non-man-made parts of the park. I started to resonate with the living spirit of Gaia. I looked at all of the benches, fences, concrete paths, no-littering-signs as absurd man-made objects amidst a much deeper, ancient ecosystem. This concrete path didn't seem to honor the primordial wisdom and intelligence of nature.

I don't believe that "man-made" things are specifically unnatural or bad; however I feel that the mainstream cultures' short-sighted goal of "conquering and controlling" "Nature" is essentially shooting ourselves in the foot. We are Nature — made of the same elements as every other life form on this planet.

It truly breaks my heart to see the domestication, disempowerment, and disconnection that is spewed by mainstream television, schooling, hospitals, etc.

I invite you to look deeper into your relationship with the wild side of yourself, and the wild side of the natural world. What social norms, laws, beliefs, and concrete paths are causing disconnection?

How can we all become more WILD and FREE?

---- September 5th, 2014 at 6:04pm :

The degree to which we've been disempowered, programmed, and domesticated by the Mainstream Strange Dream is truly astonishing. The "Average American Life" is so far out of resonance from our true nature that I am repeatedly shocked at what is considered "Normal."

I walked into a CVS pharmacy today, and realized that about 90% of that store is completely TOXIC for mind-body-spirit. The illusion of choices between shiny pink poison or creamy purple poison makes my heart hurt. This store is supposedly helping people to be healthy?! WHAT THE EFFF? Seriously, how asleep are we?

I pray for our reconnection to ourselves, each other, Earth, and the Great Spirit in all things.

---- September 3rd, 2014 at 6:07pm :

Mother Earth has been speaking to me in a language I don't quite understand with my rational mind. This language is older than words and I have to be very still and present to hear it.

Here is my translation into this funky thing called English:

"Your human species is going through a Rite of Passage from the consciousness of a Teenager to the consciousness of an Adult. As teenagers, your species has been quite unaware of your purpose and place in the greater web of life. You have wreaked havoc in hundreds of ways and gotten very, very confused.

There is a mass awakening happening as you all remember your place and purpose amongst the trees, bears, stones, and stars. Many of you are also learning from the tribes of Indigenous People who have kept the flame of INTERBEINGNESS alive for the past couple thousand years.

I am your Mother, and also your friend. I can be kind or I can be wrathful. Part of me gently invites you to find harmony, and another side of me demands it.

I want you to remember that you are all Passengers aboard this magnificent Spaceship, which is soaring through the cosmos. This planet will be in perpetual turbulence if you keep fighting with one and other. It's time to release the judgments, fears, comparisons, hatred, and grudges you hold against each other. These seemingly MINOR issues are like gigantic Dams blocking you all from working and playing together harmoniously as a peaceful planet.

The big key I want to give you today is "INSPIRED SERVICE." Find a healthy, holistic way to get inspired, and then channel that inspiration to serve the collective. When you are In-spired, that means my spirit and the spirit of the universe is flowing through you.

Saturate yourself with inspiration in the form of art, music, people, books, videos, gatherings, dancing, singing, praying, meditating, exercising, playing, massaging, giving, receiving. Take bold, courageous actions in these directions - the web of life will support you as you flap your wings. The more you fill up on inspiration, the more you can spread that spirit to others.

You've become confused largely because you only listen to your Conscious Mind. The spirit of inspiration moves through your entire body and energy field, so you must engage and listen to every cell of your being. The instruction manual for Harmonious Living with the whole web of life is deep within your cells. As you walk the path of INSPIRED SERVICE, the tools, solutions, challenges, people and places will guide you in mysterious and amazing ways. Have fun, Earthlings."

---- October 21st, 2014 at 6:37pm :

Today, Mother Earth posted in the local newspaper. This is what she wrote : "I am hiring new employees for a specific sector of the Great Web of Life. I understand that many of you humans are "unemployed" or do not feel like you are living your true purpose.

Well I have good news! The department of Earth Stewards is overflowing with job opportunities. If you are interested in becoming an Earth Steward, I will outline the credentials I am seeking:

1. I invite you to actively work on "getting the System out of your system." Mainstream society is deeply confused and out of harmony with the Web of Life. I encourage you to purge the Toxins, Old Thought Patterns, and Unhealthy Behaviors. There are many ways to do this including exercise, crying, catharsis, yoga, and fasting.

2. I invite you to connect your heart to my heart. This is no easy task. It means you must be brave enough to feel all the pain I am experiencing. I promise that every tear you shed will make you a stronger Earth Steward.

3. I invite you to set aside your hesitations, doubts, limiting beliefs, which are stopping you from stepping up into your True Self. There are thousands of opportunities waiting for you to serve the Web of Life. The time is NOW to flap your wings. Are you willing to accept the possibility of what your life can become?

If you accept this position, I cannot promise you any of the "normal" things like a steady paycheck, health insurance, or a fancy cubicle. I CAN promise you that you will experience more connection, fulfillment, joy, vitality, gratitude, and wonder than you have ever imagined.

If becoming an Earth Steward sounds like a fit for you, then I invite you to create a small ceremony for yourself. I invite you to set intentions for living as an Earth Steward and map out how you can take action towards them. I'm always here for you."

~ Pachamama

Concluding Questions : Here are a few more questions to explore on your journey with Pachamama :

1. What name resonates most with you : Gaia, Pachamama, Mother Earth, or something else?

2. What is one of your most profound experiences of connection with Pachamama?

3. How often do you appreciate the "Golden Hours?"

4. Do you already have a "Sacred Sanctuary," or perhaps multiple sanctuaries? Where would you like a new one to be?

5. When do you utilize your connection to the "7 Directions"?

6. On average, how much time do you spend barefoot or laying on Pachamama per day? What is your ideal daily amount to truly nourish this life-changing connection?

CULTIVATING COMMUNITY

INTRODUCTION

Teamwork makes the dream work! I truly believe this with all my heart. I have seen so many amazing projects, events, and healing happen when a group of like-minded / hearted people work together towards a common goal. To paraphrase a quote from Rob Hopkins, leader of the "Transition Town Movement" : "If we wait for Government to make change, it will be too late. If we try to make change only as individuals, it will be too little. But if we make changes as unified Communities, it will be just enough, just in time!"

Ever since I returned from the bike trip in late 2010, I decided to dedicate myself to "Cultivating Community" in my hometown of Pittsburgh, and anywhere else I have traveled. I've led hundreds of circles, workshops, and activities geared towards bringing together a group for a common goal. My heart and mind have been amazed at the incredible connections, friendships, and practical projects that have been birthed through this process. I will forever support the Superpowers involved with Building Community. Here are a few key insights I've gathered in my 10 or so years of practicing and studying this area :

THE KEYS TO COMMUNITY ORGANIZING

1. Make Friends First - If you are networking with people in your area, or a new zone, it's important to connect with people on a friendly, human level before trying to build a business or project together. You can still share your mission or vision, but if you bypass the basics of human connection, then I doubt many people will want to work with you. I recommend taking it slow and developing friendships with people in your community, rather than rushing into trying to transform things at a rapid rate. The best projects I've co-created have come from a group of people who are very comfortable with each other and carry a deep sense of love and trust.

2. Fake It Til' You Make It - Nobody gave me official permission - nor did I take any official training - to become a "Community Organizer." I simply saw that there was a desire within my group of friends to have regular community-building events, so I began organizing them. I contacted a local church that was open to letting groups use their space, and started scheduling "Gift Circles", which are an amazing tool for connecting people and developing practical forms of giving and receiving. (More on Gift Circles later in this chapter.)

3. Facilitate What Wants To Happen, Connect The Dots - Rather than trying to reinvent the wheel, it is important to research what projects, venues, and types of people are ALREADY in action in your community. I recommend spending a few weeks visiting "hot spots" and attending a variety of events in order to take stock of what projects are already in motion. As you visit these different places, you are assisting in weaving the web / connecting the dots of your local network.

Then, you can get a sense of what "wants to happen" and you can facilitate that process in your area. For example, you may discover that there are already 4 Community Gardens in your city, but there is no common way for those 4 groups to connect, so you could create a monthly Potluck (where everyone brings a dish or food to share and eat together). Or you could host a Film Screening and invite people from all 4 gardens.

4. Remind, Remind, Remind - When you are hosting or creating an event, it is very important to remind people several times. Although you may be afraid of annoying people with more than 1 email, I've always found that people are grateful to receive reminders. Personal calls are most effective if you want a specific person to show up. Text messages are most effective for reaching a group of people. Group emails are also very beneficial. Facebook Events are great, especially for drawing in new people and friends you've recently made. It's key to remember that not everyone checks Facebook invites, so sending a personal message can be a good addition. I recommend sending one final reminder the day before the event, because most people are quite busy nowadays and appreciate the extra mental note :)

5. Empower Others to Give Their Gifts - The best way to build a strong community is to find ways for everyone to give what they are most passionate about / skilled at. It is an amazing gift to help people develop their gifts and find ways to put them into action. The Gift Circle is a great tool for this (explained in next section).

6. Everyone Is A Participant - I believe the new paradigm of events is to have interactive settings where everyone participates. Rather than a crowd of people listening to one or two people give a lecture, I recommend finding activities that empower everyone to use their Heads, Hands, and Hearts. Sitting in a circle is a great first step, and doing a group stretching warm-up engages people in a dynamic, embodied way.

Allowing everyone to share their voice and perspective taps into the **"Collective Genius," which states that the group is always smarter than any one person is individually.**

7. Remember Why You Do The Work You Do - It is important to remember the "Why" of the project or work you are doing. This will keep you motivated and focused, while helping you to get through challenging times. If you are having Weekly Potlucks at your home, it's good to remember the time when you heard the heartfelt gratitude from one of the participants who said it was the highlight of her entire week. These little pieces of feedback are priceless and can keep you inspired to continue hosting events.

8. Keep Telling The New Story, and Brainstorming How to Keep it Growing - As you Cultivate Community in your area, you can use the power of speech to **"Speak things into Being," which means that by telling the story of what's happening you are literally making it more real, concrete, and tangible.** By going to other events and saying "Yeah, we are hosting weekly Potlucks to unify all the Community Gardens," you create a buzz in your area, which leads to more people talking about the event and ultimately more people attending the Potlucks.

It is beneficial to be an optimist, and tell the "New Story" of what is happening in your town. Rather than focusing on the status quo, or the way things have gone in the past, you can be a storyteller with a new vision of how the future can look. This "New Story" represents the "Thriving Tree" from the "Tale of the Two Trees," that I shared in an earlier chapter. The roots of the tree represent the new, holistic Cultural Beliefs, and the trees / branches represent the incredible projects and manifestations that you co-create as a community. By living and telling this story, you can be a beacon of hope and inspiration for many. This also includes doing your best to cultivate a personal lifestyle that matches this "Thriving Tree / New Story."

I invite you to engage others in brainstorming a "Best Case Scenario" for how your town could transform in one year, five years, and ten years. In 10 years of Community Building in Pittsburgh, I have seen absolutely astonishing transformation in the forms of friendships, projects, businesses, and much more. Many people doubted my efforts in the beginning, but I remained persistent, and was fueled by both my inner dedication and all the little pieces of feedback and gratitude I witnessed along the way.

9. Amplify Impact With Pictures, Videos, Social Media - To assist in telling the New Story, I recommend finding someone with a high-quality camera to take photos / videos at your events / gatherings. The precious moments and connections can be both preserved and amplified through this process. Social Media is an amazing tool for increasing the impact of your efforts. Even if only 5 people show up to an event, hundreds or even thousands can experience a taste of it if you utilize these tools properly. In a few months of Cultivating Community, I co-created around 50 YouTube videos and hundreds of photographs, which I shared regularly via Facebook and email. These photos and videos demonstrated that a group of people were "Living a New Story" and inspired many people who hadn't previously heard of what we were doing. I can't tell you how many times people came up to me and said, "I saw your video on YouTube, or photos on Facebook, and that led me to show up today!"

10. Trust The Process and Don't Get Discouraged - It is important to trust in the larger process of Cultivating Community. Sometimes I would get overwhelmed and stressed while trying to pull a big event together. In these times, I had to simply surrender and trust that everything would figure itself out. Ultimately, I believe Humanity is one super-organism, and we are each cells within this larger body. Thus, it is helpful to trust that there are larger forces at play, and that Pachamama and Great Spirit are guiding the process. We don't have to do all the work! This also helps me remember not to rush, and to savor all the subtleties and mini-miracles along the way. By trusting the process, I am able to relax into the Present Moment, and make eye contact with each person I engage with, rather than being flustered or overwhelmed.

Tying in with trust, I invite you to keep the faith. Don't get discouraged! If you step into a role as a Community Organizer, your faith will be tested time and time again. I've hosted many events where only a handful of people showed up when I expected a large group. I've also had many people upset at me for a zillion reasons, simply because I took on a role of leadership. These things can be extremely disheartening, especially when you put a lot of time and energy into serving the community. The key is to keep your heart and mind open during challenging situations and do your best to find solutions.

12. There Are No Mis-takes, only Takes, and Non-Takes - If things don't go as planned, I can guarantee you will learn something beneficial to put in your "Community Building Tool Belt." Therefore, I say there are no Mis-takes, only Takes and Non-Takes. So often, people won't take action, or hesitate to organize an event, because they are afraid that it won't turn out "perfectly." I encourage you to break through "perfectionism" and simply put your energy towards serving the community, and trust that some good will come as a result.

There are **4 Principles** related to this, which are derived from a Community Building Activity that I learned during the Transition Town Training back in 2011 :

1. **Whoever shows up are the right people for the event.**

2. **Whatever time it starts, it starts.**

3. **Whatever time it ends, it ends.**

4. **Whatever happens is good :)**

These may seem like principles for a lazy person, but they are very helpful if you tend to beat yourself up for not reaching high-expectations. Also, these 4 principles are great to apply at social events like Potlucks, Gift Circles, and Networking Events. I recommend giving organizing an event your full effort, but don't be attached to specific results. Usually, I find that the quality of the event and personal connections are more important than the quantity of people in attendance.

13. Always Seek Balance - Burnout is all too common amongst Community Organizers. Many people "bite off more than they can chew" and try to change a whole system in a short amount of time. With this in mind, it is paramount to cultivate self-care and holistic health practices so that you stay balanced in body, mind, and spirit. I recommend seeking balance in all areas of life. The inner transformation goes hand in hand with the outer transformation. I see them as a feedback loop / infinity sign, where by changing yourself, you change your community and vice-versa. Both sides are equally important.

It is also important to balance work and play while organizing events, etc. I like to say "Work + Play = the Way." Make sure your planning "coalescences" aren't overly serious, or everyone will become too stressed out. It's also key not to get too silly and lose sight of the practical, grounded action steps necessary to accomplish your goals. In all things, seek balance :)

---- For more Keys to Cultivating Community, I recommend researching the Transition Town Movement. Here is the main website : www.transitionnetwork.org/

I also invite you to watch the Mini-Documentary I co-created about Cultivating Community in my hometown of Pittsburgh : Search **"Cultivating Community Official Film"** on YouTube.

THE SPHERES OF INTERACTION, INFLUENCE, AND INTERCONNECTION

As you interact with your Community, it is beneficial to have awareness of the various different spheres that you are completely interconnected with. Ultimately the goal is to have a harmonious relationship with each aspect of these spheres. For example, if you focus too much on transforming your outer community, you can neglect your personal or close family sphere. If you are too uptight about having your direct personal life in perfect order, then you may forget about the joy and freedom of interacting with your tribe! The main keys to remember are **Awareness** and **Balance** :) Here is how I like to visualize the spheres of Interaction, Influence, and Interconnection :

AIR
(MENTAL)

FIRE
(SPIRITUAL)

1 2 3 4 5

WATER
(EMOTIONAL)

EARTH
(PHYSICAL)

THE
SPHERES
OF
INTERACTION,
INFLUENCE +
INTERCONNECTION

1. YOUR PHYSICAL - EMOTIONAL - MENTAL - SPIRITUAL
+ LOVE SELF

2. YOUR CLOSEST FRIENDS, FAMILY, RELATIONSHIPS
+ YOUR HOME ECOSYSTEM

3. YOUR WIDER NETWORK OF FRIENDS, COWORKERS,
ETC. + YOUR TOWN/CITY ECOSYSTEM

4. THE ENTIRE PLANETARY ECOSYSTEM: PLANT, MINERAL,
FUNGI, INSECT, REPTILE, ANIMAL, HUMAN + BEYOND

5. THE WHOLE ENTIRE MULTIVERSE

ASKING FOR SUPPORT

I wrote this with 4 days left in my Crowdfunding Campaign for the New Eyes Tour :

October 25th, 2014 @ 7:55pm : *I'm gonna be perfectly honest here... My life is dedicated to the service of humanity. Ever since I was hit by a car in 2010, and my life flashed before my eyes in a Near Death Experience, the only thing that has made sense is to contribute all my energy towards the upliftment of our planet.*

Every day I am grateful and humbled by the feedback I receive from people who are profoundly impacted by what I share. I can no longer shrug off the sacred responsibility and path that comes with letting the Universe work through me.

I don't need any awards, trophies, or special treatments. I am simply asking you and the Universe at large to support my basic needs so I can keep growing and walking my path. The work I do is not easily quantified in the mainstream economic system, and so it has been challenging to figure out a sustainable model of financial support.

I created the New Eyes Tour campaign to crowdfund the next phase of my journey. It has 4 days left, and I am sincerely asking for your support. Every little bit helps, and adds to the momentum. Please share the New Eyes Album as well. Even if we've never met in person, please know that I appreciate you, and I'm asking for your help too.

I felt fairly vulnerable putting myself out to the world and requesting support for this project. It was a bit like climbing out on a skinny limb of a tree. I didn't know if the tribe would support my vision, but I decided to have faith, and so I "went out on a limb." After a month of campaigning I received contributions from around 80 people from all over the world. I didn't meet my original goal, though I raised enough to complete the New Eyes Album and go on tour. Most importantly I let myself be vulnerable by asking for support, and my prayers were answered. Asking for Support is key in Building Community, because it dissolves the illusions of separation and brings the tribe together for a common purpose.

3 Questions on Asking for Support :

1. When have you received support after becoming vulnerable and asking?

2. Did the support come in the way you expected?

3. What would have been different had you not asked?

THE MAGIC OF GATHERINGS

September 23rd, 2013 @ 11:25pm : *Wowza! I just returned from the festival called Symbiosis. Nestled on a gorgeous peninsula in Northern California, thousands of beings of all ages coalesced for a truly transformative sharing of music, knowledge, outrageous foods, visionary artwork, ceremony, Permaculture, stories, and infinite inspiration!*

Experiencing the live performances of Climbing Poetree and Rising Appalachia amidst the glowing yellow moon were two of the most jaw dropping, consciousness raising hours of my entire life…

The entire audience sang along, moved in unison, and synergistically fueled the musicians on stage... My mind was blown, heart expanded, and my spirit overflowed with inspiration!

I had already loved both groups' music from listening online, but seeing them live was like a blind person regaining their perception of color :) Seriously, their music is medicine for the soul.

...Many more lessons, blessings, and inspiring information to come from this epic gathering...I love you all and it's time to take our sacred activism to the next level :)

Satnam namaste om shanti om

Here is a quote about Transformational Festivals from a friend who inspires me tremendously, Maraya Karena :

"I came to festivals from an activist background, burned out and questioning whether peace was even possible. What I saw at festivals was a way of living with others and the planet in a loving, creative, and sustainable way. Almost as if the festival was a space for enacting possibilities of what that world would look like. I saw peace, I felt peace, I was peace.

Those experiences completely shifted my motivation from reacting to the horrors of the world to becoming inspired by a vision of what could be and what already was. It made me realize that this vision, the world I had in mind, includes all of these elements that are present at festivals. Yoga, organic food, stretch fabric architecture, communication workshops. And that it could be - simply - people going forward with their lives, trusting their transformation and following their excitement that brings this world into being..."

Here is another Facebook post inspired by the magic of gatherings from **December 9th, 2014 @ 9:38pm :** *I often ponder what is the purpose of humans being on this planet. We build big skyscrapers, we get married, we go on vacation, but why are we really here?*

It is not easy to make sense of the Great Mystery of life on Planet Earth. I've been a seeker for many years, and once and awhile I feel like I'm close to an "answer." Usually this happens, when I am sitting out in the wilderness around a fire with a bunch of friends.

All the distractions of the modern age melt away as we sing songs and stare at the "ancient television" called a Bonfire. One experience where I felt true communion with the Web of Life and a deep sense of purpose was at a gathering in North Carolina this summer.

A group of 30 of us sat around a bonfire, and two phenomenal songwriters, Luke Kohen and Elah Scott led heartsongs, freestyles, and jams. Everyone in the circle was singing or drumming along, and the feeling of "tribe" was palpable.

----

3 Questions on the Magic of Gatherings :

1. What vivid memories come to you from a special gathering or event?

2. What was so special about this moment of connection with community?

3. What types of gatherings / events do you feel inspired to co-create?

COMMUNITY BUILDING ACTIVITIES

Here are a few practical and super-powerful tools / activities, which I have personally experienced and explored extensively in my 10 years of Community Building. These tools and activities have facilitated more friendships, smiles, and amazing projects than I could possibly keep track of. I am honored to be able to share what has worked so well in the communities I've been a part of, and I'm excited for you to begin implementing them in your area :)

THE COALESCENCE

Rather than a "Meeting," a Coalescence serves a very similar purpose, but has a slightly different energy and intention. The word "Meeting" often carries a certain connotation of heaviness and seriousness, whereas the word "Coalescence" is fresh and is therefore open to become something new. **A Coalescence is essentially a group of people (usually between 3 and 15) coming together for a common purpose.** Each Coalescence can have a unique intention, and depending on the group, they can decide what guidelines they would like to follow. This tool can be used to plan / organize an event, to discuss a conflict happening in your community, or for a variety of other intentions.

Here is an overview of the basic **Coalescence Steps / Guidelines** that we usually follow :

1. Designate Specific Roles : Facilitator, Scribe, Timekeeper

2. Set up the Space

3. Open the Circle / Introductions / Check-In's

4. Create the Playlist

5. Delegate Time for each Playlist item

6. Go into each Playlist item

7. Closing : Intentions / Action Steps

8. Clean - Up

Here is a bit more info on each of these Steps / Guidelines :

1. Designate Specific Roles : Facilitator, Scribe, Timekeeper : The **Facilitator**'s job is to have a "Bird's Eye View" over the entire Coalescence. This includes having a sense of each participant's mood / energy that they are emanating throughout the Coalescence. If someone is clearly burrowing a powerful emotion, it may be necessary for the facilitator to ask him or her to share what's up for them.

The **Scribe** writes down all of the Playlist items, and takes notes throughout the Coalescence, emailing them to everyone afterwards. The **Timekeeper** keeps track of the time throughout the Coalescence. This includes a 1-3 minute check-in at the beginning, and the time delegated to each Playlist item. The Timekeeper can have a bell or chime to ding in order to gently notify people if their time is up. Generally, we like to be flexible with time, though we also like to honor that some people may have other engagements planned. We usually aim for a 1-2 hr. Coalescence.

2. Set up the Space : We always sit in a circle, usually on the ground, preferably on Pachamama if it is relatively warm outside. We usually create a mini-altar and put sacred items like crystals, necklaces, or other art in the center. This helps to keep a strong center and clear intention for the Coalescence. We often share food beforehand, though we usually set it aside once the Coalescence begins.

3. Open the Circle / Introductions / Check-In's : We put our hands out and thumbs to the left, for a "Moment of Being" where we simply join energies and feel present together. Putting left hand up and right hand down allows for energy to flow around the circle. This enables us to "drop into" the space, and literally allow the magnetic field of our hearts to begin to synchronize with one another. The "Moment of Being" is usually between 30 seconds and 2 minutes. When the Facilitator feels it is over, he / she can invite everyone to raise their hands and exclaim something fun like "Happy Tuesday!"

Next, we pass around a "Speaking / Listening Object" such as a feather, stone, or stick. This object designates that whomever holding it is speaking, and everyone else is asked to give them their full attention. Each person shares their name and does a 1-3 minute "Check-In." The Check-In can answer any or all of these questions : Why are you here today? How are you feeling mentally / physically / emotionally / spiritually? What is your intention for today's Coalescence?

4. Create the Playlist : The Playlist is an alternative term for "Agenda." The Playlist covers all the topics that we want to discuss in the Coalescence, which the Scribe writes down.

5. Delegate Time for each Playlist item : First, the group decides how long they want the entire Coalescence to last. Then, they prioritize which Playlist items are most important to cover, and how much time to spend on each one. Some Playlist items can be put on a back burner until a future Coalescence, or they can be discussed by group members outside of the Coalescence.

6. Go into each Playlist item : The Facilitator guides the process of exploring and discussing each of the Playlist items. The Speaking / Listening Object is passed around to support everyone sharing their voice. It also ensures that everyone else is listening intently so they can hear other perspectives. It is so beautiful to witness the Collective Genius at play during a Coalescence. **The Collective Genius states that we are always smarter as a group than any one individual is.** It is also referred to as the "Hivemind." Often, one person's idea will build off another, which sparks a synchronistic group realization, which leads to a burst of hysterical laughter! This happened a lot when we were planning our 5th annual Peaceful Gathering of Hands in 2015. Our Collective Genius kept empowering us to co-create the most amazing event possible.

The Scribe takes notes of the key insights for each Playlist item as the Facilitator guides the overall process of allowing everyone to speak. If multiple people all want to speak, the Facilitator can create a **"Stack," where he / she keeps track of and tells the people which order they can individually speak in.**

7. Closing : Intentions / Action Steps : After the main Playlist items are covered, it is good for the Facilitator or Scribe to give a brief recap of what the group expressed /

decided. After this, the Speaking / Listening Object is passed around, as each group member does a "Check-Out." This usually includes their Intentions moving forward until the next Coalescence. It is beneficial to share specific Action Steps that you plan to take as a way to turn the Ideal into the Real Deal and make yourself accountable in front of the group. Lastly, we put our thumbs to the left again and join hands for a final "Moment of Being." This seals the Coalescence in the same way we opened it : in sacred silence and simplicity.

8. Clean - Up : It is important to "leave the space better than we found it." We make sure that everyone reclaims any items that were placed in the center. We clean up any trash / recycling / compost that was created at the Coalescence. If there is a simple way to give back to the space where we gathered, we usually do that. This way, we maintain a good relationship with any venue offering their space to us. Yay! Coalescences are so freaking awesome, because we get shit done and have fun :)

ADDITIONAL IDEAS / GUIDELINES

FOR A CIRCLE

The Coalescence and The Gift Circle (explained next in this chapter) are 2 fabulous Community Building Tools that I've experienced great success with. Both of those 2 Circles hold many of the core Guidelines that I find important, such as beginning with Check-In's and ending with Check-Outs, and using a Speaking / Listening Object. There are many other groups with tried and true techniques. I will share a few that resonate with me. These are inspired and adapted from the PeerSpirit Inc., the Millionth Circle, and the Center for Restorative Process.

1. Speak From Your Heart : The primary teaching here is to speak from your own personal experience. Rather than offering others advice, you can share what has or hasn't worked well for you.

2. Listen From Your Heart : Do your best to let go of judgments and assumptions, so that you can empathize with each person and hear their unique perspective. You are encouraged to still have your own personal preferences and perspective, but to use "discernment" rather than an emotionally charged judgment. When you practice this, it allows for the possibility of making new discoveries and connections with fellow group members. This also ties in with the next key of "No Need to Rehearse," because when you are planning out what to say next, you are usually missing out on hearing what another group member is saying.

3. No Need To Rehearse : This is a practice of trusting the moment. Rather than planning everything in advance, non-rehearsal allows you to speak from your heart. It also assists you in not getting overly analytical.

4. Without Feeling Rushed, Say Just Enough : This practice invites you to be concise, direct, and precise with what you share. This usually makes what you share more impactful, rather than a drawn-out, watered down version.

5. Use The Power of "The Pause" : If you feel like things are getting chaotic, or overly emotionally charged, you can call a "Pause," where everyone sits in silence for a minute or two until you say "Unpause." This allows for everyone to remain centered, breathing deep, and present in the circle.

6. Decide as a Group What is to be Held in Confidence : Some people may want to keep what they share in the circle confidential, so it's important to discuss this at the beginning of the circle, and make agreements so that everyone feels safe.

THE GIFT CIRCLE

A powerful Community Building Tool that fosters friendships and helps cultivate the Local Economy.

Facilitator : Keeps the overall flow of the Gift Circle on track. The Facilitator can interject different insights and perspectives that will support the group in staying focused while also keeping a playful spirit.

Time Keeper : Keeps track of the start time, end time, and lets people know when their minute or so of speaking is up. It is important for the entire group to agree on a time frame for the circle, so that everyone is on the same page. Then, the Timekeeper divides that length of time between the 4 rounds, with rounds 2 and 3 being about equal in length, and rounds 1 and 4 being about equal in length. Depending on the size of the group, we usually aim for the Gift Circle duration to be between 1.5 and 2 hours.

Scribe : This person writes down the Needs, Gifts, and Offerings, as well as the emails of everyone in the Gift Circle, and emails all the notes to everyone afterwards. The Follow-Up email is very important as a way to solidify the Gift Circle. It's also useful if you forgot to get someone's contact info. Lastly, you may discover a few days after the Gift Circle that you actually do need a new lamp, so then you can call Dolores, who was offering 3 antique lamps!

---- It is important for each person in the circle to have a small paper and pen, so they can jot down notes of whom they want to connect with afterwards and for what reason.

Round 1 : Everyone shares their name, and answers some sort of Icebreaker question such as "Why did you come to the Gift Circle tonight?" Another fun activity is for each person to share a random sound, which everyone in the group then repeats. This gets people relaxed, smiling, and helps people to get to know each other a bit more. If it feels right, you can utilize a "Speaking / Listening Object," such as a feather, stick, or stone to designate who is speaking.

Round 2 : Each person shares 1 or 2 things that they Need / Want / Would like from the Community. These can be Material or Non-Material, and Short-term or Long-term. For example, I could go to the Gift Circle looking for someone to cut my hair, or help me fix my bicycle. You can usually find someone at the Gift Circle who can directly or indirectly help you meet your Need / Want. It is truly amazing how people will show up with the most seemingly random desires and questions, and they almost always find someone to connect with about it.

Round 3 : Each person shares 1 or 2 things they have to Offer : Gifts, Skills, Resources, or Ideas. Just like the Needs, these Offerings can be Material or Non-Material, and Short-term or Long-term. For example, some people may have their time and energy as a volunteer to offer, whereas others may have a specific gift such as cooking lessons, computer maintenance, or foot massages :)

---- Rounds 2 and 3 are often intertwined because Needs and Gifts can go hand in hand. For example if Susan has a big garden in her backyard, she may need people to help her with weeding, and she also has raspberries and tomatoes to give to anyone who assists her.

During rounds 2 and 3, the Scribe writes down each person's name, what that person wants to Receive, and what they have to Give. The Facilitator holds the intention and flow of the Gift Circle in balance. It's okay if some group conversations break out for a little bit, but the Facilitator should ask people to follow-up after the circle is over if the conversation lasts more than a minute or two. Everyone in the circle should keep their paper and pen handy so they know who to exchange contact info with after the circle.

Round 4 : Each person shares intentions of who they plan to connect with and for what reason. These intentions can also pertain to day-to-day life. So, I could say, "I plan to connect with Joseph to learn about Astrology, to help Allison with her upcoming Speech, and in my daily life, I intend to exercise with more intensity!" Each person can also share 1 or 2 things they are grateful for. This centers everyone in their heart, and brings together the energy of the Gift Circle in a beautiful way. I recommend closing with a group OM, or a big group hug :)

After-Party : By the end of the Gift Circle, usually everyone has fallen in love with each other. This is the time for follow-up conversations, and for people to exchange contact info so they can take action on their Needs / Gifts. If people brought snacks or other things to share, this is a great opportunity to simply hang out. It's important to honor the venue of the Gift Circle. The Facilitator can help organize people to cleanup whatever things need to be returned to their proper place such as chairs, dishes, etc.

Summary : I've seen the Gift Circle work miracles time and time again! I've witnessed friendships blossom, deep needs be met through community, and people with amazing gifts find ways to put them into service. These are the basic guidelines, which have worked in the groups I've facilitated. I invite you to experiment with them, and potentially adapt them if you find it necessary. Have fun :)

OVERVIEW

From biking across America to growing an epic tribe in my Hometown of Pittsburgh, I've learned over and over again, that "It takes a tribe." The times of trying to do everything alone are over. The age of Collaboration and Co-creation is upon us. Festivals, Collaborative Workspaces, Networking Events, etc. are becoming more popular every day, as we realize the power of the Collective Genius. I believe that the Golden Key to accelerate the Evolution of Humanity is "Cultivating Community." Although sometimes I get depressed at the state of the World, I have seen and participated in the incredible Power of Community too many times to give up. I know that WE CAN CHANGE THE WORLD!

My vision is for a Global Village Network of Conscious Change Agents. The great news is that this Network and Movement already exists! The secret is that we go by so many different names, that we don't always collaborate or co-create in the best way.

My vision is that each town / city will have a Core Council of Leaders / Experts in a variety of fields. Community Organizers, Permaculturalists, Healers, Elders, Web Designers, Indigenous Representatives and more will make up this Core Council that will be the "steering committee" for each town.

This Network / Movement will be rooted in a foundation of New and Ancient Cultural Beliefs and Values. We will still honor the richness and diversity of local cultures, while prioritizing...

key common values of Interconnectedness, Co-Creation, Ecological Balance, Non-Violence, and Indigenous Wisdom throughout our global network.

Each town / city will have a Directory (both online and in print) that lists all the Groups, Leaders, Businesses, Projects, and Events that embody the New Cultural Values. This way, each town will have a unified sense of "THIS IS REAL. THIS IS HAPPENING. WE ARE ACTUALLY DOING THIS." This way, College Students, Filmmakers, Philanthropists, Traveling Musicians, etc. can easily plug into the Network of each town, and lend their unique skills towards this collaborative mission.

There will also be a connected network of Intentional Communities, Retreat Centers, and Permaculture Farms all around the world, for people of all ages to lend their gifts and skills to. This is already in action and continuing to develop through an amazing group called "Project Nuevo Mundo." (www.numundo.org)

I sincerely invite and encourage you to link up with like-minded people and groups in your area. (Check out the list of Movements / Groups in the last chapter of this book "Web of Infinite Inspiration") If you can't find very many people in your town, then perhaps you are meant to be the Web-Weaver! It is such a blessing to weave community, and I hope that the tools in this chapter can be of service to you and your tribe!

~ Unlocking Our Superpowers ~
Part Six
Tying it all Together :)

THE GREAT INTEGRATION

Throughout Human History, our species has always had a special connection to the planet as a whole. Essentially every Indigenous Culture has revered Mother Earth (Pachamama) as the giver of life ; providing food, water, shelter, and everything else for the tribe.

As humans evolved, some sections of Humanity began to build Civilization. This was a huge change because it distanced humans from the natural world and the spirit of Pachamama. As they began to build big cities, the sense of the wilderness began to disappear. Rather than foraging and hunting for food, they used farming and domesticated animals.

As generation after generation of children were raised in Civilization, many people forgot what it was like to be deeply connected to the spirit of our living planet. We began to see Mother Earth as a resource to be used, rather than a being to be in harmonious relationship with. This process of Separation from Nature has continued to accelerate at an exponential rate since the dawn of Modern Civilization some 10,000 years ago. All over the planet, human culture evolved and developed many incredible inventions, which were intended to "improve our quality of life."

It is important to note that not all humans decided to pursue the development of Civilization. Thousands of unique tribes all around the world chose to remain in their Indigenous Ways, staying deeply connected to Pachamama. These cultures were usually pushed to far corners of the globe, often to remote locations, in order to avoid the encroachment of civilization. They chose to preserve their ancient ways and generally live a more simple life. It's not to say they were always in utopia, but many Anthropologists document that these Tribal Peoples experienced hardly any warfare, rape, and had quite remarkable health.

As these tribes stayed in their own traditions, Civilization pressed forward full speed. In some sense, things like Christianity, Higher Mathematics / Science, and the Printing Press did enhance people's lives. There was also usually a shadow side to this "Progress." Christianity put "God" in an external realm, far away from the previously sacred Earth. Higher Mathematics / Science made it possible for humans to use "rationality" to objectify, control, and dominate the forces of nature to our benefit. The Printing Press helped accelerate the spread of information, yet also contributed to the already increasing deforestation. It is tough to say whether these changes were "good" or "bad," but whatever was happening, we can see that human consciousness was shifting, and evolving in many ways.

When coal and oil were discovered, humans were able to harness even more of the forces of nature, and eat up the "resources" of Mother Earth with lightning speed. By the early 1900s, human population had exploded to almost 2 billion people. In the 20th century, human evolution drastically increased again, as cheap coal and oil made it easier to grow more food and build civilization on nearly every corner of the globe. As Technology evolved, wars went from being fought on horseback with rifles, to planes dropping bombs. In World War 2, when the U.S. dropped two Nuclear Bombs on Japan, this drastically impacted Human Consciousness.

For the first time in the history of our planet, many people grappled with the possibility that we could wipe ourselves out! Many people realized, "If we keep blowing up nukes, we are gonna destroy our only home." I believe this marked a turning point in the awakening of greater consciousness in our species.

In the 1960s, we'd reached upwards of 3 billion people, and we were ravaging the resources of this planet at an astonishing rate. The 1960's had many other milestones in the Awakening of Humanity. We saw the rise of the Civil Rights Movement, with Martin Luther King Jr. stirring the hearts of people with his powerful speeches and passion. All over the country, people utilized Civil Disobedience and Boycotts to rally for justice and equality. This coincided with the massive Anti-War Movement, where people of all ages, colors, and backgrounds unified for a more peaceful planet. After seeing the potential destruction of Nuclear Weapons, it became more urgent and important to vote for a world with less Military Conflicts, and protest the Vietnam War.

The 1960s also gave rise to the popularity of "Psychedelics" in mainstream culture. LSD and Psilocybin Mushrooms catalyzed new shifts in consciousness in young people all across the U.S. The results varied, though overall I would say that it led to more people breaking Cultural Norms and thinking outside the box. In conjunction with this,

Shamanism began to rise in popularity as Anthropologists discovered some of the "Tribal Peoples" who had preserved the ancient ways and sacred plant medicines. For example, researcher Gordon Wasson connected with the Mazatec Indigenous People of Mexico, and spread the knowledge of shaman Maria Sabina, who taught the healing properties of Psilocybin Mushrooms. This led to many people experimenting with Sacred Mushrooms and potentially experiencing the profound healing and awakening of consciousness as a result.

One final milestone in Human Consciousness took place in the 1960s. This was the birth of the "Environmental Movement." Author Rachel Carson helped spark this stride to preserve wilderness and all Earth's creatures with her book "Silent Spring." Another big step occurred on Christmas Eve of 1968, when US Astronaut William Anders took a photo called "Earthrise" from the moon! This image was sent back to our planet, and had a profound impact on many people, because it gave a sense of "Spaceship Earth," suspended in Outer Space. Finally, we were able to see clearly that "We are all in this together." With a backdrop of darkness, and distant stars, we could now see our precious planet as one unified whole, with no visible man-made borders.

Overall the 1960s were a decade of profound transformation in Humanity's collective consciousness. Many seeds were planted, literally and metaphorically. Some of these continued to grow steadily, while others withered out, or perhaps went underground to sprout later. Let's fast-forward to the 1990s with the birth of Humanity's collective brain. Oops — I mean the Internet!

The Internet has been both a cause and an effect of accelerated Interconnection and Integration. With this world-wide-web, many of the best solutions in every field of study can be cross-referenced, compared, and discussed between people anywhere on the globe. Two doctors looking for a cure for a disease on opposite sides of the planet can now easily share data, and even have a Skype chat! The times of "Trial and Error" and "Doing It Alone" are minimized because we are working to solve challenges more as a collective species!

With the Internet growing more connected every single day, it is clear that we are in the "Age of the Great Integration." All of these historical events shifts in consciousness that I've highlighted can now be studied from anywhere on the planet, at the click of a button. It is as if the Human Brain is growing new neurons, and increasing in connectivity, which leads to even more awareness. Countless breakthroughs, inventions, collaborations, and miracles have come as a result of this World-Wide-Web!

It is a priceless gift to have such an amazing tool and pool of resources and knowledge at our fingertips.

Personally, I am most blown away by YouTube and Social Media, and how these two things have revolutionized the lives of billions of people! Whereas before the Internet, you were lucky if you could find someone in your hometown that shared the same interests as you; now you can join a Facebook Group or a chat room and connect with people five thousand miles away who also love studying Bird Migrations or Gluten Free Cupcakes : Also, the sheer amount of data and content being created daily is astounding. Every single day, there are 4 million hours of content uploaded to YouTube and 4.3 billion Facebook messages posted!

With all this data streaming past us and into us every day, many would argue that we are becoming distracted from what truly matters. I can definitely see this trend, as some toddlers are glued to their iPads before they are in Kindergarten. When so much around is mediated, we can lose touch with the realities right before our eyes. Our planet is truly at a tipping point. Deforestation, Species Extinction, Desertification, Factory Farms, Topsoil Loss, Plastic Pollution, Climate Change, and many more issues are getting worse by the day. Pachamama is calling us to wake up from the Mainstream Strange Dream, which has most people in a Consumerist trance, which is devouring her precious resources. The Tribal Peoples that never became "civilized" are reminding us that it is still possible to live in harmony with nature, and reconnect to the Web of Life.

These monumental times we are living in are calling forth the best in us. It's time to utilize all the information and resources available to us to transform our planet into the harmonious Spaceship Earth that we all dream of. To do this, we've gotta use our Superpowers! So many solutions exist, and are visible on the Internet. It is simply a matter of implementing them on a mass scale. The world needs more Web-Weavers, Village-Builders, Truth-Speakers, Art-Makers, Movers and Shakers! Are you going to answer the call?

If you do, I can promise you it will not be easy. But you will be saying YES to a life of previously unimaginable Beauty, Adventure, Magic, Service, Love, and Transformation. You will be saying YES to one of the most important missions in Human History. You will be saying YES to preserve and continue the magic of life for future generations. Let's do this!

PLUGGING INTO THE MOVEMENT

If you are choosing to answer this call to action, then you are stepping into your role as an **"Evolutionary" : someone who is dedicated to Conscious Evolution as a way of life both personally and collectively.** Here are 3 main ways to "Plug into the Movement" :

1. Join and collaborate with one or multiple Social Movements / Conscious Projects in your area. (There are a bunch listed in the upcoming chapter "The Web of Infinite Inspiration.")

2. Work on building community in your area and networking with other Evolutionary People, Projects, and Places. (Tools for this are found in the "Cultivating Community" Chapter.)

3. Participate with the "Sacred StoryWeavers." We are a Brand and Business focused on creating a positive Social and Environmental impact. Our mission is to Inspire Individual and Collective Empowerment. We provide Transformational Tools, Media, and Workshops at Live Events and through a variety of Online and Printed Materials. Our website is www.SacredStoryWeavers.net and we would love to connect with you :) Please email us with any questions or ideas : SacredStoryWeavers@gmail.com

MY PRAYER FOR THIS BOOK

The way I see it, a big part of my soul purpose is to be a "Medicine Keeper." By this, I mean that Great Spirit has entrusted me to be a steward of many new and ancient teachings. If applied, these "Medicine Teachings" can Unlock your Superpowers and bring you into a greater state of harmony, awareness, and incredible amazement of life! To be a part of bringing these teachings to the world is a tremendous honor, and a big responsibility.

Have you ever been at a festival or event and seen a live, collaborative painting? Several artists each have their own brush and set of paints, and as the music plays, they co-create an amazing piece of art moment by moment. Every artist has their own unique style and when they work together with other artists, the result is **"Synergy," where the end result is exponentially more awesome than the sum of the individual parts.**

This book is essentially a Collaborative Painting, which has been a work in progress for thousands of years. As the saying goes, "I am standing on the shoulders of giants." It is impossible for me to thank and honor everyone throughout space and time that has preserved, propagated, and evolved these Sacred Teachings and Superpowers. There are countless cultures, tribes, and communities to thank for practicing and cultivating the wisdom, which has evolved over time to become this current version.

Many brave revolutionaries, healers, shamans, renegades, visionaries, and mystics all over the world have given their lives or put their lives on the line to both preserve and propagate these messages. I pray that this spirit of truth continues to live in me, so that I can do my part in sharing this wisdom with anyone who is open to it.

In my heart of hearts, I want this "medicine" to be available to anyone who needs it. After all, everyone deserves medicine when they are not well. How can anything or anyone stand in the way of this?! It is our sacred birthright to have access to the knowledge, tools, and Superpowers that can set us free. I created a story that I will share here that articulates these concepts :

The Story of Nesreen

The year is 1904. A woman named Nesreen is walking through the desert with her kids, Tareq and Marwa. They fled their local town in Libya after a military invasion from another country. They escaped the chaos with only the clothes on their backs and a large jug of water. Nesreen walks through the desert with them for 3 days in search of food and shelter. On the morning of the third day, her children are tired of walking, and very hungry. Marwa asks, "Momma, are we going to die out here?" Nesreen replies, "Great Spirit is going to provide for us. We are being tested. We must be strong."

Finally they reach a town with a big marketplace. Nesreen does not have any money, but she is absolutely determined to find a way to feed her kids.

She approaches a Merchant with a big, braided beard who stands beside a vast array of colorful fruits and vegetables. She can't contain herself and quickly exclaims "Sir, we have traveled 3 days in the desert. We have no money. My children are extremely hungry, can we please have some food?" The merchant hesitates, and says, "I'm sorry, but I must make a living. I cannot just give away food for free!"

Nesreen pleads, "Sir, don't you trust that Great Spirit will replenish your supply if you give to us?" The merchant is taken aback. He looks from side to side.

She continues, "The birds do not worry about where they will find food tomorrow! It is only in this human society of greed and fear that we find this artificial scarcity!" He can feel the truth of her statement. He stares into the eyes of Marwa and Tareq, and then he looks over at his big supply of food. Reluctantly, he grabs a bag and fills it with fresh fruits and vegetables.

In this situation the Mental Story of money and societal norms dissolves into the "Immediacy of the Moment." The children burst into smiles, and run up and hug this old, bearded man. Nesreen dances around with the fruit and begins peeling an orange for the kids. The three of them break out into song, giving thanks and praise for the nourishment.

Nesreen bows to her knees beside a large tree and thanks Great Spirit for the blessing of this food. The bearded merchant begins to break into tears. He walks over to Nesreen, who is now sitting with Marwa, who's enjoying a big green apple. The man looks ashamed. He stutters, "I'm sorry. I'm sorry for holding back the food at first. I guess I was scared that it would leave me and my family with less. But after the words you spoke, and seeing your kids in joy, I have now realized that, "Everything balances out. Great Spirit provides when we are in the flow of giving and receiving." Then the bearded man starts laughing. "I was under the illusion that I actually owned the food! That is just a story of the mind!"

"Yes, now you can see," Nesreen replies. "All that we have is a gift from Great Spirit. We don't truly own anything, yet we must be good stewards on this planet. That is what I teach my children." Nesreen calls over Marwa and Tareq. They come and sit on her lap. They share a minute or two of silence with this kind merchant man. Each of them gives him a warm hug, and they continue on their way.

I share this story to articulate the spirit behind this book, Unlocking Our Superpowers. I am deeply passionate about everyone having access to the tools for healing, in the same way that Nesreen was deeply determined to feed her children. I pray that I will always have my basic needs met as I continue to put myself in service. With that said, a basic energy exchange of some sort does feel authentic to both honor the magnitude of these teachings, and the immense time and energy I've put into stewarding them. I do intend to have a system in place, so that those who don't have funds to exchange for a hard copy or the programs offered through Sacred StoryWeavers - can still have access to these Sacred Teachings. All of the chapters are available on our website : SacredStoryWeavers.net

----

With all that in mind, I hold a vision of people all over the world practicing and utilizing the tools in this book to create massive transformation in their lives. I imagine circles of people at festivals co-creating Affirmation Activations and discussing their personal Mental Advisors. I envision every town in America having at least one weekly Ecstatic Dance event, so that people can freely express themselves and utilize their whole BodyMind System! I can see thousands of new smiles on the faces of people who have reconnected with Pachamama and the immense joy and fulfillment they feel as a result.

Yay! I am so grateful to be able to share all of these tools, keys, and maps with the world. We are truly Unlocking our Superpowers :)

I feel inspired to share some more "Radical Honesty" on the topic of connecting with those of you who resonate with this book :

- I know in my heart that "Unlocking Our Superpowers" is destined to be translated into many languages and support transformation in the lives of many people all over the globe. We are currently building a team of Evolutionaries to carry this mission forward. If you are interested in collaborating, please email us : SacredStoryWeavers@gmail.com

- I know that I often feel a deep kinship with many of my favorite authors, whose books have been pivotal in my life. It feels like they know me inside and out. This is a very intimate relationship.

- I believe some of you may feel this way towards me. I am indeed a cool person, though ultimately, you are connecting to the goodness and truth of Great Spirit coming through me as a conduit.

- My sincere prayer is that you understand I am not able to keep in touch 1-on-1 with everyone who appreciates the work I do.

- If you do have a desire to thank me for what I share, I'm open to receiving letters / emails, though I cannot promise that I will be able to respond to all of them. I also invite you to send gratitude through the "Feelingnet" and know that I will energetically receive your gratitude through the amazing interconnected web we exist in.

- If you have a question for me, I ask that you spend at least 1 hour researching that topic on Google, YouTube, and the rest of the web, to see if you can find an answer. Personally, I have been conditioned to often seek the "easy way out," which is to ask a question to someone who's probably busy, rather than utilizing my "Google Search Superpower," and simply finding it on my own.

- If you do some research, and still feel like you want to ask me a question, you can send me an email (KevinMayCoaching@gmail.com) with the title "Question for Kevin"

and I will do my best to eventually answer it, or make a YouTube video on that topic :)

- I do 1-on-1 Transformational Coaching with individuals who I feel a deep resonance with, and who are ready to transform their lives in a major way by implementing the tools outlined in this book. I can only work with so many clients at a time, and I am very selective to only work with people who are deeply dedicated towards achieving profound results. If this sounds like a fit for you, please send me an email : KevinMayCoaching@gmail.com with the heading "Coaching Inquiry " and outline what you feel inspired to transform in your life. Thank you :)

- I invite and encourage you to share the tools in this book with anyone and everyone who may benefit from them. This book is destined to eventually reach millions of people, and I believe this will happen largely through word of mouth and peer to peer recommendations. You can also assist by requesting this book at your local Bookstores. Please share this book far and wide, while also realizing that it may not resonate with everyone you share it with. Please always honor each person's free will and realize that not everyone is open and/or ready to receive and apply these teachings.

- In conclusion, I emanate love for each and every one of you who connects with this book, and I'm deeply honored to be able to share all of this information and inspiration with you :)

- I send a double dose of gratitude to my friends and family who have been directly supportive of this book coming into existence : Samuca Flows for masterful editing and proofreading, and eternal friendship. Casey House for designing the epic front and back covers. Chelsey Crandell for painting the magnificent Rainbow Lion. Niffer Desmond for ongoing graphic design support and encouragement. Travis Kennedy for epic website design. Andrea Sarcos for capturing my 1st ever official photoshoot in the jungles of Delray Beach. Will Morgan for being a jedi and keen discernment in proofreading. Amanda, Charlie, Tina, Chris, and all my epic Cultural Recyclist homies! Charles Eisenstein for continued inspiration and for allowing me to include the Invisible Path essay. Luna Marni Mana Moonchild for the infinite love, support, and massages that kept me flowing and growing. Jean Carlo Tavarez for Reiki and encouraging me even when my Mental Advisors were tormenting me. Thank you Sol Shanti, Bobbi (Smokifantastic) Williams, Jesse Carrier, Parker Webb, Travis (Natural) Huntley, Jenna Maloney, Christopher Hills, Sagely Willow Tribe, and everyone else who has offered healing / massage to me along my journey.

Thank you Maharaji, Amma, Ram Dass, Eckhart Tolle, Wayne Dyer, Chris Uhl, Luke Kohen, Amateo Ra, Preston Smiles, Ralph (Infinite Waters) Smart, Elliott Hulse, Teal Swan, Tai Lopez and all my other teachers, mentors, and guides. Thank you to Linda Polansky, John Slicker, Patrick (Kernel LoveJoy) Hennessy, Matthew and Brian Monahan, and everyone else who held a loving, supportive space for this book to come into being. Thank you to Tony Moss, Miranda Rondeau, Haize Hawk, Sunny Solwind, Tara Karina / Dylan James Byrne, David Brown, and all my other Bird Tribe / Luvfest homies. Thanks to my housemates who encouraged me, honored my night owl tendencies, and all my other quirks. Thank you to my amazing mom (Linda May), dad (Brian May), and sister (Melissa May) for so much love, encouragement, and support along my entire journey. Thank you to all my amazing Grandparents, Aunts, Uncles, Cousins, and beautiful relatives!

So much love and gratitude to all my friends in Pittsburgh, Asheville, Delray, all my West Coast soul-fam, all my Facebook / Youtube homies, and everyone in between! Deep thanks to all the Indigenous Tribes and Wisdomkeepers who fought and still work so hard to keep the sacred ways alive. Thank you to my incredible teacher, lover, and support system : Pachamama :) Thank you to all my insect, plant, fungi, rock, crystal, lizard, animal, tree, and bird friends who have been blessing my life with wonder, wisdom, and amazement. Thank you to my cloud friends, Mama Luna, Father Sun, Mama Ocean, and all the beautiful Star Nations. Thank you to my Spirit Guides, Ancestors, and Guardian Angels who make me feel loved, supported, and protected. Thank you to the 5 elements and the 7 directions which are all interconnected into the center of my being. Thank you Great Spirit, Wakan Tanka, Gitchi Manitou for guiding and loving me every step of the way. Wow, what a beautiful life :)

THE WEB OF
INFINITE INSPIRATION

During the bike trip across America exploring Sustainable Living, we met a tremendous amount of "Solutionaries". We visited eco-villages of all shapes and sizes. Some were powered largely by hydro and solar power and surrounded with fruit trees. Many homes were built from local materials by the residents of the communities.

We realized that many of the Permaculture Solutions are already in motion and working in places all over the world. The technologies for humans to live in a harmonious balance with Natural Law already exist. There are many cutting edge Facilitation, Conflict Mediation, and Community Organizing techniques that are tried and true. Also, First Nation representatives from tribes all over the world are coming to the forefront and sharing wisdom and traditions teaching how to live in "Right Relation".

It boggles my mind how much of collective human consciousness is put towards analyzing problems, diseases, sickness, when many of the cures are already available.

This is why I firmly believe that the **CURE is CURATION!!!!**

Curation, meaning to gather and highlight pieces of artwork. The artwork we must gather and share includes : healers, philosophers, writers, activists, teachers, artists, musicians, Permaculture experts, builders, organizers, and visionaries who have so much to offer towards this new paradigm. If we highlight all of the beauty that already EXISTS, then we will see a lot more consciousness SHIFTS.

Imagine an ancient Egyptian pyramid. The innermost chamber is deep below the outer surface. A small opening in the outer wall has a mirror which catches a beam of light from the sun, which then ricochets to another mirror, and light consecutively ping pongs its way to yet another mirror, until finally SHAZAAM! — the entire inner chamber is illuminated! This technique of directing, harnessing, and utilizing a beam of light is a powerful metaphor. We can also harness the best art and solutions in the world and ricochet them through the Internet with the power of Curation. This is the work I feel called to do, and I invite you to do the same. Be a Curator, and help cure the widespread drought of inspiration and hope!

Intertwined with being a "Curator," I also invite you to be a **Lighthouse. This involves sharing information and inspiration on a local and global level. As you shine the light of positive solutions into the world, you will become a beacon of optimism for many people who you are connected to.** If you imagine a big web stretched over our planet, there are certain "nodes" or "intersection points" on the web where people and groups are broadcasting light and positive information to the rest of the web. As you begin to spread more inspiration throughout your section of the web, you will also attract more new info to share, and it becomes a beautiful snowball effect. As more of us step into the roles of Curators and Lighthouses, we are strengthening the Web of Infinite Inspiration. Also, going back to the Tale of the Two Trees, we are putting our energy into the Thriving Tree, which is based on Holistic Cultural Values. It's a huge honor to have the opportunity to play a part in this Planetary Evolution Revolution!

Within this Infinite Web of Inspiration, I will now highlight some of my favorite consciousness shifting musical artists. My life has been enriched in countless ways by these artists. May they inspire, captivate, and motivate you to be creative, expressive and fully alive!

MY FAVORITE CONSCIOUS MUSICIANS

CHANCES R GOOD

I believe Chances to be one of the most gifted lyricists in the known Universe. He weaves words like a wizard with a tongue faster than a lizard... hahah. My utmost favorite album is *Earth Tones*, followed by *What's That Smell*, *Boomerangs*, and *A Billion Years*.

If you truly absorb his lyrics, messages, and vibrations, I am confident that your DNA will be activated and rearranged in a wondrous and beneficial way. I memorized many of the lyrics to his songs while driving from Pittsburgh to Ojai in November of 2014. I had so much fun jamming out while simultaneously upgrading my DNA :

Favorite Songs : Yawanawa, Tru U, Good Morning, No Worries No Hurries ft. Ri , Sweat, Catch The Spiral, IOL, and Passion N Bliss

- www.chancesrgood.bandcamp.com/album/earth-tones

TREVOR HALL

The first time I ever heard Trevor Hall's music was at a live show at the Troubadour in L.A. I was honestly blown away by his sincere, heartfelt music. After the show I bought his album called *E3* (*Everything, Everytime, Everywhere*) and it became like a new close friend. I listened to it almost every day, and it was funny because I was living on the top of a mountain in Ojai, and in one of my favorite songs on the album, the chorus repeats "Way Up On The Mountain - woah, a woaaaaahhhh"

Trevor also shares a close connection to Neem Karoli Baba (Maharaji), who is near and dear to my heart.

Favorite Songs : Who Am I, Lime Tree, Volume, My Baba

I also highly recommend watching a live performance of "Unity" w/ Cas Haley on YouTube. I've jammed to this TRULY EPIC 'prayerformance' countless times.

- www.trevorhallmusic.com

SANTIPARRO

When I first heard his song called "Rainbows in the Night", I could feel the depths and truths of his heart coming through the music. His unique voice and style took me a little bit to get used to, AND once it clicked, I was fully groovin'. His album called "True Prayer" became my soul-ally and upliftment as I went through a 2 month long "Dark Night of the Soul" in early 2015.

Favorite Songs : Total Freedom, Where We're From, Universe Strand, and Darkness with Darkness

- www.santiparro.com

AUDIAFAUNA

I was gifted their album called "Grow Down" from a dear friend in Santa Cruz. As I drove down the California coast, I jammed out to this new music. At first, I thought "this isn't really my style." As I cruised into the night, it started to grow on me.

When I heard the song Heartwood, I became one with this band. The chorus goes "I am a lion – hear me roar" and this deeply resonated with me. I began listening to the entire album every time I would drive anywhere. I learned the lyrics quickly and deeply appreciate all of the love this band infused into "Grow Down". It has resuscitated my soul during many challenging times. I also love Audiafauna's 3-song demo called "The Leaflet".

Favorite songs : Roots, Heartwood, Going There Strong, Present, and Fallen

- www.audiafauna.bandcamp.com

AYLA NEREO

In my opinion, Ayla's album *Hollow Bone* is a masterpiece. The album feels like a direct transmission from a realm that has a harmonious balance of Angelic and Earthly energies. Her music often gives me a sense of self-empowerment, connection to Spirit, and the childlike wonder of life.

Favorite Songs : Show Yourself, Seeds, From the Ground Up, Eastern Sun, Let It In

- www.aylanereo.com

CORA FLORA

For a while, one of my friends had recommended Cora's music to me, though for some reason I never checked it out. About a year later, out of the blue, her name kept coming into my head. I decided to listen while I was practicing self-massage. This was perfectly fitting, because a lot of Cora's message is about healing our relationship with our inner child and deeper self.

I am so grateful for Cora's courage and vulnerability that she expresses in her music. I can tell she has overcome many challenges and is sharing the glorious joy which can be found on the other side of trauma.

Favorite songs: This Bliss, Flower, I Choose Love, Oh Night Divine

- www.coraflora.com

KELLEE MAIZE

Kellee is a dear friend and fellow Pittsburgher. She gifted me her album "Owl Time" and I jammed to it in my car for much of 2012. She is a gifted lyricist with a potent message, embracing the Sacred Feminine and taking action to protect our planet. Some songs carry a gentle flowing energy, while others embody the fire of transformation.

Favorite Songs : Caterpillar, Peaceburgh, Gotta Love Me, Third Eye

- www.Kelleemaize.com

FLORENCE AND THE MACHINE

When I first heard the song "Dog Days Are Over", it was like a blast of warmth and joy during a cold winter. I listened to it consistently for a week or two, until it became part of me.

For me, this band embodies a beautiful synthesis of very dark and light energies. I have been moved to tears several times listening to this powerful music. I absolutely love the epic orchestra instruments infused into many of the anthems.

Favorite Songs : Never Let Me Go, Heartlines, Cosmic Love, Dog Days Are Over, Leave My Body

- www.florenceandthemachine.net

KEVIN YAZZIE

I first heard Kevin Yazzie's song called "Love" as the soundtrack to a video created by a fellow activist, Lyla June. I literally burst into tears at the end of the video.

As I found more of his songs online, I listened to them whenever I needed help to cry and/or pray. He carries a very profound and healing medicine in his music.

Favorite Songs: Hope, Love, Charity, Ways of Life

- Search "Kevin Yazzie" on YouTube or Amazon.com

ECSTATIC UNION

This is an epic, jamming folk band with sing along melodies galore. Their music instantly puts me in a good mood. I feel more connected to the Earth and all its magic when I listen to them. Gee wiz, I am deeply grateful for these amazing musicians. Their debut album "Sundog" is packed with my favorite songs.

-        www.ecstaticunion.bandcamp.com

DAVE MATTHEWS BAND

I got introduced to Dave's music in my senior year of high school because many of my close friends were loyal fans. At first I was repelled by his voice, but as I heard some of his songs containing a deeper message, I opened up more. Eventually, I discovered my deep appreciation for the spontaneous jams in the recorded live shows. I love how the energy builds and crescendos in such magnificent ways. I don't really listen to his studio albums because the live shows are just on another level. Although not every song has the most "conscious" message, I truly believe that Dave is spreading many positive, uplifting vibes throughout the world.

Favorite Songs : Die Tryin, Crush, When the World Ends, Eh Hee, The Maker

-   www.davematthewsband.com

GROUNDATION

This is one of my favorite Reggae bands. They have a wide variety of musicians, which creates a dynamic synergy that moves my spirit. The lead singer, Harrison Stratford, channels an extremely potent and motivating vibration. This music gives me strength and determination to keep embodying love and unity.

I highly recommend the live performance on YouTube of "Undivided" at the La Nuit de l'Erdre Festival.

Favorite Songs : Mighty Souls, Here I Am, Smile, Music Is the Most High

-   www.groundation.com

YAIMA

Wow! What can I say to properly honor these amazing musicians? Their music has seeped into my soul and catalyzed profound inspiration, motivation, and celebration in my life for the past 3 years.

Pepper Proud, the lead singer in Yaima seems to speak an ancient language that my mind can't fully grasp, but my soul understands. Their music is amazing for spiritual communion, deep meditation, sacred sexuality, and for connecting to nature.

Favorite Songs : Gajamaru, Our Game, Force

- www.YaimaMusic.com

BEAUTIFUL CHORUS

I was blessed to meet this amazing group of women at a festival called Three Days of Light in Asheville in 2015. I gathered in a cabin with about 10 other friends and my heart soared as they serenaded us with their phenomenal melodies, lyrics, and harmonies.

All of these woman are channeling angelic, healing, musical frequencies, in my humble opinion. They are pioneers in the realm of Affirmation Songs, with repetitive self-empowering and self-healing mantras. I cannot recommend their magical music enough. May it open your heart and increase your joy :)

Favorite Songs : Inner Peace, Pachamama, Infinite Universe

- www.beautifulchorus.bandcamp.com

MAMUSE

This dynamic of bike-touring empowered women are two of the most soulful singers I've ever heard. Their music is both heavenly and very down-to-Earth. I have cried my eyes out many times listening to their music on YouTube. I hope to hear them live someday soon, and get to share hugs with each of them.

Favorite Songs : Hallelujah, Chico Gospel, Great Big World

- www.Mamuse.org

MATISYAHU

Matisyahu was one of the first "Conscious Musicians" that I started to enjoy listening to. I first heard his song "King Without A Crown" around my freshman year of high school, and I could feel the deep truth and wisdom in both his lyrics and his voice. Since his first album, I have been captivated, inspired, and guided by his other musical releases, particularly the album "Light," which served as a light in the darkness after my heart was deeply hurt through a relationship with a girl I was dating during the winter of 2009. May his music soothe your soul and raise your spirits!

Favorite Songs : I Will Be Light, King Without a Crown, Sunshine, Lord Raise Me Up

- www.matisyahuworld.com

LUVAMP PROJECT

Straight up, if you want to connect to the vibration of LOVE, this is the band for you. These are my dear friends, and they are the real deal :)

Favorite Songs : Be Luv, This Love, Limit Is The Sky, All Love United

- www.theluvampproject.bandcamp.com

EARTHWAKE

Tara Karina aka Dylan James Byrne, the lead singer of Earthwake is one of the most incredible, imaginative, and masterful musicians I have ever met. I am deeply grateful to be friends with them, and to have witnessed their musical evolution since 2011 when we first met. I have shed tears of gratitude, love, sadness, and forgiveness countless times while listening to their profoundly healing music. Tara also catalyzes laughter, playfulness, and joy every time they picks up their guitar to play. I cannot recommend their music enough. I am excited to see how the world transforms as the Earthwake moves through collective consciousness!

Favorite Songs : Johnny Appleseed, Dear Me, Get There, Cosmos

- www.youtube.com/user/TheEarthWake

SHINING LION

Shine Rilling aka Shining Lion is a friend of mine who I met while traveling in Ojai back in 2012. One day, I was chatting with Shine outside the local Rainbow Bridge Grocery. I started to beatbox, and he began freestyling - weaving words together off the top of his head. It was so natural for him to freestyle, though I was totally captivated and inspired. "How can he keep rhyming words without rehearsing?" I thought to myself. Deep down I really wanted to be able to do freestyle like Shine. Several years later, I have honed my skills, and learned to get into "the flow," and so I am able to freestyle fairly well. I am forever grateful for Shine's musical medicine — both his freestyles, and his written songs.

If you like authentic, grassroots, Reggae-style musical magic, then check out Shining Lion's most recent album, *One Love Vibration*. His older albums with Black Feet Music are also filled with amazing rhymes and a message of honoring the Web of Life.

Favorite Songs : Oneness, Simplify and Unify, Water of Life, High Horse

- www.shininglionmusic.com

JORDAN WALKER

I met Jordan in August of 2015 as we were both preparing to attend the 3 Days of Light Festival in Asheville, NC. I heard his sweet melodic singing and ukulele music from afar, but didn't get to fully absorb it in person. He left one of his CDs with my friend David, who let me burn a copy. This was a 5-song demo CD, and in all honesty, the sound quality was below average. But the pure love that I felt through this music blew me away, so I listened to these 5 songs over and over again. I am extremely excited to hear more of Jordan's music, as he continues to share with the world. As far as I know he has not recorded a full album yet, so I invite you to search "Jordan Children of Jah" on YouTube.

Favorite Songs : Children of Jah, Miracles, Freedom (Lion's Roar Away)

- Search "Jordan Walker Children of Jah" on Youtube

KEVIN MAY

Last but not least, is a magical human bean that I am pretty familiar with. My album "Evolution In Motion" is a fun and interactive mixture of beatboxing, singing, and Spoken Word. For a long time, my Mental Advisors have tried to convince me my songs aren't awesome, though the hundreds of heartfelt reflections I've received from friends have provided some great alternative perspectives. I recommend jamming out to these albums while driving in your car :)

Favorite Songs : Go Inside, Breathin Life, Pachamama Lullaby

-        www.KevinMay.Bandcamp.com

Here are a few more ways to explore the realms of Infinite Inspiration. I list some of my favorites in several different areas. All these lists are in no particular order :)

MY FAVORITE YOUTUBE CREATORS

1. **SKY LIFE** - I discovered Sky while watching a documentary about training with Wim Hof, with the Youtube Channel "Yes Theory." Sky participated in many intense cold exposure challenges and I was inspired by her outlook on life. Since then, I have kept up with her awe-inspiring weekly uploads. Sky has a wide range of videos exploring everything from medicinal mushrooms to hypnosis. Check out her channel!

2. **MARAYA KARENA** - Maraya cracks me up! She is so sweet, funny and creative She is honestly one of the most brilliant and articulate philosophers I have ever come across. She is as wise as Socrates, yet radiates love and compassion from her heart like a devotional singer. She has great insights on everything from healing codependency to psychedelic eroticism.

3. **ASTARIUS MIRACULII** - Astarius is one of the most amazing Sound Healers I've ever come across. I had the honor of meeting him and experiencing a

personal Didgeridoo Healing at the Conscious Life Expo in 2013. He has many profound insights on spirituality, astrology, and life in general. His eternal soul shines through every video he creates. I love one of his mantras which says, "Up at the top, there's room for all, it's just the bottom that's crowded, ya'll!"

4. **BREEZY SPREADLOVE** - I met Brianna aka Breezy at the 3 Days of Light Festival in 2015. I appreciate her playful spirit, high energy enthusiasm, and dedication

to inspire others. She is pioneering the "Golden Gaia Adventure" all across the country :)

5. **ELIZABETH DIALTO** - She leads the "Truth Telling with Elizabeth Dialto" Podcast. I love her authenticity, empowerment, and ability to apply discernment on a wide range of topics. I have learned sooo much from listening to her and her amazing guests.

6. **YES THEORY**- I have received tremendous inspiration from these fellahs. Their motto is "Seek Discomfort" and in each video they challenge themselves and/or other people to entertaining social experiments which push them outside their comfort zone. Whether it is bungee jumping out of a helicopter or going on a blind date, their videos are super intriguing and catalyze me to LIVE SPONTANEOUSLY and COURAGEOUSLY.

7. **AMATEO RA** - He is a friend of mine who greatly inspires me with his passion, insight and ability to speak on a wide range of topics. He hasn't recorded many videos since 2015, though his channel is packed with precious golden nuggets of wisdom!

8. **LILOU MACE** - Lilou has been traveling the globe interviewing cutting edge Leaders, Teachers, Authors, and other awesome people for over 5 years. I've watched hundreds of hours of her interviews and she is incredibly gifted at holding a loving, receptive space to draw forth the beauty and wisdom of each person she interviews.

9. **PATRICK HAIZE** - Patrick is one of the most brilliant integrative philosophers I have ever across. I have watched nearly all of his videos on his Youtube channel, and every one is packed with powerful insights. He has a gift for explaining complex esoteric concepts and translating them into digestible nuggets of wisdom. He's also a phenomenal Hip-Hop artist. Check out his channel!

MY FAVORITE ELECTRONIC ARTISTS

(Listed in no particular order. Also, I don't feel inspired to share a description of each artist, though I am grateful for each of their unique styles and wizardry that they craft into their music!)

1. **Bluetech**
2. **Gramatik**
3. **Kaminanda**
4. **Kalya Scintilla**
5. **Numatik**
6. **Papadosio**
7. **Clozee**
8. **Lotus**

FAVORITE HEALING MUSIC

All of these are the exact titles as they are listed on YouTube (I add the quotations. The name after is the title of the YouTube channel.) I have listened to many of these hundreds of times. They are superb and magnificent!

1. **"Merlin's Magic : 1 HOUR Healing Meditation Music" - ZenSpiritLight**
2. **"Meditation (Zen Music)" - fearless2435**
3. **"Relaxation Music / 432 Hz Dna Healing/ Chakra Cleansing Meditation" - EJ Boxing Live**
4. **"528Hz Music / Bring Positive Transformation - Meditative Mind**

5. The Channel "Ask Angels with Melanie Beckler" on YouTube has many amazing Guided Meditations / Angel Healing Meditations. I have listened to these hundreds of times, and had many deeply profound experiences. I am so grateful for Melanie who channels these messages from the Angelic Realms. I invite you to explore this multitude of magical meditations!

FAVORITE SOCIAL GROUPS / MOVEMENTS

1. **SURVIVAL INTERNATIONAL -** www.survivalinternational.org
2. **PARADIGM SHIFT CENTRAL -** www.paradigmshiftcentral.com
3. **PROJECT NUEVO MUNDO -** www.numundo.org
4. **PERMIES -** www.permies.com
5. **PACHAMAMA ALLIANCE -** www.pachamama.org
6. **I AM LIFE PROJECT -** www.iamlifeproject.org
7. **ESALEN INSTITUTE -** www.esalen.org
8. **5 RHYTHYMS DANCE -** www.5rhythms.com
9. **BIONEERS -** www.bioneers.org
10. **FESTIVAL FIRE -** www.festivalfire.com
11. **THE BLOOM SERIES -** www.thebloom.tv
12. **CITY REPAIR PROJECT -** www.cityrepair.org
13. **PEACE-LOVE-UNITY MOVEMENT -** www.peace-love-unity.org

All of these musicians, movements, meditations, and more have contributed so much inspiration to my life! They have all assisted me in tapping into and amplifying my Superpowers. I am grateful to potentially open your eyes and ears to some of these new doorways for the first time :) I encourage you to support all these projects as you feel inspired; to keep growing and strengthening the Great Web of Inspiration! To close the circle of this magical book, I feel inspired to share one of my favorite pieces of Poetry that came through my "Hollow Bamboo" back in 2014. May these lyrics inspire you to feel the Infinite Potential that lies within you. Without further ado, I'll say Scoobally doo, and let you read on through :

WHAT IF?

The Cosmos - AKA - The Big "What IF" ?
I.-F.
Infinite Form - Intertwined Flawlessly - with the
Infinite Form-less

G-O-D dancing delicately with divine GODD-ESS

One day God winked at his beloved, and Goddess smiled
9 months later - they had a child
They named their kid "IF" - and now the story gets wild

See, IF... could take on Incredible Facades!
could be male, female, visible or mirage

IF – simply put is the INFINITE FRACTAL
Fresher than fruit and older than a Pterodactyl

IF is a being - who bestows Instantaneous Forgiveness
For our Inevitable Forgetfulness
IF is the Imagination Factory…
And the portal to Inconceivable Fantasy

IF! - look at it one way and you say :
I'm Flying!

From another view, you're In Fear and you're dying
See, we've been programmed to be profoundly pessimistic
But I flip the IF like a kickflip - So I say Fuck Impossible!

Ganesh in the flesh, we're hoppin over obstacles
cuz when we're empowered by IF - We… are unstoppable...

And though we are just an Infinitesimal Fragment
We can align with the Ineffable Flow
Perhaps we are strongest
when we just ...let ...GO?

What if What IS

Is What IS
because of all the past What IF's ?
I said "What if What IS
Is What IS
because of all the past What IF's?"

Perhaps the key to sharing our greatest gifts
Is to expand our what IF's?
Holy shift, it's time to make some What IF lists!

Anyways, back to God and Godd-ess
All of you, they wish to bless
They bestow this gift - for you to use on your quest

This! is the gift of LIFE
L. - I. - F. - E.
You're given Love ... and Energy
The IF is up to thee!

(((<3)))

Made in the USA
Columbia, SC
23 October 2021